An Index of Ideas for Writers and Speakers

SCOTT, FORESMAN AND COMPANY Chicago Atlanta Dallas Palo Alto Fair Lawn, N.

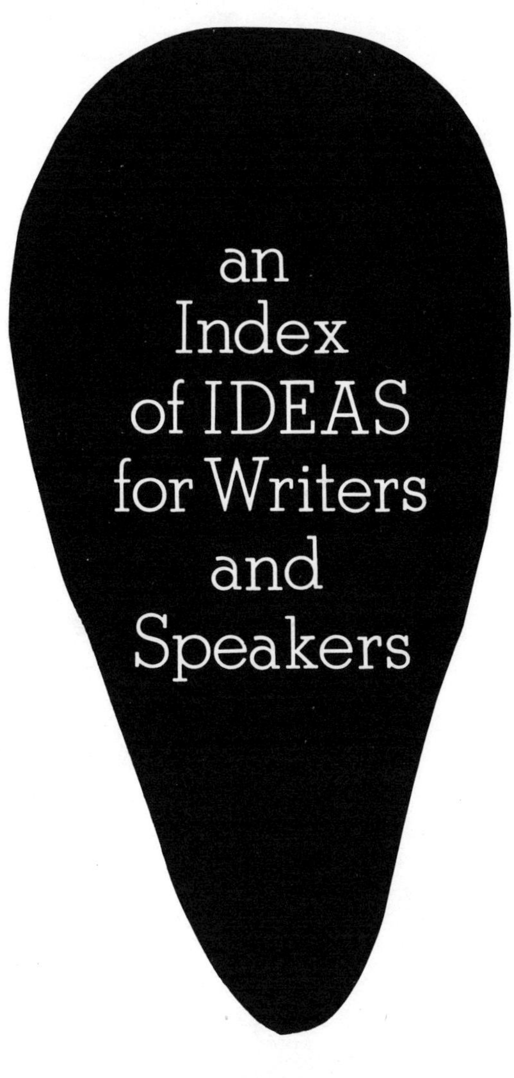
an
Index
of IDEAS
for Writers
and
Speakers

Zebulon Vance Hooker II
Roanoke College

If any Person dislike what I offer,
let him publish his own Sentiments.

Lord Herbert of Cherbury,
De Religione Gentilium

Library of Congress Catalog
Card No. 65-24445

FOREWORD

I am honored that Professor Z. V. Hooker, II, has invited me, his long-time colleague in the Department of English at Roanoke College, to write a few words for the beginning of his book, *An Index of Ideas for Writers and Speakers.*

I am also particularly pleased to do this because I believe this book will fill a real need for people who must write something but have trouble deciding what to write about. I remember my own difficulties as a freshman many years ago, and I remember also the difficulties of hundreds of my composition students who were wont to say, "I wish you would just assign me a topic. I don't know what to write about"! I also take a vicarious pleasure in the publication of this book, because, unlike a book I once planned about expository writing, this one lives in print to be used and enjoyed.

It has been interesting to me, and I hope of some usefulness to Professor Hooker, to serve as his sounding board during the conception and gestation of *An Index of Ideas for Writers and Speakers.*

P. F. K.

Salem, Virginia

ACKNOWLEDGMENTS

In Shakespeare's Troilus and Cressida, Pandarus observes "Words pay no debts." Even so, words may help to acknowledge one's indebtedness, especially in compiling an index.

Accordingly, it is my pleasure to acknowledge my debt to those individuals at Roanoke College who, by their advice and encouragement, have helped me turn words into a book. The list below could be extended, but I am particularly indebted to:

Mrs. Lucile D. Snow, Head Librarian, who, with her able staff, has given me invaluable assistance;

my colleagues in the English Department, especially Professor Matthew M. Wise, Chairman; Professor William J. Deegan; and Professor William R. Coulter—all of whom labor with me in Freshman English (Composition and Rhetoric), and from whom I have learned much;

President Perry F. Kendig, who, as former Professor of English and Dean of the College, and now in his present capacity, has continually demonstrated by word and by deed his enthusiasm for the project; and to

the spirit of Melvil Dewey, whose brilliant system of classification of books in libraries furnished me with the initial inspiration for my book.

To all of these ladies and gentlemen, and to others unnamed, I owe a great debt—and my thanks.

Z. V. H., II

Salem, Virginia

CONTENTS

TO THE USER

This INDEX OF IDEAS was originally intended exclusively for students of English composition and rhetoric at a hypothetical institution unimaginatively but deliberately called *Utopia*. The material in the work was geared to students at all levels and in all branches of education, beginning with high school or preparatory school. Thus, it was hoped, students attending Utopia High and Utopia Prep would find this INDEX useful, as would the students in Utopia's other branches: Utopia Junior College, Utopia College, Utopia Polytechnical Institute, Utopia Seminary, and, finally, the capstone of the system, Utopia University.

This INDEX is still recommended for the students of Utopia. But as the work of compiling it moved from idea to paper, it became apparent that anyone with the compulsion or need to express himself in words should find such an INDEX useful: the businessman asked to give speeches before civic groups; the journalist searching for ideas for feature stories; the clergyman desiring fresh ideas for sermons. In fact, anyone concerned with the written or spoken word should find within the pages of this book stimulating and interesting ideas.

A businessman, for instance, might find suitable topics in sections devoted to ECONOMICS or BUSINESS. The newspaper man or woman might find ideas in the section devoted to the profession of JOURNALISM. The clergyman might find it worth while to consult the sections devoted to RELIGION or PHILOSOPHY. It is perhaps superfluous to point out that Utopia's students, who will one day be businessmen, journalists, clergymen, doctors, lawyers, etc., will also find these subjects of interest. In short, it is hoped that everyone who wishes to express himself in language, written or spoken, will find new subjects to write or speak about in the pages of this INDEX.

INTRODUCTION

In any work involving, theoretically, All Knowledge, one must employ some system of classification if the material contained in the work is to be usable. Accordingly, this INDEX has brazenly borrowed from a system that has proved itself by its use in approximately 95 per cent of the college libraries in the United States: the deservedly famous Dewey decimal system. Published by the ingenious Melvil Dewey in 1876, the *Dewey Decimal Classification* is now in its seventeenth edition.

The Dewey decimal system classifies virtually all human knowledge available in book form, using whole numbers and fractions thereof (decimals), from 000 through 999.99. Within the range of these numbers fall many areas of knowledge, most of them analogous to the fields of interest and concentration of the students at Utopia. In Utopia's library, as in most other libraries in this country, books are arranged according to this classification. Thus an index of ideas can probably be most helpful to the student if it is organized in the same pattern as are the materials he will use in seeking information on his chosen topic.

Words and Ideas

This book contains thirty-four sections based on fields of student interest and the Dewey classification. These range from JOURNALISM (070-079.99) through HISTORY (990-999.99). The first section under each of these general headings is titled "Thought Starters for ANALYSIS." This list contains words and phrases intended to provide germinal ideas for themes ranging in length from short paragraphs to term papers (or even full-length books).

A single word may serve as a thought starter leading in many directions. The word *alimony,* for instance, may suggest such questions as: "Why do women (get, take) alimony?" "Is the custom of alimony anachronistic in modern America?" "Should men receive alimony?"

A thought starter may also consist of more than one word; for instance, the phrase *our blue laws* could suggest the following ideas for an oral or written composition: "Are our blue laws a joke?" "Major effects of our blue laws on our community." An idea for a composition may well be suggested by a clause—e.g., "Why I would like to be a doctor"—or an entire sentence: "Should the United States try to beat Russia to the moon?"

Ideas for prose composition, therefore, begin with words, singly or in combination. This INDEX is an "idea book"—a collection of words to suggest possible topics for writers or speakers. Although it employs rhetorical principles in the arrangement of topics, it is not a handbook of rhetoric.

Let us suppose that a freshman at Utopia, a possible zoology major, is required to write a theme for his English class. Having no specific topic in mind, he turns to the section of this INDEX devoted to his main interest: ZOOLOGY (590-599.99). Starting down the list of Thought Starters, he quickly finds one to his liking: the aardvark. His English instructor, concealing as best he can his own feelings on the subject, remarks, "That's a good topic. But what *about* the aardvark? What is your purpose in writing?"

What about the Aardvark?

At this point the student must call upon his knowledge of rhetoric. If he were allowed to use his imagination, he might write a children's story about a handsome Boy Aardvark who falls in love with a beautiful Girl Aardvark. But chances are that our student's unreasonable English instructor will compel him to concentrate on nonimaginative, factual prose, whether the subject be aardvarks or zymoscopes. The topics in this INDEX, therefore, lend themselves particularly to themes of nonimaginative prose—specifically to themes of Exposition, Argumentation, and Evaluation (more commonly called Criticism).

Kinds of Exposition. The purpose of *Exposition* is to inform or explain. There are various methods that can be used to provide information or explanation. Presented alphabetically, the methods considered in this book are the following:

(1) Analysis
(2) Cause and Effect
(3) Classification
(4) Comparison and Contrast
(5) Definition
(6) Description
(7) Process

In papers of *Analysis* something is usually broken down (or divided or partitioned) into its component parts—as, for example, Julius Caesar divided Gaul into three parts; as a biologist might dissect a frog in a laboratory; as a military strategist might examine a piece of terrain or a map thereof prior to an attack; or as an economist might analyze business cycles.

The second type of Exposition, *Cause and Effect,* is but another form of Analysis—an examination of causes, effects, or both. Generally speaking, causal analysis is concerned with answering the question "Why?" "Why am I failing English?" a student at Utopia wishes to know. A student of history asks, "Why did the Roman Empire decline and fall?"

An analysis of Effects involves consideration of results, as indicated by the following questions: "What were the principal economic effects of the American Civil War?" "What are the major effects of automation—generally; in a particular community?" "What are the major effects of alcoholism—on the alcoholic; on his family; on the community?"

Classification, a third type of Exposition, is in a sense the reverse side of the coin of Analysis. Attempting to satisfy man's passion for the orderly arrangement of knowledge, Classification is concerned with categorizing. The classifier often uses words like *kinds, sorts,* and *types.* Thus the biologist classifies animals and plants; the geologist is concerned with kinds of rocks. Psychologists and sociologists frequently attempt to classify people. Once the classification of anything is established, however, each category is developed by (comparative) analysis.

A fourth type of Exposition referred to in these pages is *Comparison and Contrast,* sometimes called simply comparative analysis. Comparison is generally concerned with similarities; contrast involves differences. Thus the prospective car buyer compares and contrasts automobiles; the economist might compare communism and capitalism as economic systems. One kind of comparison involves things in space, another things in time. Using the first of these, we may compare or contrast "this and that"—e.g., a Ford and a Rolls Royce—or "here and there": Science education in the U.S.A. and in the U.S.S.R. We may also compare and contrast "then and now,"—e.g., an ante-bellum Southern plantation and a modern farm. A special type of comparison, the Analogy, is especially useful in comparing things of different classes which nevertheless have something in common. For example, in the section of this book devoted to ECONOMICS, the student will find under "Comparison and Contrast" the phrase "Bank and mattress." These two seemingly dissimilar objects may be compared and contrasted as depositories for one's savings.

Definition, a fifth type of Exposition, is in many respects the most fundamental of all, for it is involved in almost all forms of writing. Literally, *to define* means "to establish the limits of" something. Hence a dictionary definition of cow sets up limits of meaning so that one will not confuse a cow with a hen. Note that one can define two kinds of words: concrete words and abstract words. Concrete words refer to measurable objects—e.g., *desk, tree, building;* such words are fairly easy to define. But abstract words lacking what are called "referents," virtually defy precise definition—e.g., *beauty, happiness, success, truth.*

A sixth type of Exposition is *Description,* which, as considered in this book, is concerned with objective observation based on one or more of the five senses, usually the sense of sight. For example, a student of criminology or of sociology might choose to describe a jail cell or a tenement. A freshman at Utopia might train his photographic eye by describing his dormitory room or the campus rathskeller. Any object occupying space may be described—whether person, place, or thing: a wanted criminal, the scene of an automobile accident, or a block of ice.

The seventh and final type of exposition, *Process,* is another form of Analysis. Process is concerned with answering the question "How?" In composition the principal types of process can be referred to as the How-to-do-it Process and the How-it-is-done Process. Ordinarily, the How-to-do-it Process involves a process that can be executed with the aid of a few, if any, simple tools—as in the following: "How to change an automobile tire" or "How to give oneself a home permanent."

The How-it-is-done type of Process is usually more complex, involving tools or machinery that the writer or reader does not have easy access to—e.g., "How automobile tires are made" or "How cigarettes are manufactured." A variation on this type of Process involves what might be called natural or physical processes—e.g., "How the ear hears," "How the refrigerator freezes ice," and "How our seasons change."

A more general kind of Process is extremely popular among Americans concerned with self-improvement—e.g., "How to retire," "How to make friends and influence people," and "How to succeed in business without really trying." This type of Process lends itself both to trivial topics and to extremely serious ones—e.g., "How to play tiddlywinks" or "How to secure international peace."

Themes of Exposition, therefore, explain something about some specific topic, whether the method of development be through Cause and Effect, Description, or any of the other methods discussed above.

Argumentation and Evaluation. In addition to the forms of Exposition, two other types of nonimaginative writings are treated in this INDEX: Argumentation and Evaluation. Needless to say, in arguing or evaluating one frequently uses the methods of development considered above. It is chiefly in purpose that these two types of writing differ from Exposition.

Effective *Argumentation* requires the framing of propositions. These may be of two types: (1) Propositions of Fact (or Hypothesis) and (2) Propositions of Policy. A Proposition of Fact usually takes the form of a statement which, the arguer hopes, can be proved by means of evidence. Usually such a proposition is phrased to suggest that something is true, valid, necessary, beneficial, wise, etc. Consider, for instance, the proposition that "Coeducation is conducive to serious study." In order to encourage an open mind and to discourage dogmatism, one may also phrase the proposition as a question: "Is coeducation conducive to serious study?" In this INDEX, propositions are listed in the form of questions.

Whereas the Proposition of Fact seeks primarily to convince a person or to change his mind, the Proposition of Policy usually encourages some form of action. This type of proposition is further distinguished from the Proposition of Fact by the use of a word like *should.* "Should Utopia (abandon, introduce) football?" Should the United States adopt a policy of free—i.e., unrestricted—immigration?"

The final type of nonimaginative discourse provided for in this INDEX is *Evaluation.* The more familiar term *criticism* has been deliberately avoided because of its negative connotations, but the two are essentially synonymous. Evaluation involves judgment. The evaluator sets up standards (criteria) for the ideal or perfect thing, then measures the actual against these standards.

One kind of Evaluation involves the usefulness of a particular object or group of objects, including the facilities of an agency or organization. *Consumer Reports,* for example, evaluates consumer goods: automobiles, frozen foods, clothing, etc. The other kind of Evaluation treated in these pages is the evaluation of policies. The word *policy,* as used here, suggests either a course of action or a method of procedure—e.g., Utopia's admissions policy or the U.N.'s policy regarding membership. Users of this INDEX will find topics ranging from relatively simple objects to policies relating to national, international, and even interplanetary affairs.

English teachers and professors at Utopia will doubtless be quick to observe that topics suited to literary criticism have been omitted. This omission was deliberate. Members of the faculty of Utopia, with its perfect library facilities and its excellent English Department, need no suggestions concerning topics for the evaluation of literature.

Disposing of the Aardvark. Returning to our zoology student, then, we find that there are a number of ways in which he may respond to the question "What *about* the aardvark?"

1. He may *analyze* the animal, in words, more or less as a biologist would—that is, if he has a handy specimen around the house.
2. Employing the method of *cause and effect,* he may explain why the aardvark is important, or harmful, to the people of Africa.
3. Under *classification,* our student may consider kinds of ant-and-termite-eating mammals, including aardvarks.
4. Our student may, by means of *comparison and contrast,* compare the aardvark with one of the better-known anteaters.
5. If our student is asked to write a theme of *definition,* he may confine himself to a simple dictionary-definition of *aardvark,* or he may provide an extended definition.
6. If his purpose is *description,* our aardvark fancier may simply describe the animal's appearance, habits, and so forth.
7. Finally, under *process,* he may consider the aardvark in various ways—e.g., how the aardvark is bred (or exterminated) or how the aardvark uses nature to protect itself.

It should be kept in mind, of course, that this approach to the aardvark, or to any other topic, often involves overlapping. In defining the word *aardvark,* one also classifies and describes the animal.

If our student's fascination with aardvarks becomes overwhelming, he may even engage in heated debate. For example, he may decide to write a theme on one of the following propositions: "Is the aardvark a (useful, useless) animal to African natives?" or "Should the aardvark be (actively bred, exterminated) in Africa?"

Finally, if our student wishes to evaluate the aardvark as an ant or termite exterminator, he has the permission of the author of this book to do so.

Partners in Writing and Speaking

Since the topics presented in this INDEX are merely suggestions, our student should realize the wisdom of frequent consultations with at least three individuals who are in effect partners in this venture: (1) his English instructor, (2) a member of Utopia's library staff, and (3) someone more knowledgeable of his subject than he—e.g., a member of Utopia's Zoology Department, if his subject is aardvarks. His English instructor has an obvious interest in what the student writes; a member of the library staff will be invaluable in helping him find material; and a member of Utopia's Zoology Department may be able to suggest a fresh approach to the topic.

If, unlike our zoology student, one knows exactly what he wants to write about, then he is indeed among the fortunate. In fact, the person who knows what he wants to write or talk about has scant need for this INDEX, which is intended chiefly for persons in and out of school who are not quite sure or who wish to branch out beyond a given subject. Especially is this INDEX recommended for the person who, facing a deadline, is the victim of temporary "thought-amnesia" as he searches, perhaps frantically, for something to write or talk about.

JOURNALISM 070-079.99

Thought Starters for ANALYSIS

What about:

1. Art department
2. Book reviewing
3. Business journalism
4. Business news reporting
5. Canons of journalism
6. Caricatures
7. Cartoons
8. Censorship
9. Chains, journalistic
10. Child-care department
11. Children's department
12. Circulation: newspapers and magazines
13. Club news
14. Columns
15. Comic journalism
16. Comic strips
17. Commercial journalism
18. Communication systems: use in news gathering
19. Control of the press
20. Copy writing
21. Copyreading
22. Correspondents: newspaper and magazine; radio and television
23. Court reporting
24. Crime reporting
25. Defamation
26. Delivery: newspapers and magazines
27. Drama department: radio and television
28. Economics and journalism
29. Editing: newspapers and magazines
30. Editorial departments
31. Editorial rules
32. Editorial staff
33. Editorials
34. Education
35. Employees
36. Ethics in journalism
37. Fashion department
38. Feature articles
39. Fiction department
40. Financial department
41. Financial reporting
42. Food department
43. Foreign correspondents
44. Freedom of the press
45. Gardening department
46. Headlines
47. Homemakers' department
48. House organs
49. Household department
50. Humor department
51. Influence of the press
52. Interpretative journalism
53. Interviewing, journalistic
54. Journalistic writing
55. Journalists, famous
56. Labor costs
57. Laws and regulations: journalism
58. Libel
59. Literary journalism
60. Literature and journalism
61. Local news reporting
62. Location: newspapers; radio and television stations
63. Magazine journalism
64. Management, business
65. Music department
66. Names: newspapers
67. National news reporting
68. News
69. Newsboys
70. Newscasters
71. Newspaper journalism
72. Newspapers
73. Newsstands
74. Ownership of the press
75. Periodical journalism
76. Photography, press
77. Pictorial journalism
78. Political reporting
79. Political science and journalism
80. Press
81. Press bureaus

82. Press releases
83. Press syndicates
84. Printed publications
85. Printing
86. Professional journalism
87. Radio journalism
88. Real estate department
89. Recreation department
90. Reporters
91. Reporting
92. Responsibilities of the press
93. Reviews
94. Science department
95. Science news reporting
96. Sedition
97. Size: newspapers and magazines; radio and television stations
98. Slander
99. Social sciences and journalism
100. Society department
101. Sociology and journalism
102. Sports department
103. Sports reporting
104. Style, journalistic
105. Subscriptions: newspapers and magazines
106. Sunday editions
107. Syndicated news
108. Syndicates: newspaper and magazine
109. Tabloids
110. Technical journalism
111. Telephone: use in news gathering
112. Television journalism
113. Theater and movie reviewing
114. Trade journalism
115. Travel department
116. Women in journalism
117. Women's department

CAUSE and EFFECT

1. Why I (believe in, do not believe in) censorship of the press
2. (Major) Effects of (local, state, federal; private, public) censorship of the press
3. (Major) Effects of the existence of (magazine, newspaper, radio, television) chains--on the news, on the chains themselves, on the public, on "the truth"
4. Why I (like, dislike) a particular (magazine, newspaper) column(ist)
5. Why I (read, do not read) the comics
6. (Major) Effects of control of the press by (private, public; local, state, federal) agencies
7. (Major) Effects of crime upon news--generally, in a particular news medium
8. (Major) Effects of news upon crime
9. Why I consider crime news (deemphasized, overemphasized) by our news media
10. Why I (read, do not read) the editorials appearing in the ________
11. Why I consider the ethics of (magazine, newspaper, radio, television) journalism (commendable, deplorable)
12. Why I (would, would not) like to be a foreign correspondent
13. Why the Fourth Estate is so titled
14. Why I (do, do not) believe in (absolute, limited) freedom of the press
15. (Major) Effects of (absolute, limited) freedom of the press--in peace, in war

16. Why headline writing is important in newspaper publishing
17. (Major) Effects of (sensational, "scare") headlines--on individuals, on groups; on business; on war
18. Why I consider the influence of the press (underrated, overrated)
19. (Major) Effects of (responsible, irresponsible) journalism--generally, locally, on the part of a particular publication
20. Why I (would like to be, could never be) a (journalist, newspaperman, reporter)
21. Why I have a (high, low) opinion of journalistic writing
22. Why I consider the laws and regulations governing (magazine, newspaper, radio, television) journalism (adequate, inadequate; satisfactory, unsatisfactory)--generally, locally
23. Why I consider local news reporting via (newspapers, radio, television) (adequate, inadequate; satisfactory, unsatisfactory)
24. Why I consider national news reporting via (national press services, newspapers, radio or television networks) (commendable, deplorable)
25. (Major) Effects of (responsible, irresponsible) national news reporting via the mass media--generally, locally
26. (Major) Causes of (success, failure) in newspaper publishing
27. (Major Effects of newspapers--on the general public, in a particular community
28. (Major) Effects of a particular section of a newspaper--e.g., the front page--on the reading public
29. Why newspapers publish (pleasant, unpleasant) news
30. Why I believe in (private, public) ownership of the press
31. Why I (commend, deplore) the news reporting done by our (national, international) press bureaus--e.g., A.P., U.P.I.
32. Why radio continues to be an important news medium
33. Why I consider our (local, national) (magazine, newspaper, radio, television) reporters (responsible, irresponsible)
34. Why I consider the press to be (fulfilling, shirking) its responsibilities
35. Why I (read, do not read) the sports page
36. Why I consider the sports reporting of our mass media (laudable, deplorable)
37. Why I (approve, disapprove) of journalistic style
38. Why I (approve, disapprove) of syndicated news
39. Why I (approve, disapprove) of tabloid journalism
40. Why television journalism has (a great, little) obligation (to the networks, to special interests, to the public at large)
41. Why women make (good, poor) journalists
42. Why the women's departments in our (magazines, newspapers) (interest, bore) me

CLASSIFICATION

Kinds/Types of:

1. Cartoons/cartoonists
2. Censorship in journalism
3. Control of the press
4. Copy
5. Ethics in journalism
6. House organs
7. Influence by the press
8. Magazines
9. News
10. Newscasts/newscasters
11. Newspapers
12. Periodicals
13. Photography in journalism
14. Presses
15. Printing/printers/print
16. Reporting/reporters
17. Style, journalistic
18. Syndicates in journalism
19. Women in journalism

COMPARISON and CONTRAST

1. A.P. and U.P.I.
2. Censorship: of the press and by the press
3. Censorship: here and there; yesterday and today--e.g., in the USA and in the USSR
4. The Christian Science Monitor and a sensational tabloid
5. Circulation: of a daily and of a weekly or monthly publication
6. Comic journalism: here and there; yesterday and today--e.g., in America and in Europe
7. Control of the press: here and there; yesterday and today--e.g., in Colonial and modern America
8. Defamation: in law and in journalism
9. Ethics: in journalism; in business; in politics
10. Feature articles: in a "slick" magazine and in a "pulp" magazine
11. Foreign correspondents and domestic correspondents
12. Interpretative journalism and factual reporting
13. Journalism: magazine, newspaper, radio, and/or television
14. Journalism and literature
15. Journalists: male and female
16. Libel and slander in journalism
17. Literary journalism and journalistic literature
18. Business management and labor organizations in journalism
19. News coverage: magazine, newspaper, radio, and/or television
20. A news story: in a local (daily, weekly) newspaper and in a (school, college) newspaper
21. A news story and a feature story
22. Two newspapers
23. The picture and the word in journalism
24. Professional journalism and amateur journalism
25. Printing: offset and letterpress
26. Reporters: in fact and in fiction
27. Responsibilities and privileges of the press
28. Sports department: of a (school, college) paper; of a weekly; of a (small, large) daily

29. Sports reporting: for a weekly and for a daily paper
30. Style: journalistic and literary
31. Writing: journalistic and scholarly

DEFINITION

1. Censorship
2. Defamation
3. Editorializing
4. Fact
5. Freedom of the press
6. Good taste
7. Influence
8. Irresponsible journalism
9. Libel
10. Malice
11. Management of the news
12. News
13. Objectivity
14. Opinion
15. Report
16. Sensationalism in journalism
17. Slander
18. Slanting
19. Yellow journalism

DESCRIPTION

1. The art department, or part thereof, of a newspaper or magazine publisher; of a television station
2. A cartoonist's studio, or part thereof
3. The children's department, or part thereof, of a newspaper or magazine publisher; of a radio or television station
4. The circulation department of a newspaper or magazine publisher
5. A copy desk
6. A courtroom, or part thereof
7. The drama department, or part thereof, associated with a radio or television station
8. An editor's office, or part thereof
9. The food department of a magazine, a newspaper, or a television station
10. A building, or part thereof, of a magazine publisher
11. A building, or part thereof, of a newspaper publisher
12. A photographic laboratory, or part thereof, associated with one of the news media
13. A press used in magazine or newspaper publication
14. The National Press Club, or part thereof
15. A publisher's office, or part thereof
16. The news room of a local radio station
17. A reporter's beat, or part thereof
18. The sports department, or part thereof, of a magazine, a newspaper, or a television station
19. A television station, or part thereof
20. The women's department of a magazine or newspaper publisher, or of a television station

PROCESS

1. How business can (aid, frustrate) the journalist--generally, locally
2. How the journalist can (help, hurt) business--generally, locally
3. How (magazine, newspaper, television) cartoons are made
4. How the press (is censored, censors itself)
5. How to improve (magazine, newspaper) circulation--generally, locally
6. How the press is controlled--generally, locally; at home, abroad
7. How to be an effective correspondent--on a small-town weekly, on a large daily; in a foreign land
8. How to be an effective editor
9. How to improve journalistic ethics
10. How to write a headline
11. How to improve the house organ(s) of the ______ Company
12. How to influence the press
13. How the press influences
14. How to interpret (the news, a feature article, an editorial, a headline)
15. How to conduct an interview
16. How to become a journalist
17. How to (combat, commit) libel in the press
18. How to improve national news reporting
19. How to combat (erroneous, slanted) national news reporting
20. How to make news
21. How to improve our (weekly, daily) newspapers--generally, with reference to a specific newspaper
22. How to (read, misread) a newspaper
23. How newspapers (help, hurt) people
24. How to (handle, mishandle) the press
25. From press to doorstep: the morning or evening paper
26. How to be a good reporter
27. How to be a good sports reporter
28. How to improve journalistic style
29. How to increase (magazine, newspaper) subscriptions--generally, locally
30. How to be a journalist--and a woman (and vice versa)

ARGUMENTATION

PROPOSITIONS OF FACT

1. Is censorship of the press (desirable, undesirable; necessary, unnecessary; wise, unwise)?
2. Is (local, state, federal) control of the press (legal, illegal; desirable, undesirable; wise, unwise)?
3. Is the home delivery of our local newspaper (satisfactory, unsatisfactory)?
4. Can an editor function "without strings"?

5. Are our headline writers (responsible, irresponsible)?
6. Does the press exercise (too much, too little) influence upon the American people?
7. Does interpretation have a place in journalism?
8. Is journalism respectable?
9. Is journalistic writing (literature, trash)?
10. Do minority groups have (no, undue) influence on (newspapers, radio, television)?
11. Is national news reporting by our (magazines, newspapers, radio and/or television networks) (partial, impartial; thorough, superficial)?
12. (Can, Does) any newspaper print "all the news that's fit to print"?
13. Is ________'s newscast (slanted, objective)?
14. Are our local newspapers monopolistic?
15. Is the newspaper a bargain?
16. Is (public, private) ownership of the press (desirable, undesirable; necessary, unnecessary)?
17. Does the press (inform, indoctrinate, brainwash)?
18. Is the press free?
19. What's (right, wrong) with America's press?
20. Do sponsors have undue influence on American (radio, television)?
21. Is objectivity in (magazine, newspaper, radio, television) news reporting (desirable, undesirable; possible, impossible)?
22. Is tabloid a dirty word?
23. Does television in America cater to (depravity, juvenile minds)?
24. Does television journalism serve the cause of (truth, falsehood)?
25. Does the women's department of our local (newspaper, television station) foster (maturity, immaturity)?

PROPOSITIONS OF POLICY

1. Should (magazine and newspaper publishers, radio and television stations) (accept, refuse) advertising for alcoholic beverages?
2. Should the press (be censored, censor itself)?
3. Should our communication systems be nationalized?
4. Should "scare" or inflammatory headlines be banned?
5. Should interpretative journalism be eliminated from radio and/or television newscasts?
6. Should the would-be journalist major in journalism?
7. Should (magazine, newspaper; radio, television) journalists be prosecuted for (intentional, unintentional) libel?
8. Should the news media defer to special interests or groups?
9. Should (radio, television) newscasters (simply give information, editorialize, interpret)?
10. Should reporters be compelled to reveal their sources?
11. Should (radio, television) news programs be sponsored?

OBJECTS

I. The facilities of an agency, firm, or organization devoted to some phase of journalism--for example,
   A. The art department of a magazine or newspaper publisher
   B. The news room of a radio or television station
   C. The photographic laboratory of a newspaper publisher or television station
   D. The facilities, or part thereof, of a journalism school

II. An object useful in some phase of journalism--for example,
   A. A copy desk
   B. A motion picture camera
   C. A newsstand
   D. A press
   E. A press camera
   F. A telephone
   G. A teletype machine
   H. A typewriter

POLICIES

1. A canon of journalism
2. A (local, state, federal) policy regarding censorship of the press
3. A policy of a (magazine, newspaper, radio, television) chain
4. A policy of a (local, state, federal) government regarding control of the press
5. A policy of a (magazine, newspaper, radio, television) correspondent
6. A policy of a (local, state, federal) court regarding the reporting of its operations
7. A policy of a (magazine, newspaper, radio or television station) relating to the reporting of crime
8. A policy of a (magazine, newspaper) editor
9. A policy of the education department of (a magazine or newspaper publisher; a radio or television network)
10. A policy of a house organ
11. A policy of a journalism school
12. A policy of a magazine publisher
13. A policy of a (radio, television) newscaster
14. A policy of a newspaper
15. A policy of a national press bureau
16. A policy of a press syndicate
17. A policy of a radio (station, network) relating to news
18. A policy of a (magazine, newspaper, radio, television) syndicate
19. A policy of a tabloid
20. A policy of a television (station, network)

PHILOSOPHY AND METAPHYSICS 100-129.99
and PHILOSOPHICAL TOPICS 140-149.99

Thought Starters for ANALYSIS

What about:

1. Aesthetics
2. Agnosticism
3. Ancient philosophy (see under 180-189.99)
4. Animism
5. Atomism
6. Automatism: metaphysics
7. Being, nature of
8. Bergsonism
9. Cause and effect: metaphysics
10. Chance: metaphysics
11. Change and motion: metaphysics
12. Choice: metaphysics
13. Cognition: metaphysics
14. Consciousness: metaphysics
15. Comtism
16. Cosmogony
17. Cosmology
18. Cosmos
19. Criticism
20. Death
21. Design: metaphysics
22. Determinism
23. Dialectical materialism
24. Doctrines, philosophical
25. Dualism
26. Dynamism
27. Eclecticism
28. Empiricism
29. Energism
30. Energy: metaphysics
31. Epicureanism
32. Epistemology
33. Eternity
34. Evil
35. Evolution
36. Existence
37. Existentialism
38. Experience: metaphysics
39. Fatalism
40. Fate
41. Force: metaphysics
42. Fourth dimension
43. Freedom
44. Free will
45. Future life
46. Goodness
47. Humanism
48. Idealism
49. Immortality
50. Incarnation
51. Individualism
52. Intellectualism
53. Intuitionism
54. Kantianism
55. Knowledge
56. Liberalism
57. Life
58. Man
59. Materialism
60. Matter
61. Mechanism
62. Medieval philosophy (see under 180-189.99)
63. Mind
64. Modern philosophy (see under 190-199.99)
65. Monism
66. Motion and time: metaphysics
67. Mysticism
68. Naturalism
69. Nature: metaphysics
70. Nihilism
71. Ontology
72. Optimism
73. Pantheism
74. Personalism
75. Personality: metaphysics
76. Pessimism
77. Philosophers

NOTE: Dewey treats separately Ancient and Medieval Philosophy (180-189.99) and Modern Philosophy (190.99), q.v. in the stacks of Utopia's library. See also RELIGION (200-299.99).

78. Philosophy of life, personal
79. Platonism
80. Positivism
81. Power: metaphysics
82. Pragmatism
83. Pre-existence
84. Purpose: metaphysics
85. Rationalism
86. Realism
87. Reality
88. Reincarnation
89. Relativity: metaphysics
90. Romanticism
91. Scholasticism
92. Self
93. Sensationalism
94. Skepticism
95. Sophistry
96. Soul
97. Space: metaphysics
98. Spiritualism
99. Subconscious: metaphysics
100. Subjectivism
101. Symmetry: aesthetics
102. Teleology
103. Time: metaphysics
104. Traditionalism
105. Transcendentalism
106. Transmigration
107. Truth
108. Unconscious: metaphysics
109. Universe
110. Utilitarianism
111. Values
112. Will
113. World
114. Worth

CAUSE and EFFECT

1. Why agnostics don't know
2. Why I am--i.e., exist
3. Why atomic physics is (compatible, incompatible) with atomism
4. Why people crave beauty
5. Why I (believe, doubt)
6. (Major) Effects of dogmatism (on truth; on society)
7. (Major) Effects of fatalism (in war; in a dangerous occupation)
8. Why I (believe, do not believe) in free will
9. Why I consider a future life (likely, unlikely; certain, uncertain)
10. Why people are (good, evil)
11. (Major) Effects of idealism
12. Why I (rely, do not rely) on intuition
13. (Major) Effects of materialism (in the United States; in the Soviet Union)
14. Why naturalism (is, is not) enough
15. Why I consider a firm philosophy of life (necessary, unnecessary; possible, impossible)
16. Why I hold a particular philosophy of life
17. Why pragmatism (is, is not) a satisfactory philosophy of life
18. Why I (believe, cannot believe) in pre-existence
19. Why people have (good, bad) taste
20. Why men seek truth
21. Why utilitarianism (is, is not) a satisfactory philosophy of life
22. Why I believe in the (worth, worthlessness) of (every man, some men)

CLASSIFICATION

Kinds/Types of:

1. Beauty
2. Being
3. Cause
4. Choice
5. Death
6. Evil
7. Existence
8. Experience
9. Freedom
10. Goodness
11. Idealism/idealists
12. Knowledge
13. Liberty
14. Life
15. Materialism/materialists
16. Matter
17. Naturalism/naturalists
18. Philosophy/philosophers
19. Realism/reality
20. Sophists
21. Truth
22. Worth

COMPARISON and CONTRAST

1. Accident and design
2. Aesthetics: in art and in science (e.g., mathematics)
3. Agnostic, atheist, and theist
4. Animism and supernaturalism
5. Automatism and automation
6. Beauty: to the artist; to the lover; to the philosopher
7. Body and soul
8. "Book sense" and common sense
9. Cause: in philosophy and in science
10. Classicism, neoclassicism, and romanticism
11. Consciousness: in metaphysics and in medicine
12. Death and life
13. Death: to the philosopher; to the physician; to the theologian
14. Design: in aesthetics; in metaphysics; in technology
15. Doer and thinker
16. Dualism, monism, and pluralism
17. Empiricism and scholasticism
18. Energy: in metaphysics and in physics
19. Epicureanism and hedonism
20. Evil and goodness
21. Evil: to the philosopher; to the psychiatrist; to the theologian
22. Evolution: in ontology and in science
23. Evolutionism: in biology and in philosophy
24. Existence: before birth and after death
25. Experience: first-hand and vicarious
26. Faith and fact
27. Falsehood and truth
28. Fate: in metaphysics and in naturalism
29. First cause and final cause
30. Force: in metaphysics and in physics
31. Free agency: in biology; in metaphysics; in physics; in psychology; in sociology
32. Free will and predestination
33. Freedom and responsibility

34. Freedom and security
35. Freedom: in philosophy; in political science; in religion
36. Future life: in metaphysics; in science; in theology
37. Healthy doubt and unhealthy doubt
38. Humanism and supernaturalism
39. Idealism and realism
40. Immortality: in nature and in religion; in ontology and in science
41. Instinct and intuition
42. Intuition: masculine and feminine
43. Kantianism and neo-Kantianism
44. Knowledge from books and knowledge from observation and experience
45. Liberty: in metaphysics and in political science
46. Luxury and necessity
47. Man and superman
48. Man and woman
49. Mass: in metaphysics and in physics
50. Materialism and spiritualism
51. Materialism: here and there; yesterday and today--e.g., in the United States and in the Soviet Union
52. Matter: in metaphysics and in physics
53. Mechanism and teleology
54. Metaphysics and physics
55. Mind: animal and human
56. Morality and ethics
57. Motion, change, and time: in metaphysics and in science
58. Mysticism and rationalism
59. Nature: in metaphysics; in religion; in science
60. Number: in metaphysics and in mathematics
61. Pain and pleasure
62. Personality: in philosophy; in psychology; in sociology
63. Philosophers: ancient, medieval, and modern
64. Philosophers: armchair and cracker-barrel
65. Philosophy and religion
66. Philosophy: here and there; yesterday and today
67. Physical beauty and spiritual beauty
68. Physical beauty: here and there; yesterday and today--e.g., in the Orient and in the West
69. Platonism and neo-Platonism
70. Pleasure and happiness
71. Positivism, negativism, and nihilism
72. Power: in metaphysics and in physics
73. Pragmatism: in business and in philosophy
74. Rationalism and sensationalism
75. Reality: in ontology and in science
76. Relativity: in metaphysics and in physics
77. Reliance upon authority and reliance upon experience
78. Scholasticism: ancient, medieval, and modern
79. Self: in metaphysics and in psychology
80. Skepticism: ancient, medieval, and modern
81. Space: in architecture; in metaphysics; in physics
82. Spiritualism: in religion; in philosophy; in occultism

83. Supernaturalism and superstition
84. Taste: here and there; yesterday and today--e.g., among primitive and civilized societies; esoteric and popular
85. Time: in astronomy; in geology; in metaphysics; in theology
86. Truth and beauty
87. Truth: here and there; yesterday and today
88. Values: in metaphysics and in sociology
89. Values: here and there; yesterday and today--e.g., in medieval and modern times; in the Orient and in the West
90. Will: in metaphysics and in sociology
91. Worth: in aesthetics; in metaphysics; in psychology; in sociology

DEFINITION

1. Altruism
2. Classicism
3. Common sense
4. Criticism
5. Destiny
6. Determinism
7. Dogmatism
8. Egoism
9. Error
10. Evidence
11. Existentialism
12. Faith
13. First cause
14. Freedom
15. Happiness
16. Humanism
17. Incarnation
18. Intellectualism
19. Knowledge
20. Liberty
21. Man
22. Mind
23. Mysticism
24. Nature
25. Necessity
26. Neoclassicism
27. Optimism
28. Pantheism
29. Pessimism
30. Philosophers' stone
31. Proof
32. Quiddity
33. Realism
34. Reason
35. Romanticism
36. Science
37. Superstition
38. Teleology
39. Traditionalism
40. Transcendentalism
41. Truth
42. Unity
43. Will
44. Wisdom

DESCRIPTION

I. An article or object which might lead one to engage in philosophical speculation--for example,
   A. A casket
   B. A globe
   C. An infant's crib
   D. A microscope
   E. A telescope
II. A structure, or part thereof, devoted to some aspect of philosophy--for example,
   A. A library
   B. A philosopher's study

PROCESS

1. How to answer the agnostic
2. How to acquire (physical, spiritual) beauty
3. How to strengthen belief
4. How to acquire certainty
5. How to take a chance
6. How to make an intelligent choice
7. How to be a critic
8. How to (explain, face) death
9. How to handle a dogmatist
10. How to be an intelligent eclectic
11. How to (explain, recognize) evil
12. How to justify one's existence
13. How to use freedom
14. How to be good
15. How to recognize goodness
16. How to (lose, secure) one's identity
17. How to be an individual
18. How to (acquire, use) knowledge
19. How to (secure, use) liberty
20. How to enjoy life
21. How to understand man
22. How to combat materialism
23. How to explain mysticism to a nonmystic (e.g., a scientist)
24. How to know oneself
25. How to be (a person, a personality)
26. How to find a satisfactory philosophy of life
27. How to (combat, use) power
28. How to have a purpose in life
29. How to be a true scholar
30. How to be a wise skeptic
31. How to be a true sophisticate
32. How to be genuinely spiritual
33. How to (cultivate, recognize) good taste
34. How to use time wisely
35. How to separate the best from the worst in tradition
36. How to know truth
37. How to know the value of something
38. How to strengthen the will
39. How to acquire wisdom
40. How to save the world
41. How to recognize worth

ARGUMENTATION

PROPOSITIONS OF FACT

1. Are agnostics misguided?
2. Do animals have souls?
3. Does beauty lie (chiefly, only) in the eye of the beholder?

4. Is beauty only skin deep?
5. Is beauty truth (and vice versa)?
6. Does the body matter?
7. Is the body evil?
8. Does a sound body make a sound mind (and vice versa)?
9. Can common sense be cultivated?
10. Is common sense enough?
11. Can one be too critical?
12. Is death (a beginning, the end)?
13. Is there virtue in dogmatism?
14. Does organized religion (encourage, discourage) dogmatism?
15. Is doubt wrong?
16. Is empirical knowledge enough?
17. Is Epicureanism enough?
18. Is eternity eternal?
19. Does evil pay?
20. Is evil an illusion?
21. Is experience always the best teacher?
22. Is faith enough?
23. Is fatalism a satisfactory philosophy of life?
24. Is man master of his fate?
25. Is flesh evil?
26. Is God good?
27. Does goodness pay?
28. Is hedonism a satisfactory philosophy of life?
29. Are Americans (naively, realistically) idealistic?
30. Is ignorance bliss?
31. Is immortality desirable?
32. Is immortality an illusion?
33. Must individualism be rugged?
34. Do Americans (resent, respect, suspect) intellectualism?
35. Are women more intuitive than men?
36. Is knowledge always power?
37. Is there life (before birth, after death)?
38. Is man naturally depraved?
39. Is man born free?
40. Is man God's noblest work?
41. Is man born good?
42. Is man a prelude to a superman?
43. Does man have free will?
44. Are (Americans, Russians) excessively materialistic?
45. Do all men want freedom?
46. Can the philosophy of naturalism be refuted?
47. Is nature (indifferent, kind, malevolent) to man?
48. Is necessity always the mother of invention?
49. Can the philosophy of nihilism be justified?
50. Is a philosophy of (optimism, pessimism) justified in the modern world?
51. Is organized religion necessary?
52. Is pragmatism "the philosophy of America"--generally, in business?
53. Is rationalism enough?
54. Does it pay to tell the truth?

55. Is truth absolute, relative?
56. Is virtue its own reward?
57. Is the will free?
58. Is ours the best of all possible worlds?

PROPOSITIONS OF POLICY

1. Should Utopia (hire, fire) an agnostic?
2. Should death be (accepted, feared, welcomed)?
3. Should men strive actively to abolish all evil from the world?
4. Should (the United States, the United Nations) use force to free the enslaved peoples of the world?
5. Should the individual (ever, never) compromise with his ideals?
6. Should man strive for "all knowledge"?
7. Should one "eat, drink, and be merry"?
8. Should man seek to (conquer, live with) nature?
9. Should pantheism become the world religion?
10. Should Utopia require a course in philosophy for graduation?
11. Should man strive to conquer (inner, outer) space?
12. Should Utopia offer a course in taste?
13. Should man (flaunt, respect) tradition?
14. Should man strive to know the secrets of the universe?
15. Should man attempt to impose his will on others?

EVALUATION

OBJECTS

1. An object generally associated with death--e.g., a coffin
2. An object associated with both good and evil--e.g., a gun
3. An object customarily associated with goodness--e.g., a fireplace
4. An object customarily associated with the preservation of human life--e.g., a pulmotor
5. An object or article of furniture sometimes associated with philosophical speculation--e.g., a rocking chair, a pipe
6. A useful object thought to be in good taste--e.g., an article of clothing, a piece of furniture, an automobile
7. An article of value--e.g., an antique

POLICIES

1. A policy of a (local, regional, state, national) philosophical organization or society--e.g., the American Philosophical Society
2. A particular philosophy (see "Thought Starters")
3. (A, My) philosophy of life
4. A course established or proposed by Utopia's philosophy department

BRANCHES OF PSYCHOLOGY AND PSEUDOPSYCHOLOGY 130-139.99 and GENERAL PSYCHOLOGY 150-159.99

Thought Starters for ANALYSIS

What about:

1. Ability
2. Abnormal psychology
3. Adaptability
4. Adolescence
5. Adulthood
6. Alcoholism
7. Animal psychology
8. Antisocial compulsions
9. Applied psychology
10. Aptitude tests
11. Aptitudes
12. Association of ideas
13. Astrology
14. Behavior, animal
15. Behavior, human
16. Behavioristic psychology
17. Brainwashing
18. Child psychology
19. Choice
20. Clinical psychology
21. Cognition
22. Combat neuroses
23. Comparative psychology
24. Complexes: psychoanalysis
25. Conation and feeling
26. Consciousness
27. Daydreams
28. Delinquency
29. Depth psychology
30. Developmental psychology
31. Differential psychology
32. Disabled children
33. Divination
34. Dreams
35. Drives
36. Dynamic psychology
37. Educational psychology
38. Emotions
39. Environmental psychology
40. Eroticism
41. Ethnopsychology
42. Evolutional psychology
43. Exhibitionism
44. Experimental psychology
45. Fatigue
46. Fear
47. Fetishism
48. Fortunetelling
49. Functional psychology
50. Genetic psychology
51. Genius
52. Gerontology
53. Gestalt psychology
54. Ghosts
55. Gifted children
56. Graphology
57. Habits
58. Hallucinations
59. Handedness
60. Haruspication
61. Heredity and intelligence
62. Hippocrates' theory of temperaments
63. Homosexuality
64. Horoscopes
65. Hypnotism
66. Hypochondriasis
67. I.Q.
68. Imagination
69. Incentive
70. Infant psychology
71. Insanity
72. Insomnia
73. Instinct
74. Intelligence
75. Intuition
76. Kleptomania
77. Language and thought
78. Learning

NOTE: See also such related fields as SOCIOLOGY (301-309.99), SOCIAL WELFARE (360-369.99), EDUCATION (370-379.99), MEDICINE (610-619.99), and others

79. Locomotion
80. Magic
81. Magicians
82. Manias
83. Maturity
84. Memory
85. Mental health
86. Mental illness
87. Mental tests
88. Mesmerism
89. Mind-reading
90. Motivation
91. Motives
92. Neuroses
93. Nightmares
94. Numerology
95. Objective psychology
96. Occult sciences
97. Old age
98. Omens
99. Palmistry
100. Paranoia
101. Parapsychology
102. Pathological psychology
103. Perception
104. Personality
105. Phobias
106. Phrenology
107. Physiognomy
108. Physiological psychology
109. Practical psychology
110. Primitive man
111. Problem children
112. Pseudopsychology
113. Psychoanalysis
114. Psychological schools and systems
115. Psychological tests
116. Psychological typology
117. Psychologists
118. Psychology of the aged
119. Psychology of personality
120. Psychology of the sexes
121. Psychotherapy
122. Puberty
123. Rational psychology
124. Reasoning
125. Retarded children
126. Rorschach personality tests
127. Satanism
128. Schizophrenia
129. School children
130. Sensation
131. Sexual deviation
132. Sleep
133. Social pressures and mental health
134. Somnambulism
135. Speech disorders
136. Spiritualism
137. Stammering and stuttering
138. Stanford-Binet tests
139. Structural psychology
140. Subjective psychology
141. Suicide
142. Symbolism: psychoanalysis
143. Telepathy
144. Temperament
145. Thought
146. Volition
147. Will
148. Witchcraft
149. Work
150. Youth
151. Zodiac

CAUSE and EFFECT

1. Why (adolescents, adults, children) act as they do
2. (Major) Effects of adoption--on the adopted child; on the foster parents
3. Why people age
4. Why (men, women; husbands, wives) become alcoholics
5. Why some people are (ambidextrous, left-handed, right-handed)
6. Why people act like (animals, human beings)
7. Why people (do, do not) pay attention
8. Why people (behave, misbehave)

9. (Major) Effects of brainwashing on mental health--of individuals; of groups, as in Red China
10. Why people have (complexes; compulsions; fixations; phobias)
11. (Major) Causes of (adult, juvenile) delinquency
12. (Major) Effects of (physical, mental) disability--in children; in adults
13. Why people dream--during the day; at night
14. Why people drink
15. Why (men, women) (display, do not display) their emotions
16. (Major) Effects of (release, suppression) of emotions
17. (Major) Effects of environment on (intelligence, motivation, personality)
18. (Major) Effects of eroticism on the mass media
19. (Major) Causes of exhibitionism--among children; among adolescents; among adults
20. (Major) Causes of fatigue--among men; among women
21. (Major) Causes of fetishism--in primitive cultures; in civilized societies
22. Why geniuses (should, should not) be judged according to ordinary standards of conduct
23. (Major) (Causes, Effects) of a guilt complex--among Christians; among non-Christians; in a nation
24. (Major) Effects of a physical handicap on mental health
25. (Major) Effects of heredity on (behavior, intelligence, personality)
26. (Major) Causes of homosexuality--among men; among women
27. (Major) Causes of hysteria among (single, married) women
28. Why some people (have, do not have) inhibitions
29. (Major) Effects of inhibitions on (behavior, personality)
30. (Major) Effects of institutionalization--e.g., in a mental institution or in an orphanage--upon (those institutionalized; administrators)
31. (Major) Effects of (environment, heredity, race, sex) on intelligence
32. (Major) (Causes, Effects) of jealousy--among children; among adults
33. (Major) Causes of kleptomania
34. Why people (learn, do not learn)
35. (Major) Effects of (too much, too little) love on personality
36. Why love (destroys, preserves)
37. Why some people are incapable of (loving, being loved)
38. Why people have (good, poor) memories
39. (Major) Causes of mental cruelty
40. (Major) Causes of (high, low) motivation--e.g., among school children; among adults
41. Why motives (are, are not) often hidden
42. (Major) Effects of old age on (behavior, intelligence, personality)
43. Why problem children are problems
44. Why people are psychoanalyzed

45. Why I have (great, little) faith in psychological tests
46. Why psychology interests me
47. (Major) Causes of pyromania
48. (Major) Effects of race on (behavior, intelligence, personality)
49. Why race differences are (meaningful, meaningless)
50. Why people act (rationally, irrationally)
51. Why God gave man the power to (reason, think)
52. Why school children (like, dislike) school
53. Why people smoke
54. (Major) Causes of (stammering, stuttering)
55. Why people commit suicide
56. Why people are superstitious
57. Why man thinks
58. (Major) Effects of thought control on mental health
59. Why a girl becomes a tomboy
60. (Major) Effects of war on mental health
61. Why women (do, do not) act like women
62. Why people (work, loaf)
63. Why youth (must; should not) be served

CLASSIFICATION

Kinds/Types of:

1. Ability
2. Abnormality
3. Addiction/addicts
4. Aptitude tests
5. Aptitudes
6. Animal/human behavior
7. Brainwashing
8. Cognition
9. Complexes
10. Conflicts
11. Consciousness
12. Drives
13. Imagination
14. Immaturity
15. Inferiority
16. Inhibitions
17. Insanity
18. Instincts
19. Intelligence
20. Intelligence tests
21. Learners/learning
22. Mania
23 Maturity
24. Memory
25. Mental cruelty
26. Mental disorders
27. Mental tests
28. Motives
29. Neuroses/neurotics
30. Occultism
31. Perception
32. Personality
33. Phobias
34. Psychoanalysis/psychoanalysts
35. Psychological tests
36. Psychologists/psychology
37. Psychoses/psychotics
38. Reflexes
39. Sensation
40. Temperament
41. Traits
42. Volition

COMPARISON and CONTRAST

1. Ability: among individuals; in men and in women
2. Abnormality and normality
3. Adaptability: of primitive and of modern man; of animal and of human; of men and of women

4. Age and youth
5. Alcoholic and social drinker
6. Alcoholism: among men and women; among different social classes
7. Aptitudes: among individuals; between the sexes; among different social classes
8. Astrologer and astronomer
9. Attention: among children and adults; between the bright and the not-so-bright
10. Behavior: animal and human; primitive and civilized; normal and abnormal
11. Brainwashing and indoctrination
12. Childhood: first and second
13. Clairvoyance and intuition
14. Comprehension: among age groups (infants, children, adolescents, adults, the aged); between the sexes
15. Consciousness and unconsciousness
16. Delinquency: among children, adolescents, and adults
17. Divining rod and Geiger counter
18. Drives: biological and psychological
19. Electra complex and Oedipus complex
20. Emotions: among the races; between the sexes
21. Environment and heredity
22. Exhibitionism: acceptable and unacceptable
23. Extrovert and introvert
24. Exorcism and psychiatry
25. Free will: in psychology; in philosophy; in religion
26. Free will and predestination
27. Genius and moron
28. Geomancy, astrology, and/or numerology
29. Handedness: left, right, and ambidextrous
30. Homosexuality: in male and in female
31. Hypochondriasis: in male and in females
32. Idiots, imbeciles, and morons
33. Illusion and reality
34. Imagination and reason
35. Imagination: among animals and among human beings; among men and among women
36. Immaturity and maturity
37. Inferiority and superiority
38. Inhibitions: desirable and undesirable; among age groups; between the sexes; between primitive and civilized people
39. Insanity and sanity
40. Instinct and intuition
41. Intelligence and memory
42. Intelligence: among individuals; between the sexes; between primitive and civilized people
43. Intuition: masculine and feminine
44. Kleptomaniac and thief
45. Knowledge and wisdom
46. Learning from books and learning by experience and observation
47. Love and hate
48. Love: among animals and among human beings

49. Love and instinct
50. Mania, compulsion, and phobia
51. Memory and understanding
52. Memory: among animals and among human beings
53. Motivation: between the bright and the not-so-bright; among the races; between the sexes; between different social classes
54. Motives: masculine and feminine; real and apparent
55. Natural/Physical sciences and occult sciences
56. Neuroses and psychoses
57. Passion: in men and in women; in primitive and civilized people
58. Physician and witch doctor
59. Pity: in men and in women
60. Preconscious, subconscious, and unconscious
61. Preference and prejudice
62. Pseudopsychology and psychology
63. Psychologist and psychiatrist
64. Psychology: of boys and girls; of men and women; of children and adults
65. Quackery: in occultism and in medicine
66. Reliability and validity in psychological tests
67. Rote learning and conceptual learning
68. Satanism and Christianity
69. Sickness and sin
70. Sin: in psychology; in religion
71. Subjective psychology and objective psychology
72. Thought control: in education; in the mass media
73. Will and instinct
74. Work and play

DEFINITION

1. Amnesia
2. Animal magnetism
3. Apparition
4. Black magic
5. Brain
6. Catharsis
7. Compulsion
8. Conditioning
9. Cruelty
10. Delirium tremens
11. Deviation
12. Dipsomania
13. ESP
14. Ego
15. Epilepsy
16. Feeblemindedness
17. Feeling
18. Freedom
19. Guilt complex
20. Humours
21. Hysteria
22. Id
23. Imagery
24. Inhibition
25. Jealousy
26. Judgment
27. Libido
28. Masochism
29. Morality
30. Norms
31. Nymphomania
32. Poltergeist
33. Primitivism
34. Psyche
35. Psychosomatic
36. Sadism
37. Sin
38. Split personality
39. Sublimation

DESCRIPTION

1. A crystal ball
2. A divining rod
3. A piece of equipment used in a psychological experiment
4. An institution, or part thereof, devoted to psychological experiments
5. A home for the aged, or part thereof
6. A mental hospital or sanitarium, or part thereof
7. The office of a psychoanalyst
8. The setting of a séance
9. A piece of equipment used in administering an aptitude or intelligence test
10. A piece of equipment used in testing sensation or perception (hearing, tasting, etc.)

PROCESS

1. How (ability, aptitude) is determined
2. How to cure absentmindedness
3. How (animals, human beings) adapt to their environments
4. How to cure alcoholism
5. How to (acquire, sublimate, use) animal magnetism
6. How to (subdue, treat) antisocial compulsions
7. How aptitude tests are (used, misused)
8. How astrology originated
9. How to help backward children go forward
10. How to cure bed-wetting
11. How biology affects (behavior, intelligence, personality)
12. How the body influences the mind (and vice versa)
13. How to understand (boys, girls; men, women)
14. How the brain functions
15. How people are brainwashed
16. How to make the right (choice, decision)
17. How to improve community services for mental health--generally; locally
18. How to (acquire, lose) a complex
19. How to make daydreaming constructive
20. How to (help, understand) delinquents
21. How physical disease affects mental health
22. How to interpret dreams
23. How to (understand, treat) drug addiction
24. How to (display, control) one's emotions
25. How environment affects mental health
26. How to treat the epileptic
27. How to combat (physical, mental) fatigue
28. How fatigue affects mental health
29. How to tell fortunes--e.g., with cards; by palmistry
30. How we grow (physically, mentally, spiritually)
31. How to (nourish, starve) a guilt complex
32. How to cultivate good habits
33. How to understand the handicapped

34. How heredity affects (behavior, intelligence, personality)
35. How to behave like a human being
36. How hypnotism (helps, hinders) mental health
37. How to treat hypochondria
38. How to live (with, without) an imagination
39. How incentive is killed--e.g., among school children
40. How to treat (an inferiority, a superiority) complex
41. How to understand (infants, children, adolescents, adults)
42. How to live (with, without) inhibitions
43. How to treat insomnia
44. How to (cultivate, recognize) intelligence
45. How to (pass, fail) an intelligence test
46. How to treat kleptomania
47. How to acquire (knowledge, wisdom)
48. How we learn
49. How to learn (with, without) books
50. How to promote maturity
51. How to improve one's memory
52. How to combat mental cruelty
53. How to promote mental health
54. How to treat mental illness
55. How to motivate (school children, workers)
56. How to cure nail-biting
57. How the nervous system functions
58. How to (enjoy, live with, understand) old age
59. How to develop one's personality
60. How to cure a phobia
61. How to interpret bumps in phrenology
62. How a physical incapacity affects mental health
63. How to help problem children solve their problems
64. How to (pass, fail) a psychological test
65. How one of the five senses functions
66. How to explain sex (to a young child, to an adolescent)
67. How psychologists explain sin
68. How to stop (smoking, drinking)
69. How to stop snoring--in oneself; in others
70. How to cure (stammering, stuttering)
71. How we think
72. How to cure thumb-sucking
73. How to understand (oneself, others)
74. How to strengthen the will

ARGUMENTATION

PROPOSITIONS OF FACT

1. Can animals (reason, think)?
2. Are aptitude tests (reliable, unreliable; meaningful, meaningless)?
3. Is character a result of (design, fate)?
4. Are children naturally (good, bad)?

5. Is conscience (a reliable, an unreliable) guide for human conduct?
6. Are delinquent (children, adults) to blame?
7. Are there significant psychological differences between (the races, the sexes)?
8. Are dreams (meaningful, meaningless)?
9. Is ESP bunk?
10. Do (evil, good) spirits exists?
11. Does man have free will?
12. Is genius one tenth inspiration and nine tenths perspiration?
13. Are geniuses (born, made)?
14. Is (heredity, environment) of (major, minor) importance in determining (behavior, intelligence, personality)?
15. Can human (behavior, intelligence, personality) be (controlled, predicted)?
16. Are inhibitions (beneficial, harmful; necessary, unnecessary)?
17. Are intelligence tests (reliable, valid)?
18. Is intuition (a reliable, an unreliable) guide to (action, behavior, conduct)?
19. Are women (more, less) intuitive than men?
20. Can anyone learn anything?
21. (Can, Does) love conquer all?
22. Is everyone capable of (loving, being loved)?
23. Does an elephant have a (good, poor) memory?
24. Is a (good, bad) memory (acquired, inherited)?
25. (Can, Do) men and women really understand each other?
26. Are mental tests (reliable, valid)?
27. Is occultism a science?
28. Are psychological tests (reliable, valid)?
29. Is psychology a science?
30. Is man (a rational, an irrational) animal?
31. Is suicide an act of (courage, cowardice)?
32. Is thought (a blessing, a curse)?
33. Are the American people the victims of thought control (in education; in the mass media)?
34. Are women naturally (inferior, superior) to men?

PROPOSITIONS OF POLICY

1. Should abnormal (adults, children) be kept at home, institutionalized)?
2. Should adopted children be told?
3. Should (backward, superior) children be segregated in our schools?
4. Should boys and girls be taught separately in our (schools, colleges)?
5. Should brainwashed ex-servicemen be (hospitalized, tried for treason)?
6. Should children be "seen and not heard"?
7. Should parents be "pals" to their children?
8. Should the parents of delinquent children be (punished, held liable for the misdeeds of their offspring)?

9. Should one marry a genius?
10. Should a genius marry?
11. Should illegitimate children be discriminated against (in law, by society)?
12. Should intelligence tests be required by law before (entering school; applying for a job, applying for a driver's license; marriage; running for public office; voting; making a will)?
13. Should primitive emotions be (released, repressed) by civilized (man, woman)?
14. Should psychological tests be required before one (goes to school; marries; gets a job; seeks public office)?
15. Should (reason, instinct) be the final guide in human (behavior, conduct)?
16. Should school children be (segregated, integrated) on the basis of (ability, race, religion, sex)?
17. Should women court men--obviously?
18. Should all (men, women, children) work--in the home; outside the home?
19. Should youth be served (before, at the expense of) age?

EVALUATION

OBJECTS

I. Equipment used in the study or practice of psychology or psychotherapy--for example,
   - A. A piece of equipment used in a mental institution--e.g., a strait jacket
   - B. A piece of equipment used in a psychological test or experiment--e.g., a maze; a Skinner box
   - C. A piece of equipment used in testing perception or sensation

II. Facilities of an institution or organization engaged in the promotion of mental health or devoted, directly or indirectly, to some aspect of psychology--for example,
   - A. An institution devoted to the treatment of alcoholism
   - B. A mental hospital
   - C. A corrective school
   - D. Utopia's psychology department

POLICIES

A policy in effect or proposed by an agency, institution, or organization--local, state, or federal; public or private--devoted to some aspect of mental health or to psychology or pseudopsychology--for example,

- A. A policy of a local adoption agency
- B. A policy of a local children's home or orphanage
- C. A policy of a (local, regional, national) Psychological Association
- D. A policy of Utopia's psychology department
- E. A policy of a local sanitarium

ETHICS 170-179.99

Thought Starters for ANALYSIS

What about:
1. Adultery
2. Alcoholic beverages
3. Altruism
4. Amusements
5. Animal fighting
6. Animals, cruelty to
7. Authoritarian ethics
8. Behavior
9. Betting
10. Bullfighting
11. Business ethics
12. Caste
13. Celibacy
14. Charity
15. Chastity
16. Cheating
17. Children, cruelty to
18. Chivalry
19. Christian ethics
20. Church and state
21. Cockfights
22. Comic strips
23. Conduct of life
24. Conscience
25. Continence
26. Conversation, social
27. Corruption, political
28. Courtesy
29. Courtship
30. Dancing
31. Dice games
32. Disarmament
33. Discrimination
34. Divorce
35. Dog racing
36. Drug addiction
37. Dueling
38. Duties, political
39. Duty
40. Egoism
41. Entertainment
42. Espionage
43. Ethical theories
44. Euthanasia
45. Evolutionary ethics
46. Fair play
47. Family ethics
48. Gallantry
49. Gambling in business
50. Gambling games
51. Games
52. Golden Rule, the
53. Graft, political
54. Happiness
55. Hedonism
56. Heroism
57. Honesty
58. Hospitality
59. Humane societies
60. Intemperance
61. International relations
62. Liberty of conscience
63. Lotteries
64. Loyalty, political
65. Modesty
66. Morality
67. Morals
68. Moral philosophy
69. Motion pictures
70. Nagging
71. Narcotics
72. Obscenity
73. Pacifism
74. Philanthropy
75. Pleasure
76. Politeness
77. Political ethics
78. Pornography
79. Prejudice
80. Pride
81. Prize fighting
82. Profanity
83. Professional ethics
84. Prohibition
85. Prostitution
86. Public officials
87. Pugilism
88. Racial discrimination
89. Racing
90. Recreation
91. Revolution, political
92. Right and wrong
93. Roulette
94. Salacious art and literature

95. Segregation
96. Sexual ethics
97. Smoking
98. Social drinking
99. Social ethics
100. Sportsmanship
101. State ethics
102. Success
103. Suicide
104. Swearing
105. Tax payment
106. Television programs
107. Temperance
108. Theater
109. Tolerance
110. Truth
111. Vanity
112. Vices
113. Virtues
114. Vivisection
115. War
116. Wrestling

CAUSE and EFFECT

1. Why our state abortion laws (need, do not need) changing
2. Why (men, women) commit adultery
3. Why our (local, state, federal) laws pertaining to the (manufacture, sale, use) of alcoholic beverages (need, do not need) changing
4. (Major) Effects of the (manufacture, sale, consumption) of alcoholic beverages--generally; locally
5. Why I consider Sunday amusements (proper, improper)
6. Why I (approve, disapprove) of ethical codes based upon authority
7. Why people bet
8. Why I consider our community blue laws (beneficial, harmful)
9. (Major) Effects of the (strict, loose) enforcement of community blue laws
10. Why our state (needs, does not need) revised regulations governing boxing
11. Why I (applaud, deplore) business ethics--generally; in a particular business
12. Why I consider card playing (moral, immoral)--generally; on Sundays
13. Why I consider social caste in America (right, wrong; avoidable, unavoidable)
14. Why I (give, do not give) to charity
15. Why I consider chivalry (dead, dying, still alive) in modern America
16. Why I consider Christian ethics (vital, archaic) in the modern world
17. Why I (approve of, disapprove of) cigarette smoking
18. Why I consider many comic strips (moral, immoral)
19. Why compromise is (good, bad; right, wrong; moral, immoral)
20. (Major) Causes of political corruption--generally; in (local, state, federal) politics
21. Why I consider dancing (moral, immoral)
22. Why I consider discrimination based on (ability, income, race, religion, sex) (good, bad; moral, immoral; right, wrong)
23. Why our state divorce laws (need, do not need) changing

24. Why (men, women, adolescents, children) dress as they do
25. Why I consider the dress habits of our (men, women, adolescents, children) (good, bad; right, wrong; moral, immoral)
26. Why I consider our (state, federal) laws relating to drug addiction (good, bad; moral, immoral; right, wrong)
27. Why I consider euthanasia (moral, immoral; right, wrong)
28. Why I (approve of, disapprove of) the concept of free love
29. Why I consider gambling (moral, immoral; right, wrong)
30. Why I consider the Golden Rule (a possible, an impossible) ideal
31. (Major) Causes of political graft--generally; in local, state, national politics
32. Why Americans (belittle, worship) heroes
33. Why honesty (is, is not) the best policy
34. Why I consider our state's laws governing horse racing (good, bad; moral, immoral)
35. Why we (need, do not need) a national lottery
36. Why our state laws governing marriage (need, do not need) revision
37. Why people are (moral, immoral, amoral)
38. Why I consider motion pictures (a good, a bad) influence on public morality
39. (Major) Effects of motion pictures on public morality--generally; locally
40. Why I consider pacifism (good, bad; moral, immoral; right, wrong)
41. (Major) Effects of universal peace--internationally; nationally; locally
42. Why I have (a high, a low) opinion of political ethics
43. Why people have prejudices
44. Why I have (a high, a low) opinion of professional ethics (in what profession(s)?
45. Why I (consider, do not consider) state laws regarding prostitution in need of revision
46. Why right is right
47. Why I consider (racial, religious, sexual) segregation (good, bad; moral, immoral; right, wrong)
48. Why I consider the sexual ethics of our society (good, bad; moral, immoral; right, wrong)
49. Why sin appeals
50. Why our (local, state, federal) tax laws (encourage, discourage) immorality
51. Why I consider our television programs (good, bad; moral; immoral)
52. (Major) Effects of (too much, too little) tolerance
53. Why wrong is wrong

CLASSIFICATION

Kinds/Types of:
1. Behavior
2. Bigotry/bigots
3. Caste
4. Courage
5. Cruelty

6. Discrimination
7. Ethics
8. Graft/grafters
9. Happiness
10. Honesty
11. Justice
12. Loyalty
13. Modesty
14. Prejudice
15. Pride
16. Sin(s)
17. Tolerance/toleration
18. Vanity
19. Vice(s)
20. Virtue(s)
21. Wrong(s)

COMPARISON and CONTRAST

1. The ethics of abortion: here and there; yesterday and today--e.g., in the United States and in a foreign country
2. Adultery: to the man of God and to the social scientist
3. The ethics of alochol: here and there; yesterday and today--e.g., in ancient, medieval, and modern times
4. Amorality, immorality and morality
5. Amusements: Christian and non-Christian; civilized and uncivilized
6. Animal fighting and prize fighting
7. Art: salacious and "pure"
8. Blue Laws: here and there; yesterday and today--e.g., in Puritan and in modern America
9. The ethics of boxing: here and there; yesterday and today--e.g., in ancient Rome and in modern America
10. The ethics of card games: for fun and for profit.
11. Social caste: here and there; yesterday and today--e.g., in India and in Russia
12. The ethics of chastity: here and there; yesterday and today; among men and among women
13. Cheating: in business; in school; in marriage; in politics; etc.
14. Chivalry: here and there; yesterday and today--e.g., in Medieval England and in modern America
15. Chivalry: in theory and in practice
16. Christian ethics and non-Christian ethics
17. Christian ethics: in theory and in practice
18. Civility: between men and women; among men; among women; between youth and age
19. Class ethics: lower, middle, and upper
20. Compromise: right and wrong
21. Conscience: among Christians and among non-Christians; in primitive and civilized societies
22. Conversation: at home and in business; at a hen party and at a stag party; before marriage and after marriage
23. Corruption: in politics and in business
24. The ethics of dancing: here and there; yesterday and today--e.g., in primitive and modern societies
25. The ethics of divorce: here and there; yesterday and today--e.g., among Christians and among non-Christians
26. The ethics of dress: here and there; yesterday and today--e.g., in ancient, medieval, and modern times

27. Duty: to oneself; to one's family; to one's country
28. Duty: to oneself and to God
29. The ethics of espionage: by one's own country and by an enemy country
30. Ethics: business and political and/or professional
31. Exposure, personal: decent and indecent
32. Fair play: in love and war
33. Family ethics: in ancient, medieval, and modern times; in primitive and civilized societies
34. Filial duties: here and there; yesterday and today--e.g., in Europe and in America
35. Gambling: on Wall Street and in Reno
36. Graft: honest and dishonest
37. Heroism: here and there; yesterday and today--e.g., in ancient Greece or Rome and in modern America
38. Honesty: in business; in politics; in government; in the professions
39. Integration: by force and by persuasion
40. The ethics of international relations: here and there; yesterday and today; during the age of Napoleon and today
41. Political loyalty: here and there; yesterday and today--e.g., in the United States and in Russia or Communist China
42. Lust and love
43. The ethics of marriage: in Christian and non-Christian lands; in ancient, medieval, and modern times; among primitive and civilized peoples
44. Modesty: false and true
45. Morals: of animals and of primitive peoples; of the leisure class and of the working class; of the sexes
46. Moral law and natural law
47. The ethics of pleasure: here and there; yesterday and today--e.g., among Christians and among non-Christians
48. Pride: sinful and commendable
49. Pornography and art
50. Prostitution: legal and illegal
51. Sexual ethics: here and there; yesterday and today--e.g., in ancient, medieval, and modern times; among primitive and civilized societies
52. The ethics of sportsmanship: here and there; yesterday and today--e.g, in the ancient and modern Olympic Games
53. Success: here and there; yesterday and today; e.g., in the Orient and in the West
54. The ethics of suicide: in the Orient and in the West
55. The ethics of war: in ancient, medieval, and modern times; among primitive and civilized societies; before and after the A-bomb

DEFINITION

1. Amorality
2. Casuistry
3. Class
4. Compromise

5. Ethics
6. Evil
7. Freedom
8. Goodness
9. Graft
10. Honor
11. Integrity
12. Justice
13. Loyalty
14. Sin
15. Wrong

DESCRIPTION

1. A store, or part thereof, selling alcoholic beverages
2. A local amusement park, or part thereof
3. An enclosure, or part thereof, devoted to animal fighting (e.g., bulls, cocks)
4. A local boxing arena, or part thereof
5. Headquarters, or part thereof, of a local charity
6. A local dance hall, or part thereof
7. A pair of dice
8. A track where dog racing takes place
9. A weapon used in dueling
10. A fairgrounds, or part thereof
11. A gambling casino, or part thereof
12. A gaming table
13. Headquarters, or part thereof, of a local humane society
14. A lawyer's office, or part thereof
15. A prize fighter's dressing room, or part thereof
16. A race track, or part thereof
17. Racing stables, or part thereof
18. A sporting goods store, or part thereof
19. Local headquarters, or part thereof, of the Women's Christian Temperance Union
20. A local theater, or part thereof
21. A tobacco warehouse, or part thereof
22. A wrestling arena, or part thereof

PROCESS

1. How to improve our abortion laws
2. How to improve (local, state, federal) laws or regulations governing (manufacture, sale, use) of alcoholic beverages
3. How to combat betting--generally; locally
4. How to (enforce, live with) local blue laws
5. How to be ethical in business
6. How to improve business ethics--generally; locally
7. How to (eliminate, control) social caste in the United States
8. How to make Christian ethics work--in a Christian country; in a non-Christian country
9. How to combat the harmful effects of the comics
10. How to compromise--and still keep one's principles
11. How to be a good conversationalist

12. How to (deal with, eliminate) political corruption--generally; locally
13. How to discriminate (intelligently, unintelligently)
14. How to improve our divorce laws
15. (How, How not) to drink
16. How to be ethical--and successful
17. How ethics evolved
18. How to hear, see, and speak no evil
19. How to obey the Golden Rule
20. How to be good--and have fun
21. How to (find, recognize) happiness
22. How to (secure, eliminate, clean up) horse racing--generally; in our state
23. How to promote voluntary (racial, religious, sexual) integration--generally; in our community
24. How to love wisely and well
25. How to distinguish between love and lust
26. How to improve (public, private) morals or morality--generally; locally
27. How to improve the morality of our motion pictures
28. How to be an ethical politician
29. How to (detect, combat) pornography
30. How to combat the evils of prize fighting--generally; locally
31. How to promote professional ethics (In what professions?)
32. How to combat the evils of prostitution--generally; locally
33. How to eliminate social rank in the United States
34. How to distinguish right from wrong
35. How to stop smoking
36. How to improve our television programs
37. How to obey the Ten Commandments
38. How to improve the morality of the theater
39. How to be tolerant
40. How to (recognize, tell) the truth
41. How to inculcate a sense of values

ARGUMENTATION

PROPOSITIONS OF FACT

1. Do our (local, state, federal) laws relating to the (manufacture, sale, use) of alcoholic beverages (encourage, discourage) immorality?
2. Are Sunday amusements (good, bad; moral, immoral; right, wrong)?
3. Is animal (e.g., bull, cock) fighting (good, bad; moral, immoral; right, wrong)?
4. Are our (local, regional) blue laws (good, bad; right, wrong)?
5. Is professional boxing "organized murder"?
6. Can a successful businessman also be a good Christian?

7. Is capital punishment (right, wrong; moral, immoral; good, bad)?
8. Is a caste system in the United States (good, bad; right, wrong; avoidable, unavoidable)?
9. Is chivalry (dead, vital) in modern America?
10. Are Christian ethics feasible in a Communist world?
11. Does everyone have a conscience?
12. Does courtesy pay?
13. Is the art of courtship (dead, still alive) in modern America?
14. Is dancing (moral, immoral)?
15. Is discretion the better part of valor?
16. Is discrimination on the basis of (ability, income, race, religion, sex) (good, bad; moral, immoral; right, wrong)?
17. Is divorce (moral, immoral; right, wrong)?
18. Is the double standard of morality--one for men, one for women--(good, bad; moral, immoral; right, wrong)?
19. Do women dress (for men, for other women)?
20. Is free love free?
21. Is free love love?
22. Is gallantry old-fashioned?
23. Is horse racing (good, bad; moral, immoral; right, wrong)?
24. Is modesty (natural, unnatural)?
25. Is morality (absolute, relative)?
26. Are American motion pictures (good, bad; moral, immoral)?
27. Is nature (moral, immoral, amoral)?
28. Can one love his neighbor as himself?
29. Is pride (a sin, a virtue)?
30. Is a classless society (possible, impossible, desirable, undesirable) in modern America?
31. Does television in America contribute to the (morality, immorality) of the people?
32. Are the Ten Commandments (vital, old-fashioned)?
33. Is the American theater (moral, immoral)?
34. Can one be too tolerant?
35. Is truth (relative, absolute)?
36. Is all fair in love and war?

PROPOSITIONS OF POLICY

1. Should salacious (art, literature) be removed from news and magazine stands?
2. Should professional boxing be abolished--generally; in our state?
3. Should Christian ethics be revised?
4. Should indecent shows be barred from our carnivals and circuses?
5. Should indecent or "horror" comic strips be banned from magazine and newsstands?
6. Should dancing be abolished at church functions?
7. Should adolescents be taught at home to drink alcoholic beverages?

8. Should the double standard of morality be abolished?
9. Should a couple "go dutch"?
10. Should euthanasia be legalized?
11. Should our state (legalize, outlaw) gambling?
12. Should our state (legalize, outlaw) horse racing?
13. Should our state legalize lotteries?
14. Should loyalty oaths be mandatory as a requirement for (public, private) (employment, tenure)?
15. Should marriage be made hard, divorce easy, to obtain?
16. Should suggestive newspaper advertising for motion pictures be outlawed?
17. Should pornographic material be removed from (news and magazine stands, libraries)?
18. Should professional men and women--doctors, lawyers, etc.--advertise?
19. Should prostitution be legalized in the United States?
20. Should Utopia require courses in sex education for graduation?
21. Should persons who commit suicide be denied Christian burials?
22. Should the (stocks, whipping post) be reinstated?
23. Should television programs be censored in the interest of public morality?

EVALUATION

OBJECTS

I. Equipment usually associated with ethical conduct--i.e. with right and wrong:
   A. An article used in boxing--e.g., gloves
   B. An article used in playing cards--e.g., a card table
   C. An article of use to a cigar, cigarette, or pipe smoker--e.g., a can of tobacco; a lighter
   D. An article used in gambling--e.g., a roulette wheel
   E. An article used in racing--e.g., a sports car
   F. An article of use in conducting a war--e.g., an H-bomb

II. Facilities of a business or organization engaged, directly or indirectly, in matters pertaining to ethics or matters of right and wrong--for example,
   A. Facilities of an amusement park
   B. Facilities of a gambling casino
   C. Facilities of a local church
   D. Facilities of a local horse-racing establishment
   E. Facilities of a local theater

POLICIES

A policy of an establishment, institution, or organization relating to ethical conduct--for example,
   A. A policy, in effect or proposed, of the local Better Business Bureau

B. A policy of a (local business, church, community) relating to blue laws
C. A church's policy on celibacy
D. A policy of Christian ethics--e.g., turning the other cheek
E. A policy embodied in the Hippocratic oath
F. The honor system of a school or military academy
G. A policy of a local or national racial organization--e.g., the Ku Klux Klan, the Black Muslims
H. A policy of a temperance organization--e.g., the WCTU
I. One of the Ten Commandments

RELIGION 200-299.99

Thought Starters for ANALYSIS

What about:
1. Amish churches
2. Ancestor worship
3. Angels
4. Anglican churches
5. Animal worship
6. Ante-Nicene church
7. Anthems
8. Antiquities, Biblical
9. Apocalypses
10. Apocrypha: Bible
11. Apostles
12. Apostles Creed
13. Archeology, Biblical
14. Arminianism
15. Art: Christian ecclesiology
16. Asceticism
17. Atheism
18. Augustinians
19. Baptism
20. Baptist churches
21. Bazaars, church
22. Beatitudes
23. Bel and the dragon
24. Bible: authorship
25. Bible as literature
26. Biblical characters
27. Book of Common Prayer
28. Brahmanism
29. Brotherhoods, monastic
30. Buddhism
31. Burial rites
32. Business and Christian religion
33. Calvinist churches
34. Campbellite churches
35. Capitalism and Christian religion
36. Christ, Jesus
37. Christian church
38. Christian doctrines
39. Christian life
40. Christianity
41. Christology
42. Chronology, Biblical
43. Church administration
44. Church history
45. Church of Christ, Scientist
46. Church of England
47. Church of Jesus Christ of Latter-Day Saints
48. Church of the Brethren
49. Church and state
50. Civilization and Christianity
51. Classical religion and mythology
52. Clergy
53. Communism and Christianity
54. Comparative religions
55. Confucianism
56. Cosmogony and cosmology
57. Creation
58. Crusades
59. Death
60. Deism
61. Democracy and Christianity
62. Demonology
63. Demoninations
64. Dietary laws: judaism
65. Disciples of Christ churches
66. Divinity
67. Douay Bible
68. Druidism
69. Dunkards
70. Ecclesiology
71. Economic problems and Christianity
72. Ecumenical councils
73. Education, Christian
74. Ethics, religious
75. Evangelism
76. Evil
77. Fall of man
78. Free thought
79. Free will
80. Freedom of man
81. Freedom of religion
82. Friends, Society of (Quakers)
83. Funerals

84. Future life
85. Geography, Biblical
86. Germanic mythology and religion
87. God(s)
88. Good
89. Gospels
90. Heaven
91. Hebrew religion
92. Hell
93. Heresies
94. Hinduism
95. Holy Family
96. Hussites Christian church
97. Icons
98. Immortality
99. Indian (American) religion
100. Inquisition
101. Islam
102. Jainism
103. Jehovah's Witnesses
104. Jesuits
105. Judaism
106. Judgment, Last
107. King James Bible
108. Koran
109. Latter-Day Saints Church
110. Liberty of conscience
111. Magi
112. Mahomet
113. Man
114. Mariology
115. Marital problems and Christianity
116. Marriage rites
117. Mary, Virgin
118. Mazdaism
119. Mecca
120. Mennonite Church
121. Missions, foreign
122. Mithraism
123. Mohammedanism
124. Monasteries
125. Monophysite churches
126. Moravian Church
127. Mormon Church
128. Mosaic law
129. Moslems, religion of
130. Natural religion
131. Nestorian Church
132. Non-Christian religions
133. Norse religion and mythology
134. Oriental Christian churches
135. Origin of man
136. Original sin
137. Pacifism and Christianity
138. Pantheism
139. Parseeism
140. Phallicism
141. Predestination and free will
142. Presbyterian churches
143. Primitive Christian churches
144. Protestantism
145. Psuedepigrapha
146. Psychology of religion
147. Puberty rites
148. Puritanism
149. Race relations and Christianity
150. Reformations
151. Religious art
152. Religious education
153. Religious festivals
154. Religious wars
155. Revised Standard Bible
156. Roman Catholic Church
157. Sacraments
158. Saints
159. Salvation Army
160. Science and religion
161. Science and the Bible
162. Second coming
163. Sects
164. Seminaries, theological
165. Seventh Day Adventist Church
166. Shaker churches
167. Shintoism
168. Sin
169. Sisterhoods
170. Slavery and Christianity
171. Socialism and Christianity
172. Socinianism
173. Socioeconomic problems and Christianity
174. Soul
175. Statuary, religious
176. Sunday
177. Swedenborgian Church

178. Symbolism, religious
179. Taboos
180. Taoism
181. Theism
182. Unitarian Church
183. Universalist Church
184. Virgin birth
185. War and Christianity
186. YMCA/YWCA
187. Young people's Christian groups
188. Zoroastrianism

CAUSE and EFFECT

1. Why people (are, become) atheists
2. (Major) Effects of the Bible on my life
3. Why I (would like to, could never) belong to a monastic (brotherhood, sisterhood)
4. Why I (wish, do not wish) to be (buried, cremated) when I die
5. Why churchmembers "backslide"
6. (Major) Effects of business (capitalism) on Christianity
7. (Major) Effects of Christianity on business (capitalism)
8. (Major) Effects of Christianity on some phase of American life--e.g., recreation, sex
9. Why I (am, am not) a Christian
10. (Major) Effects of (Communism, socialism) on Christianity
11. Why I (go, do not go) to church
12. Why I (belong to, do not care to belong to) the ________ Church
13. Why people violate (any one of) the Ten Commandments
14. Why people become conscientious objectors
15. Why man has a conscience
16. Why the Dead Sea Scrolls are important
17. Why I (believe in, do not believe in) denominational religion
18. Why I (like, detest) the Devil
19. Why the Jews have dietary laws
20. Why I consider divorce (consistent, inconsistent) with Christianity
21. (Major) Effects of Christianity on education
22. Why evil exists
23. Why foreign missions are (desirable, undesirable; necessary, unnecessary)
24. Why I (am, am not) a free-thinker
25. Why Christian funeral customs (are, are not) barbaric
26. Why I (believe in, do not believe in) God
27. Why I (believe in, do not believe in) the Immaculate Conception
28. Why I (believe, do not believe) in the immortality of man
29. Why God is invisible
30. Why I (gladly accept, cannot accept) Jesus Christ as my personal savior
31. Why I (accept, reject) the concept of ministerial authority
32. Why I (would, would not) like to be a minister

33. Why I (would, would not) like to be a minister's (wife, child)
34. Why I (believe in, do not believe in) foreign missions
35. (Major) Effects of foreign missions--on Christianity; on the missionaries; on those ministered to
36. Why the Mormon Church (practised, abandoned) polygamy
37. Why I (believe in, do not believe in) the concept of Original Sin
38. Why I (accept, do not accept) the doctrine of papal infallibility
39. Why I (believe in, do not believe in) parochial schools
40. Why people (pray, do not pray)
41. Why people need religion
42. Why I consider the qualifications for the clergy (adequate, inadequate)--generally; in my church
43. (Major) Causes of antagonism between science and religion
44. (Major) Effects of science on religion
45. Why people sin
46. Why Sunday School (does, does not) appeal to me
47. Why my church considers (smoking, drinking, dancing) taboo
48. Why I consider the Ten Commandments (timeless, outdated)
49. Why I consider the unity of all Christians (desirable, undesirable; necessary, unnecessary; possible, impossible)
50. Why I (did, did not; would like to, would not like to) join the (YMCA, YWCA, YMHA, YWHA)

CLASSIFICATION

Kinds/Types of:

1. Angels
2. Art, religious
3. Authority/authorities
4. Charity
5. Charlatans
6. Christians
7. Church government
8. Churches
9. Churchgoers
10. Clergymen
11. Congregations
12. Death
13. Discrimination (in the church)
14. Evidence (of God)
15. Evil
16. Faith
17. Freedom
18. Good/goodness
19. Grace
20. Hell
21. Heretics/heresy
22. Idols/idolatry
23. Love
24. Prayer(s)
25. Puritans
26. Religion
27. Religious orders
28. Sin(s)/sinners
29. Taboos, religious
30. Temptation
31. Truth

COMPARISON and CONTRAST

1. African religion: primitive and modern
2. Amusements: Sunday and weekday--generally; locally

3. Anglo-Saxon law and Hebraic law
4. Bible and Koran
5. Bible: Revised Standard Version and King James Version
6. Burial rites, Christian and non-Christian
7. Religion in business and business in religion
8. Christianity in communism and communism in Christianity
9. Creation: Genesis and geology
10. Death: in religion and in science
11. Depravity in Christian doctrine vs. depravity in naturalism
12. Economics: in the Bible and on Wall Street
13. Election: in religion and in politics
14. The end of the world: according to the Bible and according to science
15. Eve and Mary
16. Evil: in ancient, medieval, and/or modern times
17. Faith and knowledge
18. Free will and predestination
19. Genesis and genetics
20. God's view of man and man's view of God
21. Group religion and private religion
22. Heaven: as a place and as a state of mind
23. Heaven: in Christian doctrine and in other religions
24. Hell: as a place and as a state of mind
25. Images: Christian and pagan
26. Joseph and Mary
27. Life after death in Christian doctrine and in non-Christian religions
28. Lord's Day and man's day
29. Divine love and human love
30. Mahomet/Mohammed and Christ
31. Marriage rites: in and out of Christianity
32. Mythology and religion
33. Original sin and original innocence
34. Puritanism: in Old and New England
35. Purpose: divine and human
36. The right to believe and the right not to believe
37. The Jewish Sabbath and the Christian Sunday
38. Salvation: via self and via God
39. Satan and God
40. Sin: to the minister, to the physician, and/or to the psychiatrist
41. Sin: to the Christian and to the non-Christian
42. Socialism in Christianity and Christianity in socialism
43. Symbolism: Christian and pagan
44. Unpardonable sin and pardonable sin
45. World's end: to the theologian and to the scientist

DEFINITION

1. Authority
2. Blasphemy
3. Brotherhood
4. Death
5. Disestablishmentarianism
6. Eternity

7. Evil
8. Faith
9. Freedom
10. Fundamentalism
11. Good
12. Grace
13. Heathen
14. Heresy
15. Idolatry
16. Immortality
17. Infallibility
18. Liberty
19. Limbo
20. Myth
21. Predestination
22. Salvation
23. Sin
24. Superstition
25. Truth
26. Wisdom

DESCRIPTION

I. A useful or ornamental article or object associated with some phase of religion, Christian or non-Christian, past or present--for example;
   A. An altar
   B. A baptismal font
   C. A coffin
   D. A pulpit
   E. A statue of a religious figure
   F. A tomb or tombstone

II. Facilities of an institution or organization associated, directly or indirectly, with religion--for example;
   A. Facilities of a church
   B. Facilities of a funeral home
   C. Facilities of a monastery or convent
   D. Facilities of a parochial school
   E. Facilities of a seminary
   F. Facilities of a Sunday School

III. A building or other structure, or part thereof, devoted to some phase of religion--for example;
   A. A Buddhist temple
   B. A cathedral, or part thereof
   C. A minister's study
   D. A mosque
   E. A Quaker meeting-house, or part thereof
   F. A synagogue
   G. The Taj Mahal

PROCESS

1. How archaeology aids the theologian
2. How saints are beatified
3. How to (interpret, misinterpret) the Bible
4. How to conduct a vacation Bible school
5. How to put on a church bazaar
6. How to know Christ
7. How to lead a Christian life
8. How to join the right church
9. How to make money for one's church
10. How to make an article of church furniture

11. How churches (gain, lose) members
12 How civil government (interferes with, protects) religion
13. How various denominations select their clergymen
14. How Christianity (aids, thwarts) communism
15. How to explain death to a child
16. How to prepare for death
17. How ecumenical councils function
18. How to find evidence of God in nature
19. How to explain evil in the world
20. How to strengthen one's faith (within, without) the church
21. How to promote freedom of religion (within, without) the church
22. How to give to the church
23. How to find God (within, without) the church
24. How to do good
25. How to love one's neighbor as oneself
26. How to become a minister
27. How to interest young men in entering the ministry
28. How Popes are chosen
29. How to be a good pastor
30. How to improve race relations in our churches
31. How to reconcile religion and science
32. How to reconcile religious freedom and Christianity
33. How God reveals himself
34. How the Salvation Army saves
35. How to achieve salvation (within, without) the church
36. How to recognize sin
37. How to improve (Sunday, Sabbath) School--generally; locally
38. How religious taboos originated
39. How torture has been used in the Christian church
40. How to achieve Christian unity
41. How to worship (in private, in public)
42. How to improve the local YMCA

ARGUMENTATION

PROPOSITIONS OF FACT

1. Are Sunday amusements--e.g., bowling, card-playing, etc.--sinful?
2. Is the Bible the Word of God?
3. Is vacation Bible school (beneficial, superfluous)?
4. Am I my brother's keeper?
5. Can one succeed in business and remain a true Christian?
6. Is capitalism reconcilable with Christianity?
7. Does charity begin (at home, abroad)?
8. Are children the primary purpose of a (Christian) marriage?
9. Is Christ the Son of God?
10. Is Christianity the only way to salvation?

11. Do organized churches (enslave, liberate) mankind?
12. Is there evidence of God in nature?
13. Does Christianity (encourage, discourage) freedom of religion?
14. Are Christian funeral rites (Christian, barbaric)?
15. Is God (evil, good, jealous, just, perverse)?
16. Is Christian church government (autocratic, democratic)?
17. Does God help those who help themselves?
18. Are Kosher laws obsolete?
19. Do missionaries serve (a beneficial, a harmful) purpose?
20. Are modern versions of the Bible "perversions"?
21. Are all non-Christians damned?
22. Is personal religion enough?
23. Is man (perfect, perfectible)?
24. Should prayer be (allowed, required) in our public schools?
25. Are the qualifications for our clergy (adequate, inadequate)--generally; in our church?
26. Is religion "the opiate of the people"?
27. Does religious education educate?
28. Is salvation possible for non-Christians?
29. Does science (confirm, deny) the existence of God?
30. Is man born in sin?
31. Is Sunday made for man or for God?
32. Are Sunday Schools (worthwhile, worthless)?
33. Is unification of Catholic and Protestant churches desirable, undesirable; possible, impossible)?
34. Do our churches discriminate against women?
35. Is the worship of nature enough?

PROPOSITIONS OF POLICY

1. Should (agnostics, atheists) be allowed to teach at Utopia?
2. Should children in our church(es) be required to learn the catechism?
3. Should chapel attendance at Utopia be (optional, required)?
4. Should Christians spread the Gospel among peoples in other lands who do not actively seek the Word?
5. Should our church(es) be (given, denied) the responsibility of sex education for the young?
6. Should our church(es) accept "tainted money" (e.g., money contributed by a whiskey distiller)?
7. Should our church(es) advertise?
8. Should clergymen be paid for doing the Lord's work?
9. Should a clergyman have an eight-hour day, with time-and-a-half for overtime?
10. Should a college education be required for all clergymen?
11. Should one send flowers at funerals?
12. Should our church(es) (abandon, promote) foreign missions?
13. Should gambling--e.g., bingo games--be (encouraged, discouraged) in our church(es)?

14. Should everyone be his own interpreter of the Bible?
15. Should (priests, monks, nuns) be allowed to marry?
16. Should rank be abolished in the ministry of our church(es) in the interest of democracy and equality?
17. Should a person who commits suicide be (given, denied) a Christian burial?
18. Should all Protestant churches unite?
19. Should Christians go to war?
20. Should women become ministers?

EVALUATION

OBJECTS

I. Facilities of an institution or organization engaged in the practice, promotion, or study of religion--for example,
   A. Facilities of a church or other place of worship
   B. Facilities of a school or college chapel
   C. Facilities of a convent
   D. Facilities of the local YMCA

II. An object useful in the practice of promotion of religion--for example,
   A. A translation of the Bible
   B. A collection plate
   C. A Communion vessel
   D. A confessional
   E. A hymnal
   F. An organ
   G. A clergyman's vestments

POLICIES

Evaluation of a policy, in effect or proposed, of an agency, institution, or organization devoted to the practice, promotion, or study of religion regarding one of the following:

Abortion	Marriage
Adultery	Missions
Birth control	Prayer
Blood transfusions	Ritual
Censorship	Sacraments
Dancing	Salvation
Divorce	Science
Drinking	Sex
Euthanasia	Sin
Evolution	Smoking
Funerals	War
Gambling	Women

SOCIOLOGY 300-309.99

Thought Starters for ANALYSIS

What about:
1. Adolescents
2. Adultery
3. Age groups
4. Anti-Semitism
5. Assimilation
6. Automation
7. Bastardy
8. Beliefs, cultural
9. Bionomics
10. Career women
11. Caste
12. Censorship
13. Child Development
14. Childhood
15. Cities
16. City planning
17. Classes, social
18. Cliques
19. Companionate marriage
20. Competition
21. Compromise
22. Conflict
23. Control, social
24. Counseling, marriage
25. Courtship
26. Crowds
27. Cultural sociology
28. Culture
29. Dating
30. Degeneration
31. Demography
32. Discrimination
33. Divorce
34. Domestic relations
35. Ecology
36. Economic and social planning
37. Engagement
38. Environmental sociology
39. Ethnic groups
40. Evolutional sociology
41. Family
42. Fashion movements
43. Gangs
44. Gerontology
45. Group behavior
46. Habits
47. Home life
48. Homosexuality
49. Human relations
50. Husband-wife relationship
51. Illegitimacy
52. Indians, American
53. Industrialization
54. Institutions, social
55. International planning
56. Jews
57. Leadership
58. Longevity
59. Loyalty, group
60. Male role in society
61. Malthusian theory
62. Marital relations
63. Marriage
64. Mass communication
65. Mate selection
66. Middle age
67. Migrations, human
68. Minorities
69. Miscegenation
70. Mobs
71. Monogamy
72. Mores
73. Motherhood
74. National planning
75. Nomads
76. Old age
77. Parent-child relationship
78. Parenthood
79. Pathology, social
80. Planned communities
81. Polygamy
82. Population
83. Prejudice
84. Premarital relations

NOTE: See also such related fields as SOCIAL WELFARE (360-369-99), EDUCATION (370-379.99), CUSTOMS and FOLKLORE (390-399.99), and others

85. Pressure groups
86. Propaganda
87. Prostitution
88. Public opinion
89. Race discrimination
90. Race relations
91. Racial minorities
92. Rank, social
93. Reform movements
94. Regional planning
95. Retirement
96. Revolutionary movements
97. Riots
98. Rumor
99. Rural sociology
100. Segregation
101. Senescence
102. Sexes, roles of
103. Slavery
104. Social change
105. Social discrimination
106. Social dynamics
107. Social ecology
108. Social evolution
109. Social problems
110. Social psychology
111. Social sciences
112. Society
113. Sociologists
114. Suburban sociology
115. Taboos
116. Technology and family life
117. Technology and social change
118. Traditions
119. Trial marriage
120. Urban sociology
121. Urbanization
122. Women
123. Youth groups

CAUSE and EFFECT

1. Why I (approve of, disapprove of) reservations for our American Indians
2. (Major) Effects of automation--on business and industry; on labor; on society at large--generally; locally
3. (Major) Effects of the practice of birth control--on the principals involved; on society at large
4. (Major) Causes of broken homes
5. (Major) Effects of the career woman--on herself; on her family; on a community's economics; on society
6. Why I (approve of, disapprove of) censorship as a means of social control (kinds of censorship?)
7. (Major) Effects of the centralization of population--generally; locally
8. Why cities (grow, die)
9. (Major) Causes of class conflict--generally; locally
10. Why I (believe in, do not believe in) class distinctions
11. Why I (believe in, do not believe in) companionate marriage
12. (Major) Causes of social conflict--generally; locally
13. (Major) Causes of (adult, juvenile) delinquency
14. Why people discriminate
15. Why I (approve of, disapprove of) divorce
16. (Major) Effects of divorce--on the principals involved; on their families; on society
17. Why I (approve, disapprove) of the double standard
18. (Major) Effects on the employment of women (outside of home)--on women themselves; on their families; on society
19. Why people go in for fads

20. (Major) Effects of feminism--on women; on men; on children; on society in general
21. (Major) Causes of homosexuality
22. Why I consider income (a valid, an invalid) basis for discrimination
23. (Major) Effects of industrialization on the family--generally; locally
24. (Major) Causes of infidelity (among men, among women)
25. Why Americans (are, are not) "anti-intellectual"
26. Why (leaders, followers) are necessary to society
27. (Major) Effects of too much (leading, following) on society
28. (Major) Causes of longevity
29. Why I (consider, do not consider) ours a man's world
30. Why men discriminate against women
31. (Major) Effects of mixed marriages--on husband and wife; on children; on society at large
32. Why I consider monogamy (moral, immoral; natural, unnatural)
33. Why our church (approves, disapproves) of planned parenthood
34. Why pressure groups pressure
35. (Major) Effects of retirement--on the person(s) retired; on a family; on society at large
36. Why I (believe in, do not believe in) compulsory retirement
37. (Major) Causes of suicide
38. Why I (approve of, disapprove of) trial marriages
39. (Major) Effects of urbanization on the family
40. Why wives go astray
41. Why women work (outside the home)

CLASSIFICATION

Kinds/Types of:

1. Aristocrats/aristocracy
2. Class conflict
3. Communities
4. Conformity/conformists
5. Discrimination
6. Fads/faddists
7. Groups
8. Prejudice
9. Pressure groups
10. Propaganda
11. Status/status seekers
12. Taboos, sociological

COMPARISON and CONTRAST

1. The American family and the (African, Asian, European) family
2. American Indians: in fact and in fiction
3. Aristocracy: here and there; yesterday and today--e.g., in America, and in Europe
4. Birth control and death control
5. Brainwashing and indoctrination

6. Careers for women: here and there; yesterday and today--e.g., in the United States and in the Soviet Union
7. Caste: here and there; yesterday and today--e.g., in Africa and in India
8. Class distinction: here and there; yesterday and today--e.g., in ancient, medieval, and modern times
9. The Colonial American family and the modern American family
10. The Colonial American (husband, wife) and the modern American (husband, wife)
11. Courting customs: here and there; yesterday and today--e.g., in America and in a foreign country
12. Culture and civilization
13. Domestic service: here and there; yesterday and today--e.g., in America and in Europe
14. Factory system: here and there; yesterday and today--e.g., in nineteenth-century England and in modern France
15. Fad and fashion
16. Fads: here and there; yesterday and today--e.g., in eighteenth-century France and in modern America
17. Family customs: here and there; yesterday and today--e.g., in a primitive and in a civilized society
18. Feminism vs. femininity
19. A house and a home
20. Husband-wife relationship: here and there; yesterday and today--e.g., in ancient (Greece, Rome) and in modern America
21. Man's role in the family: here and there; yesterday and today--e.g., in nineteenth- and twentieth-century America
22. Mass demonstrations and tantrums
23. Mate selection: among humans and among animals
24. Minorities in America and minorities in (Asia, Africa, Europe, Russia)
25. Nomads: in America and abroad
26. Parent-child relationship: in America and abroad--e.g., in (China, Japan)
27. Prejudice and preference
28. Prejudice: among white and among non-whites
29. Racial discrimination: in the United States and in the Union of South Africa
30. Slavery: here and there; yesterday and today--e.g., in ancient Greece and in the nineteenth-century South
31. Social evolution and social revolution
32. Status symbols: lower class; middle class; and/or upper class
33. (Racial, religious, social, sexual) taboos: here and there; yesterday and today--e.g., in primitive and in civilized societies

DEFINITION

1. Change
2. Civilization
3. Class
4. Collectivism
5. Conformity
6. Cooperation
7. Culture
8. Custom
9. Ecology
10. Equality
11. Ethnology
12. Eugenics
13. Fad
14. Family
15. Feminism
16. "Group-think"
17. Heredity
18. Heritage
19. Incompatibility
20. Indoctrination
21. Matriarchy
22. Maturity
23. Mores
24. Myth
25. Normality
26. Ostracism
27. Patriarchy
28. Patriotism
29. Popularity
30. Preference
31. Propaganda
32. Responsibility
33. Right(s)
34. Status
35. Success
36. Value(s)

DESCRIPTION

An area, enclosed or open, associated with the interaction of people or groups of people--for example,

A. A classroom
B. A clinic
C. A community center, or part thereof
D. A factory, or part thereof
E. A home for the aged or disabled
F. A jail, or part thereof
G. An orphanage, or part thereof
H. An Indian reservation, or part thereof
I. A slum or tenement

PROCESS

1. How to live (with, without) the <u>aged</u>
2. How to live with <u>automation</u>
3. How homes are <u>broken up</u>
4. How to choose a <u>career</u>
5. How to handle (one's own; the neighbors') <u>children</u>
6. How <u>cities</u> (grow, decay)
7. How to eliminate <u>class conflict</u>
8. How society compels <u>conformity</u>
9. How to curb (adult, juvenile) <u>delinquency</u>
10. How to eliminate <u>discrimination</u> based on (money, race, religion, sex, other)
11. How to be an individualist in a <u>group</u>
12. How to improve <u>human relations</u>--generally; locally
13. How to keep up with the <u>Joneses</u>
14. How to make the <u>Joneses</u> think you're ahead

15. How to promote group loyalty
16. How machinery affects social change
17. How to (curb, promote) mass demonstrations
18. How mobility affects the family
19. How to (improve, destroy) our neighborhood
20. How society ostracizes an individual
21. How to (influence, combat) public opinion
22. How to combat (economic, racial, religious, sexual, social) prejudice
23. How to eliminate racial discrimination
24. How to improve race relations--generally; in our community
25. How to retire
26. How to eliminate slums--generally; in our community
27. How to plan a town
28. How urbanization affects the family--generally; in my city
29. How war affects the family

ARGUMENTATION

PROPOSITIONS OF FACT

1. Is abortion (defensible, indefensible)?
2. Is our state's age-of-consent law (just, unjust; reasonable; unreasonable)?
3. Is alimony a racket?
4. Are American Indians "second-class citizens"?
5. Is an aristocracy (compatible, incompatible) with American democracy?
6. Is automation (a blessing, a curse)?
7. Is neighborhood "block-busting" (fair, unfair; just, unjust; legal, illegal)?
8. Is censorship (a legitimate, an illegal) method of social control?
9. Are our state's laws regulating child labor (necessary, unnecessary; sensible, foolish)?
10. Do we give our children (too few, too many) (privileges, responsibilities)?
11. Is society (fair, unfair) to illegitimate children?
12. Is a classless society (desirable, undesirable; possible, impossible)?
13. Is the common man too "common"?
14. Are Americans blind conformists?
15. Is equal opportunity (possible, impossible) in the United States?
16. Is the family becoming obsolete in the United States?
17. Are Americans "group-thinkers"?
18. Is woman's place (in, outside) the home?
19. Are Americans anti-intellectual?
20. Are leaders (born, made)?
21. Is every adult fit for (marriage, parenthood)?
22. Is (man, woman) naturally (monogamous, polygamous)?

23. Can mate selection be made scientific?
24. Is planned parenthood (moral, immoral; wise, unwise)?
25. Is human progress inevitable?
26. Is legalized prostitution (desirable, undesirable; moral, immoral)?
27. Are the sexes equal?
28. Are American teen-agers maligned?
29. Are Americans (contemptuous of, slaves to) tradition?
30. Do women belong (at home; in business; in the professions)?
31. Does youth (rule, ruin) America?
32. Is the worship of youth--i.e., the determination to stay young--in America (laudable, deplorable)?

PROPOSITIONS OF POLICY

1. Should adolescents be allowed to (buy alcoholic beverages, drive automobiles, marry, vote)?
2. Should aged relatives be (cared for at home, institutionalized)?
3. Should American Negroes be given a state of their own?
4. Should capital punishment be abolished?
5. Should class distinctions be eliminated in the United States?
6. Should the United States cooperate with (communist, socialist) countries?
7. Should parents be held legally responsible for the delinquency of their children?
8. Should all forms of discrimination be outlawed in the United States?
9. Should divorce laws be uniform throughout the United States?
10. Should the double standard of morality be eliminated?
11. Should euthanasia be legalized in the United States?
12. Should all citizens in the United States be fingerprinted?
13. Should the income tax be used to eliminate class distinctions in America?
14. Should the majority rule?
15. Should marriage be a "50-50" partnership?
16. Should the science of eugenics be used in mate selection?
17. Should the mothers of illegitimate children be sterilized?
18. Should the pillory be revived?
19. Should prostitution be legalized in the United States?
20. Should persons of different (races, religions) marry?
21. Should persons on relief be denied the vote?
22. Should the United States (discourage, actively support) revolutionary movements in other countries?
23. Should Utopia (offer, require) a course in sex education?
24. Should strikes vitally affecting the public interest be outlawed?

25. Should the United States furnish <u>technical assistance</u> to under-developed nations with communist leanings?
26. Should <u>teen-agers</u> be spanked?
27. Should <u>women</u> have "equal status" with men in (social, political, economic, religious) spheres?

EVALUATION

OBJECTS

I. <u>Facilities</u> of an institution or organization devoted to some phase of group life and human relations--for example,
   A. A home for the aged or disabled
   B. A child-guidance clinic
   C. A community center
   D. An Indian reservation
   E. A prison

II. An <u>object</u> of use to an individual or organization in carrying out a sociological purpose--for example,
   A. A piece of equipment used by a law-enforcement agency --e.g., a riot gun
   B. An electric chair
   C. A piece of equipment used in a recreation center
   D. A piece of equipment used in a rehabilitation center

POLICIES

A policy, in effect or proposed, of an agency, institution, or organization--local, state, or federal; public or private --for a sociological purpose--for example,
   A. A community policy affecting adolescents--e.g., a curfew policy
   B. A policy of an adoption agency
   C. A church's policy regarding birth control
   D. A state's law(s) governing capital punishment
   E. A firm's policy relating to the employment of (middle-aged persons, minorities, women)

POLITICAL SCIENCE 320-329.99

Thought Starters for ANALYSIS

What about:

1. Absolutism
2. Aliens: rights and privileges
3. Allegiance
4. Anticlericalism: church and state
5. Apportionment, legislative
6. Aristocracy
7. Assembly, right of
8. Association, right of
9. Asylum, right of
10. Autocracy
11. Autonomy of state
12. Balance of power
13. Ballot
14. Bills: legislative procedure
15. Campaigns, political
16. Censorship
17. Church and state
18. Cities and state
19. Citizenship
20. Civil liberties
21. Civil rights
22. Cold war
23. Colonies and colonization
24. Communist Party: U.S. politics
25. Communist state
26. Communities and state
27. Congresses, legislative
28. Congressional immunity
29. Democracy
30. Democratic Party
31. Diplomacy
32. Diplomatic history
33. Disfranchisement
34. Divine right of kings
35. Drafting bills
36. Due process of law
37. Elections
38. Electoral College
39. Electoral districts
40. Electoral systems
41. Electorate
42. Emigration
43. Equal protection of law
44. Espionage, diplomatic
45. Expression, freedom of
46. Farm communities and state
47. Fascist State
48. Feudalism
49. Foreign policy
50. Forms of state
51. Four Freedoms
52. Freedom
53. Fugitive slaves
54. Ideal state
55. Immigrants: rights and privileges
56. Immigration
57. Imperialism
58. Individuals and state
59. Inequality, individual
60. Information, freedom of
61. International politics
62. International relations
63. Investigations, legislative
64. Jurisdictionalism: church and state
65. Lawmaking
66. Laws: enactment
67. Legislative bodies
68. Loyalty, political
69. Marriage and citizenship
70. Minorities and state
71. Monroe Doctrine
72. Monarchy
73. National Socialist State
74. Natural rights
75. Naturalization
76. Nazism
77. Oligarchy
78. Parliamentary law
79. Petition, right of
80. Political parties
81. Poll tax
82. Press, freedom of
83. Pressure groups: legislative abuses
84. Primary elections

85. Property rights
86. Refugees
87. Religion, freedom of
88. Representative government
89. Republican Party
90. Revolution
91. Riots
92. Rules of order (parliamentary)
93. Self-determination
94. Self-government
95. Senates, legislative
96. Separation: church and state
97. Socialist Party
98. Sovereignty
99. Speech, freedom of
100. Statelessness: citizenship
101. States' rights
102. Suffrage
103. Syndicalism
104. Taxation, power of
105. Totalitarianism
106. Towns and state
107. United Nations trusteeship system
108. Utopias
109. Veto
110. Voters' qualifications
111. Voting
112. Whig Party
113. Woman suffrage
114. World state

CAUSE and EFFECT

1. Why I consider a man's first allegiance to be (to himself, to his country, to the United Nations)
2. Why I consider a particular amendment to (the federal, state) constitution (necessary, unnecessary; wise, unwise)
3. Why I consider South Africa's policy of apartheid (defensible, indefensible)
4. Why government by an aristocracy (is, is not) proper in democracy
5. Why the right of assembly must be (absolute, qualified) in a democracy
6. Why the right of association in a democracy must be (absolute, qualified)
7. Why I consider the ballot (a right, a privilege)
8. Why the bicameral legislature is (effective, ineffective)
9. Why I (approve of, disapprove of) a particular bill (proposed, enacted) by (our State Legislature, Congress)
10. Why the caucus is (necessary, unnecessary) in political elections
11. Why I (believe in, do not believe in) censorship of the press (by itself, by government) in a democracy
12. Why the church is necessary to the state
13. Why the state is necessary to the church
14. Why the city needs the state
15. Why the state needs the city
16. Why I (would, would not) like to be a citizen of a country other than the United States
17. Why I (would, would not) like to be a citizen of the world
18. Why I (embrace, reject) the philosophy of civil disobedience
19. (Major) Effects of complete acceptance of the philosophy of civil disobedience--generally; effects on local, state, national government

20. (Major) Effects of ethnic groups on civil government--generally; locally
21. Why additional civil rights legislation is (necessary, unnecessary; beneficial, harmful) in the United States at the present time
22. Why the Communist Party (should, should not) be outlawed in the United States
23. Why the Communist state (is, is not) the answer to the (economic, social, political) problems
24. (Major) Causes of political corruption--generally; locally
25. Why I (am, am not) a (Democrat, Republican)
26. Why I (believe in, do not believe in) the democratic form of government
27. Why I (would, would not) like to be a career diplomat
28. Why due process of law is essential to our form of government
29. Why I (believe, do not believe) in (compulsory, voluntary) voting by citizens in a democracy
30. Why I consider the educational qualifications for voting (adequate, inadequate) in (State, national) elections--
31. Why the ______ Party (won, lost) the (18--, 19--) election
32. Why I consider the Electoral College (still vital, obsolete)
33. Why I have (great, little) faith in the American electorate
34. Why President Lincoln emancipated the slaves--generally; only in those parts of the Confederacy occupied by Union troops
35. Why Americans become expatriates
36. (Major) Causes of (the rise, the decline) of feudalism
37. Why the filibuster serves (a harmful, a useful) purpose in modern American government
38. (Major) Causes of (the success, the failure) of American foreign policy--generally; at a particular time in history; during a particular Presidential administration
39. (Major) Effects of the complete realization of the Four Freedoms--internationally; nationally; regionally; locally
40. Why I look upon the franchise as (a right, a privilege) to be (restricted, unrestricted)
41. Why I consider our immigration laws (fair, unfair; just, unjust)
42. Why I (do, do not) subscribe to certain sentiments expressed in the Declaration of Independence
43. Why laws are necessary
44. Why I (approve of, disapprove of) a literacy test as a requirement for voting
45. Why lobbies serve (a useful, a harmful) purpose in government
46. Effects of marriage on citizenship
47. Why I consider minority rule (beneficial, harmful) to the state
48. Why I consider the Monroe Doctrine (dying, very much alive) in the world today

49. Why I consider nationalism (a sign of strength, a sign of weakness) in the modern world
50. Why our naturalization laws (need, do not need) revision
51. Why I consider man's rights (natural, man-made)
52. (Major) Causes of Negro slavery--outside the United States; in the United States
53. Why I consider ownership of property a sacred right
54. Why I consider political parties (a positive good, a pernicious evil) under our form of government
55. Why I (approve of, disapprove of) the poll tax
56. Why everyone deserves the right of privacy
57. Why I consider property rights (more, less) important than human rights
58. Why I consider present qualifications for suffrage (sound, unsound)
59. Why I consider the qualifications for (state, federal) legislators (satisfactory, unsatisfactory)
60. Why I consider the quota system for immigrants (necessary, unnecessary; wise, unwise; just, unjust)
61. Why I consider self-government (desirable, undesirable; possible, impossible)
62. (Major) Effects of complete social equality--internationally; nationally; locally
63. Why I believe in (absolute, restricted) freedom of speech
64. Why I believe in separation of church and state
65. (Major) Effects of statelessness
66. Why I consider the concept of states' rights to be (alive, dead) in the United States today
67. Why one should (always, never) vote a straight ticket
68. Why I (approve of, disapprove of) syndicalism
69. Why town meetings are (important, unimportant)--generally; in our town
70. Why voting is (a meaningful, a meaningless) gesture
71. Why I (believe in, do not believe in) compulsory voting
72. Why I (support, do not support) the principle of woman suffrage
73. Why I (approve of, disapprove of) a world government or world state

CLASSIFICATION

Kinds/Types of:

1. Allegiance
2. Alliance(s)
3. Amendments
4. Aristocracy/aristocrats
5. Ballots/balloting
6. Bills
7. Censors/censorship
8. Citizens/citizenship
9. Conservatism/conservatives
10. Constitutions
11. Dictatorship/dictators
12. Freedom
13. Government(s)
14. Liberalism/liberals
15. Monarchy/monarchs
16. Politics/politicians
17. Pressure groups
18. Representation
19. Rulers
20. Statesmen
21. World government

COMPARISON and CONTRAST

1. Absentee voting and voting in person
2. Aristocracy: Natural and artificial; in ancient, medieval, and modern times
3. Bicameral legislatures and unicameral legislatures
4. Colonialism: debits and credits
5. Communism: in theory and in practice
6. Congress and Parliament
7. Conservative and Liberal
8. Constitutions: Confederate States of America and United States of America
9. Delegated powers and implied powers
10. Democracy: in ancient Greece and in modern America
11. Democracy and republic
12. Democratic Party and Republican Party
13. Dictatorships: ancient, medieval, and modern
14. Elections: here and there; yesterday and today--e.g., the election of 1864 and that of 1964 in the United States
15. Election campaigns: here and there; yesterday and today
16. Emancipation: de facto and de jure
17. Espionage: in fact and in fiction
18. Ethnic groups and the state: here and there; yesterday and today--e.g., in Hitler's Germany and in Stalin's Russia, etc.
19. Feudal manor and ante-bellum Southern plantation
20. Ancient Greek city-state and modern American state
21. Human rights and human responsibilities
22. Imperialism: here and there; yesterday and today--e.g., in the Communist World and in the West
23. Laboring classes and the state: here and there; yesterday and today--e.g., in modern Russia and in modern America
24. Liberty and license
25. Loyalty: to self, to State, to nation; to U.N.
26. Monarchy: here and there; yesterday and today--e.g., during the reign of Elizabeth I and that of Elizabeth II
27. Nationalism and internationalism
28. Nationalism: here and there; yesterday and today--e.g., in the United States in the 1770's and in emerging African nations today
29. Natural rights and civil rights
30. Negro slavery: here and there; yesterday and today--e.g., in the ante-bellum South and in modern Africa
31. Passive resistance: here and there; yesterday and today--e.g., in India and in the United States
32. Passport and visa
33. Patriotism: true and false
34. Political parties: here and there; yesterday and today--e.g., in England and in the United States
35. Politician and statesman
36. Pure communism and (Russian, Chinese) communism
37. Pure democracy and American democracy
38. Revolutions: here and there; yesterday and today--e.g., American, French, and Russian

39. Senates: here and there; yesterday and today--e.g., in ancient Rome and in modern America
40. Slavery: here and there; yesterday and today--in the (Middle, Far) East and in the West; in ancient Greece or Rome and in (Czarist, Communist) Russia
41. Tyranny: by the few and by the many
42. Utopias: in theory and in practice--e.g., in Scandinavian countries, in Russia, in the United States, elsewhere
43. Voting procedures: here and there; yesterday and today--e.g., manually and by machine

DEFINITION

1. Civil disobedience
2. Cloture
3. Cold War
4. Colonialism
5. Coup d'état
6. Equality
7. Expatriation
8. Franchise
9. Frank
10. Gerrymander
11. Immunity
12. Initiative
13. Liberty
14. Literacy
15. Lobby
16. Matriarchy
17. Nepotism
18. Patriarchy
19. Patriotism
20. Politics
21. Proletariat
22. Recall
23. Referendum
24. Republic
25. Satellite
26. Suffragette

DESCRIPTION

I. An enclosure devoted to political or governmental activities--for example,
   A. Local campaign headquarters, or part thereof, before, during, or after a political campaign
   B. The office of a (local, state, federal) legislator
   C. The Senate or House of Representatives, or part thereof
   D. The U.N. Building, or part thereof
   E. The White House, or part thereof
II. An object used in or related to governmental activities --for example,
   A. A ballot
   B. A gavel
   C. A passport
   D. A voting booth
   E. A voting machine

PROCESS

1. How to cast an absentee vote
2. How to cast a ballot
3. How the bicameral legislature works

4. How a bill becomes a law (in our state legislature, in Congress)
5. How to campaign for (local, state, federal) public office
6. How the caucus operates
7. How to become a citizen of the United States
8. How to keep the Cold War cold
9. How to colonize
10. (How, How not) to write a letter to your (Congressman, Senator)
11. How to be (a good, a bad) Congressman
12. How (our state, the Federal) Constitution is amended
13. How to combat political corruption--generally, locally
14. How to tell a Democrat from a Republican
15. How aliens may avoid deportation
16. How to prepare for a career in diplomacy
17. How to be a successful diplomat
18. How bills are drafted in (our state legislature; Congress)
19. How the Electoral College functions
20. How to educate the electorate for citizenship
21. How to (conduct, thwart) a filibuster
22. How foreign populations (were, are) absorbed in America
23. How to secure the Four Freedoms--in the United States; throughout the world
24. How immigrants to the United States are (selected, rejected)
25. How public officials are impeached--e.g., the President of the U.S.
26. How Congress (investigates, is investigated)
27. How (local, state, federal) laws are made
28. How nations (rise, fall)
29. How Nazism (rose, fell)
30. How to (practise, thwart) noncooperation with government
31. How to (administer, take) an oath of (allegiance, office)
32. How the British Parliament functions
33. How to (apply for, secure) a passport
34. How to (draw up, circulate) a petition
35. How to distinguish a politician from a statesman
36. How the poll tax originated
37. How to secure legislation through Referendum
38. How public officials may be removed via Recall
39. How the requirements for our legislators are determined
40. How to achieve Utopia
41. How to vote
42. How to bring about (a world government, a world state)

ARGUMENTATION

PROPOSITIONS OF FACT

1. Was the abolition of slavery in the United States possible without war?
2. Are our age qualifications for suffrage (fair, unfair; reasonable, unreasonable)?

3. Is one's first allegiance to oneself?
4. Are church and state separate in modern America?
5. Is world citizenship (desirable, undesirable; wise, unwise)?
6. Is Communism (doomed, inevitable)--in the United States; in the world?
7. Was the Southern Confederacy a legal government?
8. Is the principle of Congressional immunity (wise, unwise)?
9. Is the Federal Constitution (vital, obsolete)?
10. Is a world democracy (possible, impossible; desirable, undesirable)?
11. Is our government (a democracy, a republic)?
12. Are American diplomats (adequately, inadequately) trained for their jobs?
13. Are our methods of electing our (state, federal) legislators (effective, ineffective; old-fashioned, up-to-date)?
14. Is the Electoral College obsolete?
15. Is the American electorate (competent, incompetent; responsible, irresponsible), by and large, in the selection of (local, state, national) public officials?
16. Are all men created equal?
17. Does the filibuster (hinder, help) the cause of liberty in America?
18. Is America's foreign policy likely (to ruin, to save) our country?
19. Is every citizen entitled to the franchise?
20. Do our legislators (abuse, deserve) the franking privilege?
21. Is complete human freedom (possible, desirable)?
22. Are our immigration laws (fair, unfair; just, unjust; discriminatory, nondiscriminatory)?
23. Is an Independent political party (desirable; possible) in the United States?
24. Is inequality (a fact of nature, the work of man)?
25. Is ours a government (of laws, of lawyers)?
26. Can legislative bodies be truly impartial?
27. Is death preferable to loss of liberty?
28. Are mass demonstrations in violation of (local, state, federal) law (ever, always) justified?
29. Is the Monroe Doctrine dead?
30. Is nationalism a sign of (weakness, strength)?
31. Are natural rights (natural, man-made)?
32. Are our naturalization laws (just, unjust; wise, unwise)?
33. Is noncooperation with government (defensible, indefensible)?
34. Is the parliamentary system superior to ours?
35. Are political parties (a positive good, a necessary evil) in the United States?
36. Is patriotism "the last refuge of the scoundrel"?
37. Are political conventions a joke?
38. Are political parties (necessary, unnecessary)?
39. Is political science a science?
40. Is the poll tax (fair, unfair; democratic, undemocratic)?

41. Is privacy (a right, a privilege)?
42. Is private property sacred?
43. Are our qualifications for suffrage on (the local, the state, the national) level (adequate, inadequate; satisfactory, unsatisfactory)?
44. Is the quota system (fair, unfair; beneficial, harmful) to (immigrants, the United States)?
45. Are (State, federal) requirements for legislators (adequate, inadequate; satisfactory, unsatisfactory)?
46. Are requirements for naturalization (fair, unfair; wise, unwise)?
47. Is the so-called right of association (a right, a privilege)?
48. Is the so-called right of revolution--as outlined, for example, in the Declaration of Independence--(a right, a risk)?
49. Was the secession of West Virginia from Virginia legal?
50. Are people capable of self-government?
51. Is the spoils system (just, unjust; wise, unwise)?
52. Is the gradual (evolutionary) abolition of the state (desirable, undesirable; possible, impossible)?
53. Is the doctrine of states' rights obsolete in modern America?
54. Has (our state, the federal) government (abused, used wisely) the power to tax?
55. Does the United States need a strong third party?
56. Is the United Nations merely a debating society?
57. Can the United Nations be saved?
58. Is Utopia (possible, desirable)?
59. Is compulsory voting (wise, unwise)?
60. Has woman suffrage benefited (womankind, mankind)?
61. Is a world (government, state) (desirable, possible)?

PROPOSITIONS OF POLICY

1. Should allegiance to the United Nations take precedence over national allegiance?
2. Should the right of association be guaranteed by Constitutional amendment?
3. Should the ballot be granted to all citizens in good standing in the United States?
4. Should citizenship in the United Nations have priority over national citizenship?
5. Should Congress pass additional civil rights legislation?
6. Should the Communist Party be outlawed in the United States?
7. Should the United States become a communist state?
8. Should avowed communist sympathizers be sent to communist countries at the expense of the federal government?
9. Should members of Congress be appointed for life?
10. Should Congress establish an Academy for Diplomats?
11. Should the Electoral College be abolished?
12. Should Congress remove all (racial, national) exclusions from its immigration laws?

13. Should the United States have a plural executive?
14. Should the filibuster be outlawed?
15. Should the United States adopt a policy of free (i.e., unrestricted) immigration?
16. Should our immigration laws be (relaxed, tightened)?
17. Should (the President, some other public official) be impeached?
18. Should the United States actively support insurrections for freedom (within the United States itself; throughout the world)?
19. Should Supreme Court Justices be appointed for life?
20. Should all lawmakers be lawyers?
21. Should loyalty oaths be (required, optional) as prerequisites for (employment, tenure)?
22. Should the majority always rule?
23. Should Congress encourage mass migrations within the United States in order to bring about a more even distribution of the population?
24. Should the minority rule in the United States?
25. Should all nations relinquish (some, all) of their sovereignty to the United Nations in the interest of world peace?
26. Should all political parties have equal right to be heard (e.g., on national television)?
27. Should politicians take (intelligence tests, mental maturity tests) before they are allowed to assume office?
28. Should property rights come (before, after) (civil, human) rights?
29. Should our qualifications for suffrage be revised?
30. Should Congress establish uniform voting laws?
31. Should our laws pertaining to voting qualifications be revised?
32. Should (literacy, maturity, intelligence) tests be required of all would-be voters?

EVALUATION

OBJECTS

I. Facilities of an agency or organization--local, state, or federal; public or private--devoted to the study or promotion of government--for example,
   A. Facilities of the local City or Town Hall
   B. Facilities of a hall in which political conventions are held
   C. Facilities available to legislators in a state capitol--e.g., for communication or transportation
   D. Facilities of the Senate Office Building
   E. Facilities of the United Nations or one of its agencies
II. An object of use to individuals and/or institutions devoted to the study or promotion of government--for example,
   A. An attaché case

B. A campaign button or poster
C. A passport holder
D. A tax form
E. A voting booth
F. A voting machine

POLICIES

A policy in effect or proposed by an individual, institution, or organization--local, state, or federal; public or private--devoted to the study or promotion of government--for example,

A. A policy of the federal government affecting aliens
B. South Africa's policy of apartheid
C. A policy of (a state, the federal) government regarding asylum
D. A policy of the United States government relating to the Cold War--e.g., a policy concerning trade with communist countries
E. The policy of (diplomatic, legislative) immunity
F. A policy of the federal government regarding the loyalty oath
G. A political party's platform
H. A political party's policy regarding "disloyal" members
I. A policy of the United Nations--e.g., a policy concerning membership

ECONOMICS 330-339.99

Thought Starters for ANALYSIS

What about:

1. Accidents, industrial
2. Agricultural economics
3. Arbitration: labor economics
4. Automation
5. Balance of trade theory
6. Bankruptcy
7. Banks and banking
8. Barter instruments
9. Bolshevism
10. Brokers: investment economics
11. Brook Farm Community
12. Budgets, national
13. Building and loan associations
14. Business crises and cycles
15. Business forecasting
16. Buyers' guides
17. Capital
18. Capitalism
19. Checks
20. Child labor
21. Christian socialism
22. Coinage: metals
23. Coins: mint practices
24. Collective bargaining
25. Collectivism
26. Collectivist farms
27. Commercial geography
28. Common land
29. Communism
30. Communist infiltration: labor organizations
31. Communist Manifesto
32. Community ownership of land
33. Company unions: labor economics
34. Competition
35. Compulsory labor
36. Conservation policies: land; natural resources
37. Consumer education
38. Consumer goods
39. Consumption
40. Controlled economics
41. Convict labor
42. Corporations
43. Cost of living
44. Costs and prices
45. Credit, public and private
46. Credit institutions
47. Credit instruments
48. Crop production
49. Currency
50. Customs duties
51. Debts, public and private
52. Deflation
53. Democracy, social
54. Deposits: banks and banking
55. Depressions
56. Dialectical materialism: Marxian economics
57. Dictatorship of the proletariat: Marxianism
58. Diminishing returns
59. Disability pensions
60. Discrimination in employment
61. Disputes, labor-management
62. Distribution of wealth
63. Distributive economics
64. Dividends: investments
65. Economic geography
66. Economic history
67. Economic planning
68. Economists
69. Eminent domain: land
70. Employers
71. Employment

NOTE: See also such related fields as SOCIOLOGY (300-309.99), SOCIAL WELFARE (360-369.99), HOME ECONOMICS (640-649.99), and BUSINESS (650-659.99)

72. Employment agencies
73. Exemptions, tax
74. Fabian Socialism
75. Factory systems: production
76. Fair trade
77. Farm industries
78. Farm land
79. Farm products: marketing
80. Farmers' cooperatives
81. Fascism
82. Federal debt
83. Finance, public and private
84. Financial panics
85. Food supply
86. Foreign aid
87. Free trade: tariff policy
88. Fringe benefits
89. Gangsterism in labor unions
90. Gold and silver standards
91. Gross national product
92. Guaranteed annual wage: labor
93. Guilds: production
94. Health facilities: industrial
95. Hygiene, industrial
96. Ideologies
97. Immigrants: labor
98. Income
99. Income tax
100. Industrial accidents
101. Industrial credit
102. Industrial economics
103. Industrial fatigue: industrial hygiene
104. Industrialists
105. Industrial sociology
106. Industrial welfare
107. Inflation
108. Injunctions: labor
109. Interest: finance
110. International trade
111. Labor
112. Labor unions
113. Land, public and private
114. Landlordism: land
115. Large industries: production
116. Layoffs: labor
117. Legal tender
118. Loan institutions
119. Loans, public and private
120. Lotteries: public revenues
121. Luxury taxes
122. Machinery in industry
123. Manpower: labor
124. Manufacturing industries
125. Marginal utility theory
126. Married women in labor
127. Marxian socialism and communism
128. Mass production
129. Mediation: labor
130. Mercantilism
131. Minimum pay: labor
132. Minority groups, employment of
133. Money
134. Money substitutes
135. Monopolies: labor unions
136. Monopolies: production
137. Mortgages: finance
138. National debt
139. Nationalization: industries and land
140. Natural resources
141. Nonmetallic money
142. Occupational diseases
143. Old age pensions
144. Open door policy
145. Open shop: labor
146. Overtime
147. Ownership of land
148. Paper money
149. Parities
150. Partnerships
151. Pawnbroking
152. Pay
153. Physically handicapped, employment of
154. Picketing: labor
155. Planned economy
156. Political action: labor
157. Political economy
158. Portal-to-portal pay: labor
159. Poverty
160. Price control and determination

161. Price supports, agricultural
162. Prices
163. Prison labor
164. Private enterprise
165. Production
166. Professions
167. Property theories
168. Prosperity
169. Protective tariff
170. Public borrowing
171. Public domain
172. Racketeering: labor unions
173. Real estate business
174. Reciprocal trade agreements
175. Recruitment, personnel: labor
176. Reform movements, socio-economic
177. Regional planning
178. Rehabilitation: industrial sociology
179. Rent: land
180. Resources, national
181. Retirement
182. Revenues, public
183. Right to work
184. Saint-Simonism
185. Salaries: labor
186. Sales taxes
187. Savings
188. School and work programs
189. Sharecropping
190. Small industries
191. Socialism
192. Space rights
193. Specialization: labor
194. Standard of living
195. State socialism
196. Stock exchanges
197. Stockbrokers
198. Strikes: labor
199. Subversive activities: labor organizations
200. Supply and demand
201. Syndicalism
202. Take-home pay
203. Tariff duties
204. Tariff policy
205. Taxation and taxes
206. Technocracy
207. Tenancy: land
208. Totalitarianism
209. Trade agreements
210. Trade unions
211. Training workers
212. Turnover, labor
213. Underconsumption
214. Underdeveloped areas, economic assistance to
215. Unemployment
216. Union-management relations
217. Union shops
218. Unions, labor
219. Utopias, economic
220. Vacations: labor
221. Wages
222. Wages for women
223. War debts, public
224. Warfare, economics of
225. Wealth
226. Welfare programs: industrial sociology
227. White collar workers
228. Women, employment of
229. Work
230. Workers
231. Working conditions: industrial sociology
232. Working day, length of
233. Working week, length of
234. Workmen's compensation: industrial sociology
235. Youth: labor

CAUSE and EFFECT

1. (Major) Causes of industrial accidents--generally; in a local industry
2. Why agriculture (does, does not) flourish under communism
3. (Major) Effects of automation (on business, on industry, on labor)--generally; locally
4. Why the Brook Farm Community (arose, fell)

5. (Major) Causes of business cycles
6. Why I (believe in, do not believe in) capitalism
7. Why I (support, do not support) the closed shop--generally; locally, in a particular industry
8. Why the coffee break is (beneficial, harmful) to (employees, employers)
9. Why coins are round
10. Why I (am opposed to, support) the Common Market
11. (Major) Effects of the Common Market--on the United States; on European members; on European nonmembers; on others
12. (Major) Effects of communism on labor--e.g., on the productivity or on the welfare of labor
13. Why communism (appeals, does not appeal) to (the workers, the intellectuals)--at home, abroad
14. (Major) Effects of competition on prices--nationally; locally
15. Why American consumer goods are (inferior, equal in quality, superior) to those of foreign countries (cf. American and German automobiles; American and Swiss watches, etc.)
16. Why I believe in (controlled, uncontrolled) economics
17. Why everything costs so much
18. Why credit is (a blessing, a curse)
19. Why crop supports are (necessary, unnecessary)--generally; locally
20. (Major) Causes of discrimination in employment--generally; locally; in a particular business or industry
21. Why economics (deserves, does not deserve) to be called "the dismal science"
22. Why businessmen (employ, do not employ, dislike employing) women
23. Why I consider our laws on tax exemptions (reasonable, unreasonable; just, unjust)
24. Why export trade is (necessary, unnecessary) to the economy of the United States
25. (Major) Effects of foreign labor--generally; regionally; locally
26. (Major) Effects of a policy of free trade--at home; abroad
27. Why the guaranteed annual wage for industry is (a wise, an unwise) idea
28. Why I consider the income tax (just, unjust; constitutional, unconstitutional)
29. Why I (oppose, support) the practice of governmental intervention in strikes
30. Why I (approve of, disapprove of) labor unions
31. (Major) Effects of being (married, engaged, single) upon working women
32. (Major) Effects of mass production--upon management; upon labor; upon production; upon employment; upon the economy of a locality, a region, a country; etc.
33. (Major) Causes of the depletion of our natural resources
34. Why I believe in (private, public) ownership of land

35. Why I consider parity prices (sensible, silly)
36. Why I consider a pay-as-you-go fiscal policy (desirable, undesirable; necessary, unnecessary) for (local, state, national) government
37. (Major) Effects of a pay-as-you-go fiscal policy for the federal government--e.g., in welfare, defense, etc.
38. Why economic planning is (necessary, unnecessary; possible, impossible) in (government, business)
39. (Major) Causes of poverty--locally; regionally; in a particular state; nationally
40. (Major) Effects of (price controls; price-fixing; price supports)--by government; by private enterprise
41. Why I prefer (to rent, to buy, to build)
42. Why I consider right-to-work laws (just, unjust; sound, unsound; constitutional, unconstitutional)
43. Why I consider Social Security (a blessing, a curse)
44. Why I consider the strike (a legal, an illegal) weapon of labor
45. Why U.S. tariff policies (need, do not need) revision
46. Why I (approve of, disapprove of) the custom of tipping
47. (Major) Causes of unemployment--generally; regionally; locally; in a particular industry
48. Why I consider withholding taxes (fair, unfair; legal, illegal)
49. (Major) Effects of a shorter (working day, working week)--generally; locally; effects on management and labor; effects on employment, etc.

CLASSIFICATION

Kinds/Types of

1. Banks/bankers
2. Bankruptcy
3. Bonds
4. Capital/capitalists
5. Corporations
6. Currency
7. Income
8. Interest
9. Loans
10. Money
11. Notes
12. Prices
13. Profits
14. Property
15. Revenue(s)
16. Securities
17. Stocks
18. Tariffs
19. Unions
20. Wages
21. Wealth

COMPARISON and CONTRAST

1. Agriculture: in modern America and in modern Russia (or Red China)
2. Automation: on the farm; in business; in industry
3. Bank and mattress
4. Bankruptcy: voluntary and involuntary
5. Barter and (metallic, paper) money
6. Bear market and bull market
7. Bimetallism and monometallism

8. Blue collar and white collar
9. Bonds and stocks
10. Budgets: national and family
11. Business forecasting and weather forecasting
12. Closed shop and open shop
13. Coffee break and British tea-time
14. Coins: counterfeit and genuine
15. Communistic economics and capitalistic economics
16. Communist enterprise and free enterprise
17. Company-controlled unions and worker-controlled unions
18. Consumer goods: here and there; yesterday and today--e.g., in modern America and in Russia
19. Direct taxes and indirect taxes
20. Discrimination: by employers and by employees
21. Distribution of wealth: here and there; yesterday and today--e.g. in medieval England and in modern America
22. Employment of women: here and there; yesterday and today--e.g., in modern America and in modern Russia
23. Enterprise: for oneself and for government
24. Fair trade and unfair trade
25. Gangsterism: in labor and in management
26. Gold standard and silver standard
27. Interest: legal and illegal
28. Labor: for need and for love
29. Lockouts and sit-down strikes
30. Manufacture: by hand and by machine
31. Pawnbroker and stockbroker
32. Payment: by cash and by check
33. Price control and wage control
34. State employees and private employees
35. Stocks: common and preferred
36. Tariffs: for protection and for revenue
37. Union shop and non-union shop
38. Vacations for labor: here and there; yesterday and today--e.g., in America and in Russia
39. Work day: here and there; yesterday and today; for labor and for management
40. Work week: for housewives and for career women
41. Working: for a man and for a woman
42. Working women: married and single

DEFINITION

1. Babouvism
2. Bank note
3. "Bankers' hours"
4. Bills of credit
5. Blacklisting
6. Bourse(s)
7. Cartel
8. Caveat emptor
9. Chattel mortgage
10. Clearing house
11. Collateral
12. Common Market
13. Communist Manifesto
14. Cottage industry
15. Counterfeiting
16. Curb exchange
17. Discount
18. Eminent domain
19. Entrepreneur
20. Fair profit

21. Fair trade
22. Fair wage
23. IWW
24. Investment
25. Laissez faire
26. Lease
27. Moratorium
28. Parity
29. Physiocracy
30. Single tax

DESCRIPTION

I. A building, or part thereof, used by an agency, institution, or organization--local, state, or federal; public or private--devoted to some phase of economics (i.e., to buying and selling of goods and/or services) --for example,
   A. An employment agency, or part thereof
   B. A local bank, or part thereof
   C. A local brokerage firm, or part thereof
   D. A customs house, or part thereof
   E. A local factory, or part thereof
   F. A federal mint, or part thereof
   G. A gold depository (e.g., at Fort Knox)
   H. A pawnshop
   I. A stock exchange (e.g., the New York Stock Exchange), or part thereof

II. A piece of equipment used by an agency, or organization devoted to some aspect of economics--for example,
   A. An adding machine
   B. A cash register
   C. A printing press used by a counterfeiter
   D. A stock ticker

III. Facilities of an agency or organization engaged in some phase of economics--for example,
   A. Facilities of a building and loan association
   B. Facilities of a local real estate firm
   C. Facilities of a local bank

PROCESS

1. How to open a bank account
2. How to get a loan from a bank
3. How to (avoid, go into) bankruptcy
4. How to borrow (from individuals; from a bank; from government)
5. How brokers help investors
6. How to succeed in business (by trying, without even trying)
7. How to invest capital
8. A check: from writing to return
9. How coins are minted
10. How cooperative school and work programs work
11. How to (safe-guard, lose) one's credit rating
12. How (metallic, paper) currency is (made, counterfeited)
13. How to (get into, stay out of) debt

14. How to make a bank deposit
15. How wealth may be distributed fairly
16. How to talk like an economist
17. How (employees, employers) are cheated
18. How to secure (full-time, part-time, temporary) employment
19. How to (apply for, get) free land from government
20. How to prevent industrial accidents--generally; locally, in a particular industry
21. How to solve the problem of industrial wastes--generally; locally, with regard to local industry
22. How to invest (a small amount, a large amount) of money--and keep one's shirt
23. How to be a lovable landlord
24. How to (make, break) a lease
25. How to make (a small, a large) killing in the stock market
26. How to marry a millionaire--generally; locally
27. How to (form, dissolve) a partnership
28. How to pay as you go--individually; in government
29. How to eliminate poverty--internationally; nationally; regionally; locally
30. How prices are (controlled, determined, fixed)
31. How to (determine, make) a fair (profit, wage)
32. How to (buy, rent, sell) real estate
33. How to curb abuses in unemployment relief--generally; locally
34. How to retire
35. How to be a considerate tenant
36. How to assure an economic Utopia
37. How to curb abuses in welfare programs--generally; locally
38. How to work--for oneself; for others
39. How to make youth work

ARGUMENTATION

PROPOSITIONS OF FACT

1. Can agriculture thrive (under communism, in a completely free economy)?
2. Does automation (eliminate, create) jobs?
3. Is the practice of "blockbusting" (ethical, unethical; just, unjust)?
4. Can the federal budget be balanced?
5. Can business cycles be leveled off?
6. Is conflict between capital and labor (avoidable, inevitable; healthy, unhealthy)?
7. Is (capitalism, communism) doomed?
8. Can capitalism and communism coexist peacefully?
9. Are our child labor laws obsolete?
10. Can a man be a good Christian and a millionaire?
11. Is money put into a Christmas savings account (well, ill) placed?

12. Is the Common Market (a threat, a challenge) to America?
13. Is communism (the friend, the enemy) of labor?
14. Are communists infiltrating our labor organizations--generally; locally?
15. Is craftsmanship (dying, dead) in America today?
16. Is credit (a blessing, a curse)?
17. Are credit cards (a blessing, a curse)?
18. Are crop supports (necessary, unnecessary)?
19. Is the equal distribution of wealth (desirable, possible)?
20. Is economics "the dismal science"?
21. (Can, Do) (employees, employers) ignore (race, sex) in employer-employee relations?
22. Do women deserve equal pay?
23. Are our tax exemptions (fair, unfair; reasonable, unreasonable)?
24. Is foreign aid worth it?
25. Is free trade (possible, improbable; desirable, undesirable)?
26. Is a general sales tax (for our community, for our state) (desirable, undesirable; necessary, unnecessary)?
27. Is the graduated income tax (just, unjust)?
28. Does labor deserve a guaranteed annual wage?
29. Is the __-hour (day, week) for labor (reasonable, unreasonable; possible, impossible)?
30. Is the income tax (necessary, unnecessary; just, unjust)?
31. Are our inheritance tax laws (just, unjust)?
32. Is American labor spoiled?
33. Is the laborer always worthy of his hire?
34. Are labor unions (the enemy, the friend) of labor?
35. Is legal interest ethical interest?
36. (Can, Does) money buy (happiness, misery)?
37. Does money talk? (What does it say?)
38. Is love of money the root of all evil?
39. Is nationalization of American industries--e.g., railroads, steel--(desirable, undesirable; necessary, unnecessary; wise, unwise)?
40. Is the open shop (beneficial, harmful) to labor?
41. Are parity prices (fair, unfair; reasonable, unreasonable)?
42. Is poverty the root of all evil?
43. Can poverty be abolished--in the United States; throughout the world?
44. Is the profit motive (good, evil)?
45. Are our property taxes (fair, unfair)--generally; locally?
46. Are protective tariffs (beneficial, detrimental) to the United States?
47. Are public employees (servants, slaves) of government?
48. Is the local evaluation of real estate (fair, unfair)?
49. Are our local real estate taxes (fair, unfair)?
50. Are the policies of _______ Company regarding the recruitment of personnel (just, unjust; sound, unsound)?
51. Does unemployment relief (discourage, encourage) unemployment--generally; locally?
52. Is it cheaper to (rent, build, buy)?

53. Do unions have the right to interfere with the right to work?
54. Is the sales tax (just, justified)--generally; locally?
55. Do the school and work programs in our community work?
56. Is a "soak the rich" tax policy (just, unjust; justified, unjustified)?
57. Are strikes a legitimate weapon of labor?
58. Is syndicalism the answer to America's (political, social, economic) problems?
59. Do our tariff policies (help, harm) the United States?
60. Do Americans have taxation (with, without) proper representation?
61. Do our (local, state, federal) tax laws (encourage, discourage) honesty?
62. Is tipping a form of legalized extortion?
63. Is free trade free?
64. Is welfare in our community a racket?
65. Are women suited to employment outside the home?
66. Are working conditions at _______ Company (satisfactory, unsatisfactory)?

PROPOSITIONS OF POLICY

1. Should absentee ownership of land be prohibited?
2. Should anti-trust laws apply to unions?
3. Should the United States grant economic assistance to countries which are (neutral; communist controlled or dominated)?
4. Should special banks be established to cater to women?
5. Should banks in America be nationalized?
6. Should collective bargaining be (compulsory, voluntary)?
7. Should one be neither a borrower nor a lender?
8. Should banks give interest on Christmas Savings accounts?
9. Should _______ Company have (a closed, an open) shop?
10. Should the coffee break be abolished?
11. Should the United States participate in the Common Market?
12. Should labor share in (the management, the ownership, the profits) of corporations?
13. Should corporation taxes be (raised, lowered)?
14. Should crop production be regulated by the federal government?
15. Should currency be (all paper, all metal)?
16. Should customs duties be (abolished, raised, lowered)?
17. Should all direct taxes be replaced by indirect taxes?
18. Should dividends be taxed?
19. Should labor be drafted in wartime?
20. Should women receive "equal pay for equal work"?
21. Should employed women receive special consideration--e.g., time off during pregnancy?
22. Should excess profits taxes be (increased, decreased, abolished)?
23. Should excise taxes be (raised, lowered, abolished)?
24. Should freedom to work be guaranteed by constitutional amendment?

25. Should the United States return to the gold standard?
26. Should all labor receive a guaranteed annual wage?
27. Should import duties be (raised, lowered, abolished)?
28. Should (state, federal) income taxes be (raised, lowered, abolished)?
29. Should the salaries of industrialists be limited in wartime to (say) $25,000 (net)?
30. Should the Federal Government fix all interest rates?
31. Should the United States join an "international labor pool"?
32. Should taxes on land replace all other taxes?
33. Should we have a (state, national) lottery?
34. Should a "Management Day" be added to the list of national holidays?
35. Should married women (with, without) children work outside the home?
36. Should members of minority groups be given preference in hiring?
37. Should the (United States government, United Nations) combat the economic problems brought about by the population explosion by disseminating information on birth control?
38. Should the federal government (control, fix) prices of all goods (in interstate commerce; vital to the national interest or welfare)?
39. Should price supports--e.g., on agricultural products--be (abandoned, continued)?
40. Should the production of crops be regulated by the federal government?
41. Should the United States (abolish, continue) reciprocal trade agreements?
42. Should sales taxes be (instituted, abolished)--generally, locally?
43. Should the United States remain on the silver standard in domestic trade?
44. Should strikes be outlawed in all industries affecting the national interest?
45. Should withholding taxes be withheld?

EVALUATION

OBJECTS

I. Facilities of an agency or organization engaged in some aspect of economics (i.e., buying and/or selling)--for example,
   A. Facilities of a local bank or small-loan concern
   B. Facilities of a local real estate firm

II. A useful object involved, directly or indirectly, in some phase of economics--for example,
   A. An object affecting industrial accidents--e.g., a ladder; a lathe
   B. An object used in agriculture--e.g., a tractor

C. An object used in a bank--e.g., a safe-deposit box; a vault
D. A checkbook

POLICIES

Evaluation of a policy, in effect or proposed, of an agency, institution, or organization--local, state, or federal; public or private--engaged, directly or indirectly, in some phase of economics--for example,

A. A policy of a local bank
B. A policy of the Common Market
C. A firm's policy relating to employment of the handicapped
D. A policy of a local or national labor union
E. A policy of a public or private firm relating to the employment of minorities
F. A policy of the New York Stock Exchange
G. A policy of (a private firm, a state agency, the federal government) relating to the employment of women

LAW 340-349.99

Thought Starters for ANALYSIS

What about:

1. Abortion: criminal law
2. Adultery: criminal law
3. Amendments, constitutional
4. Amnesty
5. Ancient law
6. Arbitration, international
7. Armaments limitation: international law
8. Arson
9. Articles of Confederation
10. Belligerants: law of war
11. Bequests
12. Blockade: law of war
13. Bribery
14. Burglary
15. Business law
16. Capital punishment
17. Cases, legal
18. Chattels
19. Church law
20. Civics
21. Civil procedure
22. Civil trials
23. Civil war: international law
24. Codes: criminal law
25. Commercial law
26. Common law
27. Community property
28. Constitutional history
29. Constitutional law
30. Constitutions, public
31. Consular service
32. Contracts
33. Coroners inquest
34. Court rules
35. Courts, law
36. Courts martial
37. Criminal law
38. Criminal libel
39. Death penalty
40. Deportation: criminal law
41. Diplomacy: international law
42. Diplomatic service
43. Disarmament: international law
44. Domestic relations
45. Due process of law
46. Embezzlement
47. Equity
48. Espionage: criminal law
49. Estate planning
50. Etiquette, diplomatic
51. European tribal laws
52. Evidence
53. Executions
54. Exile
55. Family law
56. Foreign law
57. Foreign service
58. Forensic chemistry
59. Forensic medicine
60. Forensic psychiatry
61. Forgery
62. Frauds
63. Freedom of the seas
64. Genocide: international law
65. Immunity, diplomatic
66. Imprisonment
67. Inheritance
68. Injuries
69. Inquest, coroner's
70. International cooperation: international law
71. International law
72. Interstate law
73. Judges
74. Judicial system
75. Jurisprudence

NOTE: See also such fields as POLITICAL SCIENCE (320-329.99), PUBLIC ADMINISTRATION (350-359.99), SOCIAL WELFARE (360-369.99), and others

76. Jury trial
77. Justice, administration of
78. Justices of the peace
79. Law of Nations
80. Lawyers
81. Legal antiquities
82. Lynching
83. Magna Carta: English constitutional history
84. Manslaughter
85. Maritime law
86. Marque and reprisal, letters of
87. Martial law
88. Mediation: international law
89. Medical jurisprudence
90. Medical testimony
91. Mercantile law
92. Moot courts
93. Municipal law
94. Murder
95. Mutiny
96. Napoleonic Code
97. Nations, law of
98. Natural law, theory of
99. Negligence
100. Neutrality: law of war
101. Notaries public
102. Nuclear weapons: international control
103. Nuisances
104. Numbers game
105. Nuremberg Trials
106. Oaths
107. Offenses, criminal
108. Organization of American States
109. Pacifism
110. Pardon
111. Peace: international law
112. Penal codes
113. Perjury
114. Personal property
115. Persons, legal
116. Poor laws
117. Procedure
118. Property
119. Prostitution: criminal law
120. Public law
121. Punishment
122. Racketeering
123. Real estate law
124. Rights, Bill of
125. Riots
126. Robbery
127. Roman Law
128. Sales
129. Sea warfare: international law
130. Shipwrecks: international law
131. Slander
132. Statutes, British and U.S.
133. Supreme courts: jurisdiction
134. Testimony
135. Torture: legal antiquities
136. Treason
137. Treaties: international law
138. Trial by jury
139. Trial by ordeal
140. Trials
141. Trials: martial law
142. Trials: war criminals
143. Twelve Tables
144. United Nations: international law
145. Unlawful assemblies
146. War: international law
147. War crimes: international law
148. Wills
149. World government

CAUSE and EFFECT

1. Why I (consider, do not consider) "criminal" abortion a crime
2. Why nations commit acts of aggression
3. Why women (receive, refuse) alimony

4. Why I (believe in, do not believe in) "entangling alliances"
5. Why I consider an amendment to our federal Constitution (necessary, unnecessary)
6. Why the Articles of Confederation (came about, failed)
7. Why we (have, need) a Bill of Rights
8. (Major) Effects of (local, state, federal) laws governing business
9. Why I (believe in, do not believe in) capital punishment
10. Why capital punishment (is, is not) a deterrent to crime
11. (Major) Effects of our child labor laws--generally; locally
12. Why I consider our city ordinance(s) relating to ____________ (just, unjust; legal, illegal)
13. Why I consider (local, state, federal) laws pertaining to civil rights (just, unjust; necessary, unnecessary; legal, illegal)
14. Why I look upon laws intended to regulate the conduct of war as (wise, foolish)
15. Why a contract is necessary
16. Why I (believe in, do not believe in) corporal punishment
17. Why I consider our corporation laws (fair, unfair; reasonable, unreasonable)--generally; locally
18. Why the United Nations has a Security Council
19. Why I consider our county ordinance relating to ____________ (effective, ineffective; just, unjust)
20. (Major) Causes of crime--generally; locally
21. (Major) Effects of crime--generally; locally
22. Why I would like a career in the diplomatic service
23. Why I consider our diplomatic service (a success, a failure)--generally; in a particular foreign country
24. Why I consider our (state, federal) extradition laws (effective, ineffective; just, unjust)
25. Why I (believe in, do not believe in) freedom of association
26. Why I consider the U. N. General Assembly an (effective, ineffective) organizaton
27. Why I consider the Golden Rule (vital, obsolete)
28. Why I consider our immigration laws (discriminatory, non-discriminatory; just, unjust)
29. (Major) Effects of our immigration laws (Kinds of effects? Effects upon what or whom?)
30. Why I (believe in, do not believe in) diplomatic immunity
31. Why I consider our (state, federal) income tax laws (discriminatory, non-discriminatory; just, unjust; legal, illegal)
32. Why I consider the inheritance tax (fair, unfair; legal, illegal)
33. Why I (believe in, do not believe in) the jury system
34. Why I (would, would not) like to be a lawyer

35. Why I (trust, distrust) lawyers
36. Why the League of Nations (came into being, failed)
37. Why I (approve, disapprove) of (state, federal) lotteries
38. Why the Magna Carta is important to Americans
39. (Major) Effects of our marriage laws--upon marriage; upon divorce
40. Why I (consider, do not consider) nuclear weapons legitimate weapons of war
41. Why I consider the Nuremberg Trials (just, unjust; legal, illegal)
42. (Major) Effects of the Nuremberg Trials--on international law; on international justice
43. Why I (approve of, disapprove of) the Organization of American States
44. Why I (do, do not) consider personal property sacred
45. Why I consider our laws governing prostitution (adequate, inadequate; wise, foolish)
46. Why I (approve of, disapprove of) public welfare
47. Why I (consider, do not consider) the Supreme Court supreme
48. Why I consider our (local, state, federal) tax laws (equitable, inequitable; legal, illegal)
49. Why I (believe in, do not believe in) the United Nations
50. Why a will is necessary

CLASSIFICATION

Kinds/Types of:

1. Aggression
2. Assault
3. Bankruptcy
4. Battery
5. Bequests
6. Cases, legal
7. Contracts
8. Corporations
9. Courts, law
10. Crime/crimes
11. Evidence
12. Felony/felonies
13. Injury/injuries
14. Judges
15. Juries
16. Law/laws
17. Lawyers
18. Misdemeanors
19. Murder
20. Negligence
21. Proof
22. Property
23. Rights
24. Statutes
25. Testimony
26. Wrongs

COMPARISON and CONTRAST

1. An aggressive act and a defensive act
2. Ambassador, consul, and/or minister
3. Amendment: of a State Constitution and of the Federal Constitution
4. Ancient law and modern law--e.g., law in ancient Greece and in modern America

5. Artificial persons and natural persons
6. Assault and battery
7. Bankruptcy: voluntary and involuntary
8. Barrister, solicitor, and/or lawyer
9. Burglary and robbery
10. Church law and civil law
11. Circumstantial evidence and direct evidence
12. Commonwealth and State
13. Competence and incompetence
14. Constitution: of the Southern Confederacy and of the United States
15. Crime, misdemeanor, and/or felony
16. Death: in law; in medicine; in religion
17. Extradition: interstate and international
18. Fact and opinion
19. Grand jury and trial jury
20. Grand larceny and petit larceny
21. Grounds for divorce and grounds for marriage
22. Homicide, manslaughter, and murder
23. House and home
24. Kleptomaniac and thief
25. Law: of man, of God, and/or of nature
26. Law: Anglo-Saxon, Mosaic, Napoleonic and/or Roman
27. Law and equity
28. Law, ordinance, statute, decree, and/or executive order
29. Lawyers: in fact and in fiction (e.g., on television)
30. League of Nations and United Nations
31. Libel and slander
32. Liberty and license
33. Life: in law; in medicine; in religion
34. Magna Carta and Declaration of Independence
35. Manslaughter: in peace and in war
36. Martial law and civil law
37. Nuremberg Trials and witch trials
38. Occidental law and oriental law
39. Patriotism and treason
40. Prejudice and preference
41. Religious law: Christian and Moslem
42. Seduction and statutory rape
43. Subpoena and summons
44. Trial by jury and trial by judge
45. Tribal law: European, American Indian, and/or African

DEFINITION

1. Accident
2. Act of God
3. Aggression
4. Blood money
5. Case method
6. Caveat emptor
7. Contract
8. Decency
9. Entail
10. Habeas corpus
11. Hustings
12. Illiteracy
13. Implied consent
14. Incompatibility

15. Intent
16. Justice
17. Kangaroo court
18. Mayhem
19. Malfeasance
20. Malpractice
21. Mental cruelty
22. Natural rights
23. Peer
24. Poetic punishment
25. Primogeniture
26. Privacy
27. Property
28. Sanity
29. Sheriff
30. Sovereignty

DESCRIPTION

I. A building or other structure devoted to the study and/or administration of law or justice--for example,
   A. (Local, State, National) headquarters of the American Bar Association
   B. A courthouse
   C. A prison
   D. The U.N. building, or part thereof

II. Facilities of an agency, institution, or organization--local, state, or federal; public or private--dealing with some phase of law--for example,
   A. Facilities of the (local, national) headquarters of the Federal Bureau of Investigation
   B. Facilities of a law firm
   C. Facilities of Utopia's Law School

III. An object used by an individual or organization engaged in some aspect of law or jurisprudence--for example,
   A. A briefcase
   B. A gallows
   C. A gavel
   D. A jury box
   E. A witness stand

PROCESS

1. How to adopt a child
2. How to (get, avoid paying) alimony
3. How to (raise, jump) bail
4. How to (avoid, declare) bankruptcy
5. How to (prepare for, pass) the State Bar examination
6. How to (win, lose) a case
7. How (the United States, our state) Constitution originated
8. How to become a court reporter
9. How to (prepare for, improve) diplomatic service
10. How to (avoid, secure) a divorce
11. How to plan an estate
12. How to (secure, interpret) evidence
13. How to examine a witness
14. How to prepare for foreign service
15. How to be an intelligent juror
16. How a jury is selected

17. How a (state, federal) bill becomes a law
18. How a (state, federal) law is repealed
19. How to hire a lawyer
20. How to help your lawyer
21. How to get a parole
22. How to sue
23. How to get a case before the Supreme Court
24. How to (give, interpret) testimony
25. How treaties are made
26. How to make a will

ARGUMENTATION

PROPOSITIONS OF FACT

1. Are State adoption laws (effective, ineffective; fair, unfair)?
2. Are our laws governing alimony (necessary, unnecessary; wise, foolish)?
3. Does our (state, federal) constitution need amending?
4. Is the ______ Amendment to our (state, federal) Constitution (just, unjust; legal, illegal)?
5. Are our (State, federal) laws governing amnesty (effective, ineffective; just, unjust)?
6. Are the Attorney General's opinions (invaluable, worthless)?
7. Are our laws relating to bail (effective, ineffective; fair, unfair; just, unjust)?
8. Are (state, federal) bankruptcy laws (effective ineffective; just, unjust)?
9. Is the (American, State) Bar Association (beneficial, harmful; necessary, unnecessary) to the practice of law?
10. Are (state, federal) laws pertaining to capital punishment (effective, ineffective; just, unjust)?
11. Is church law (effective, ineffective; discriminatory non-discriminatory)--generally; in our church?
12. Is our (city, town) ordinance relating to ____________ (effective, ineffective; fair, unfair; legal, illegal)?
13. Are our (local, state, federal) codes pertaining to ______________ (effective, ineffective; just, unjust)?
14. Is the United States Constitution (vital, obsolete)?
15. Is our state Constitution (adequate, inadequate)?
16. Do our (local, state, federal) courts (promote, impede) justice?
17. Do our punishments fit our crimes?
18. Does fear of the death penalty deter the would-be criminal?
19. Does our diplomatic service need revitalizing--generally; in a particular country?
20. Is the principle of diplomatic immunity (wise, unwise)?
21. Are (local, state, federal) laws pertaining to (economic, racial, religious, sexual) discrimination (discriminatory, nondiscriminatory; just, unjust)?

22. Are (state, federal) laws pertaining to divorce (effective, ineffective; just, unjust)?
23. Are (state, federal, international) laws governing extradition (effective, ineffective; just, unjust)?
24. Are our laws on habeas corpus (satisfactory, unsatisfactory)?
25. Are federal laws governing immigration (discriminatory, nondiscriminatory; just, unjust; wise, unwise)?
26. Can judges be impartial?
27. Are our methods of selecting jurors (wise, unwise)?
28. Is the jury system (effective, ineffective; fair, unfair)?
29. Is justice blind?
30. Is the language of law (necessary, unnecessary)?
31. Is law a science?
32. Are (state, federal) marriage laws (adequate, inadequate; just, unjust)?
33. Are military courts (just, unjust)?
34. Were the Nuremberg Trials (legal, illegal)?
35. Is the Organization of American States (effective, ineffective)?
36. Are (state, federal) laws governing pardons (reasonable, unreasonable; satisfactory, unsatisfactory)?
37. Are (state, federal) laws governing paroles (effective, ineffective; just, unjust)?
38. Do our (local, state, federal) laws dealing with pornography (discourage, encourage) the practice?
39. Do our diplomats have (too many, too few) privileges?
40. Is a repeal of the __________ Amendment of the (state, federal) Constitution (desirable, undesirable; necessary, unnecessary)?
41. Do our (state, federal) laws pertaining to sex crimes (encourage, discourage) such crimes?
42. Is our local sheriff (capable, incapable; honest, dishonest)?
43. Is our State Bar Association (adequate, inadequate; effective, ineffective)?
44. Is our Supreme Court (partial, impartial)?
45. Is the United Nations (an effective, an ineffective) instrument for world peace?
46. Is all fair in love and war?

PROPOSITIONS OF POLICY

1. Should the age of consent be (raised, lowered)--generally; in our state?
2. Should capital punishment be abolished?
3. Should (federal, state, union) laws relating to child labor be amended?
4. Should (state, federal) government corporations compete with private corporations--e.g., the TVA?
5. Should the (state, federal) Constitution be (amended, scrapped)?
6. Should one (take his case to court, settle out of court)?

7. Should the punishment fit the crime?
8. Should avowed Communist sympathizers--including United States citizens--be deported to Communist countries willing to receive them?
9. Should (national, international) laws relating to diplomatic immunity be amended?
10. Should Congress establish an Academy for diplomats?
11. Should (economic, racial, religious, sexual, other) discrimination be abolished by means of a Constitutional Amendment?
12. Should (state, federal) divorce laws be amended?
13. Should (local, state) laws governing domestic relations be amended?
14. Should the dowry be (abolished, continued, revived)?
15. Should federal laws governing (emigration, immigration) be amended?
16. Should the (state, federal) government guarantee freedom of association?
17. Should (local, state, federal) laws on gambling be amended?
18. Should (local, state, federal) judges be appointed for life?
19. Should the qualifications for would-be jurors be (raised, lowered)?
20. Should the jury system be scrapped?
21. Should Utopia (institute, expand) its law school?
22. Should the loyalty oath be (optional, required) as a condition of (public, private) employment?
23. Should State marriage laws be amended?
24. Should State miscegenation laws be (amended, abolished)?
25. Should an avowed pacifist be President of the United States?
26. Should the (pillory, stocks, whipping post) be revived?
27. Should (local, state, federal) qualifications for police officers be revised?
28. Should pornographic works be removed from our (local, state, federal) art galleries; book-and-magazine stands; libraries)?
29. Should prostitution be (legalized, outlawed) in the United States?
30. Should public floggings be reinstated (in our state; in the United States)?
31. Should (local, state, federal) relief laws be amended?
32. Should strikes be (permitted, outlawed) in (trades, occupations) affecting the public interest?
33. Should we have a "Super Supreme Court"?
34. Should (local, state, federal) tax laws be amended?
35. Should the United States continue its support of the United Nations?
36. Should the United Nations be removed from its present site?
37. Should we have a world government?

OBJECTS

I. Facilities of a firm or organization (local, state, or federal; public or private) devoted to law or to some aspect of jurisprudence--for example,
   A. Facilities of a law firm
   B. Facilities of Utopia's Law School--e.g., the library
   C. Facilities of a local, state, or federal court
   D. Facilities of the United Nations

II. An object of use to an individual or organization engaged in the study of law or in the administration of justice--for example,
   A. An electric chair
   B. A pair of handcuffs
   C. A lie detector
   D. A two-way police radio
   E. A state or federal tax form

POLICIES

A policy, in effect or proposed, of an agency, organization, or institution--local, state, or federal; public or private--concerned with some phase of law or of jurisprudence--for example,

   A. A policy of a private adoption agency
   B. A church's policy relating to (abortion, adultery, birth control)
   C. A policy of the American Bar Association--e.g., a policy relating to membership, disbarment, etc.
   D. A city, county, or town ordinance
   E. A policy of a court-martial
   F. The Golden Rule
   G. A policy of the United Nations--e.g., U.N. policy relating to membership, payment of dues, etc.

PUBLIC ADMINISTRATION 350-359.99

Thought Starters for ANALYSIS

What about:

1. Administration, military
2. Administration, public: central and local
3. Air warfare
4. Armed forces
5. Army department
6. Atomic warfare services
7. Bacteriological warfare, civilian protection from
8. Bases: Air Force, Army, and Navy
9. Benefits, veterans'
10. Biological warfare
11. Blackouts
12. Blockades, naval
13. Bombings
14. Budgets: government and military
15. Cabinet: U.S. Government
16. Camouflage
17. Camps, military
18. Chaplains
19. Chemical warfare
20. City government administration
21. Civil defense
22. Civil service
23. Civilian manpower mobilization
24. Coast Guard, U.S.
25. Communication services
26. Conscription: manpower and wealth
27. Corruption in public service
28. County government administration
29. Courts martial
30. Debts, public
31. Decorations, military
32. Demobilization
33. Department of Agriculture
34. Department of Commerce
35. Department of Defense
36. Department of Health, Education, and Welfare
37. Department of Interior
38. Department of Justice
39. Department of Labor
40. Disabled veterans
41. Discipline, military
42. Education of veterans
43. Employment of veterans
44. Enlisted personnel
45. Enlistment, manpower
46. Equipment: armed forces
47. Espionage, military
48. Etiquette, military
49. Examinations, civil service
50. Executive branch of government
51. Exemptions from military service
52. Expenditure, public
53. Federal employees
54. Federal government: administration
55. Financial administration: governments
56. Fleets
57. Food: armed fôrces
58. Foreign legion
59. Games, war: military science
60. Gas warfare
61. Geography, military
62. Government administration
63. Government contracts
64. Government employees
65. Government pensions

NOTE: See also POLITICAL SCIENCE (320-329.99), LAW (340-349.99), ENGINEERING (620-629.99) especially Military and Naval Engineering (623-623.9), and others

66. Government property
67. Government purchasing
68. Governments, administration of
69. Ground forces
70. Guerrilla warfare
71. Guns: military equipment
72. Hospitals, armed forces
73. Intelligence, military and naval
74. Internment: civilians and enemy aliens
75. Interstate relations
76. Jeeps
77. Justice, military
78. Law: military and naval
79. Legislative control: central government
80. Local governments, administration of
81. Logistics
82. Loyalty oaths: government personnel
83. Marine Corps
84. Medical installations: armed forces
85. Medical services: armed forces
86. Merchant marine, mobilization of
87. Merit system for government personnel
88. Metropolitan areas, administration of
89. Military defense
90. Military life
91. Military science
92. Militia
93. Municipal administration
94. Municipal governments
95. Munitions manufacture
96. Mutiny
97. National defense
98. National governments, administration of
99. National guard
100. Naval forces
101. Naval life
102. Naval science
103. Naval warfare
104. Navy
105. Navy Department
106. Nepotism in government
107. Nuclear warfare
108. Offenses: armed forces
109. Officers: armed forces
110. Officials, government
111. Ordinances, local
112. Ordinance, military and naval
113. Patronage, government
114. Pay: armed forces
115. Police: civil and military
116. Post Office Department
117. Powers, presidential
118. Powers, separation of
119. Presidency
120. Press censorship in government
121. Prisoners of war
122. Psychological warfare services
123. Public finance: central and local
124. Public health boards
125. Public officials: central and local government
126. Public property, administration of
127. Public safety
128. Public service employees
129. Public welfare, administration of
130. Public works, administration of
131. Purchasing governments: central and local
132. Quartermaster Corps
133. Quarters: armed forces
134. Recruitment, military
135. Rehabilitation: veterans
136. Religious services, military
137. Removal of public officials
138. Reserves, military
139. Retirement: armed forces
140. Rights of veterans
141. Salaries: government administration
142. Sea power
143. Sea warfare

144. Secret service
145. Shelters: civil defense
146. Spoils system: central and local governments
147. State control of local governments
148. State Department
149. State employees
150. State governments
151. Submarine warfare
152. Survival instructions
153. Taxation
154. Town government
155. Transportation facilities, military
156. Treasury Department
157. Uniforms, military
158. United States Government
159. Universal military training
160. Veterans
161. Vice-presidency, U.S.
162. Village government, administration of
163. Volunteers, military
164. WAC
165. WAF
166. WAVES
167. War Department
168. Warfare
169. Warships
170. Weapons, military
171. Welfare: public administration

CAUSE and EFFECT

1. (Major) Effects of the ______ Air Base--on local businesses; on community life; on local schools
2. Why I (consider, do not consider) the battleship obsolete in modern warfare
3. Why I consider veterans' benefits (deserved, undeserved)
4. Why the Federal blockade of the Confederacy succeeded
5. Why I (approve of, disapprove of) a United States blockade of Cuba
6. (Major) Causes of an unbalanced (local, state, federal) budget
7. Why (the President of the United States, a state governor) needs a Cabinet
8. Why I believe in (a strong, a weak) central government
9. Why I (consider, do not consider) our local civil defense program (adequate, inadequate)
10. Why I consider civil service examinations (fair, unfair)
11. Why civil service reform is (necessary, unnecessary)
12. Why we (should, should not) have a civilian Commander-in-Chief
13. Why I (believe in, do not believe in) compulsory military service
14. Why I (favor, do not favor) the conscription of (civilian manpower, wealth) in wartime
15. (Major) Causes of corruption in (local, state, federal) government
16. Why I (approve, disapprove) of the way the Department of (Agriculture; Commerce; Defense; Health; Education and Welfare; Interior; Justice; Labor; Post Office; State; Treasury) is being run
17. (Major) Causes of (inefficiency, subversion) in one of the above Departments of the Federal Government
18. Why all veterans (deserve, do not deserve) an education at government expense

19. Why veterans (deserve, do not deserve) preferential treatment in employment
20. (Major) Causes of the use of (poor, inadequate) equipment by our armed forces
21. (Major) Effects of military (life, training) on ex-servicemen
22. Why the French Foreign Legion came into being
23. Why the H-bomb is (a legitimate, an illegal; a moral, an immoral) weapon of war
24. Why our highway department (does, does not) provide (a good, a bad) highway system
25. Why I consider our local (military, naval, veterans') hospital (adequate, inadequate; satisfactory, unsatisfactory)
26. Why the infantry is (necessary, unnecessary) today
27. Why international forces are (desirable, undesirable; feasible, impractical; necessary, unnecessary)
28. (Major) Effects of leisure on servicemen
29. Why loyalty oaths (should, should not) be required of (local, state, federal) government personnel
30. Why I (do, do not) consider the Marine Corps a builder of men
31. Why I (approve of, disapprove of) the merit system for all (local, state, federal) government employees
32. Why military life (makes, breaks) men
33. Why (local, state, federal) government patronage is (fair, unfair; wise, unwise)
34. Why the powers of the President (should, should not) be restricted
35. Why government censorship of the press is (desirable, undesirable; necessary, unnecessary; wise, unwise)--in peace; in war (cold or hot)
36. Why Utopia (needs, does not need) an ROTC
37. Why separation of powers is necessary in government
38. Why the spoils system is (a positive good, a necessary evil) in government
39. Why the President's term of office (should, should not) be restricted
40. Why distinctive uniforms for servicemen are (desirable, undesirable; necessary, unnecessary)
41. Why universal military training is (desirable, undesirable; necessary, unnecessary)
42. Why I consider the weapons used by our armed forces (adequate, inadequate; obsolete, up-to-date; superior, inferior)
43. Why women are (useful, useless) in our armed forces
44. (Major) Effects of women in our armed forces

CLASSIFICATION

Kinds/Types of:

1. Ammunition
2. Bases
3. Battleships
4. Budgets
5. Charters

6. City governments
7. Contracts, government
8. Examinations, civil service
9. Financing, government
10. Martinets
11. Press censorship
12. Reserves
13. Revenues, public
14. Ships
15. Town governments
16. Warfare
17. Warships
18. Weapons

COMPARISON and CONTRAST

1. Air raid shelter and fall-out shelter
2. Air warfare: yesterday, today, and tomorrow
3. Arms: here and there; yesterday, today, and tomorrow--e.g., ancient, medieval, and modern
4. Blockading: here and there; yesterday, today, and tomorrow--e.g., during the Age of Napoleon, during the Civil War, today
5. Cabinets: official and "kitchen"
6. Camouflage: here and there; yesterday and today--e.g., in the seige of Troy and in World War II
7. Camouflage: by man and by nature
8. Cavalry: here and there; yesterday and today--e.g., horse and mechanized
9. Clothing, military: here and there; yesterday and today--e.g., in medieval Europe and in modern America
10. Coast Guard, U.S.: in peace and in war
11. Commonwealth and State
12. Detectives: in fact and in fiction
13. Entertainment: of servicemen and of officers
14. Firearms: here and there; yesterday, today, and tomorrow --e.g., in ancient, medieval, and modern times
15. Fleets: here and there; yesterday and today--e.g., in ancient Rome and in modern America; the Spanish Armada and a Japanese fleet in World War II
16. French Foreign Legion: in fact and in fiction (e.g., in motion pictures)
17. Games: war and Olympic
18. Guerrilla warfare, Indian warfare, and/or jungle warfare
19. Guns and butter
20. Highway patrols: in fact and in fiction (e.g., on television)
21. Indian fighting and street fighting
22. Jeeps: in peace and in war
23. Kings: here and there; yesterday and today--e.g., in ancient, medieval, and in modern times
24. Marine Corps: in fact and in fiction (e.g., in motion pictures)
25. Military life: here and there; yesterday and today--e.g., in ancient Sparta and in modern America
26. Mountain warfare, desert warfare, and/or jungle warfare
27. Officer and gentleman
28. Officers: here and there; yesterday and today--e.g., in ancient, medieval, and modern times

29. A police action and a war
30. Punishment, military: here and there; yesterday and today--e.g., in ancient, medieval, and modern times
31. Spoils system: here and there; yesterday and today--e.g., in the Age of Jackson and today
32. Town and city
33. War: defensive and offensive
34. Women in war: here and there; yesterday and today--e.g., in the USA and in the USSR in World War II
35. Working for (a local, a state, the federal) government and working for (oneself, a private concern)

DEFINITION

1. Aggression
2. Borough
3. Bureaucracy
4. Camouflage
5. Charter
6. City
7. Commonwealth
8. Constable
9. County
10. Cryptanalysis
11. Cryptography
12. Etiquette
13. Frogman
14. Goldbrick
15. Graft
16. Guerrilla
17. Hierarchy
18. Lobby
19. Logistics
20. Malingering
21. Municipality
22. Nepotism
23. Police action
24. Public interest
25. Suburb
26. Town
27. Urban
28. Village

DESCRIPTION

I. An area devoted to some phase of public administration or military operations--for example,
   A. A local Air Force, Army, or Navy base
   B. A concentration camp
   C. A military camp
   D. A navy yard

II. A building or other structure, or part thereof, devoted to some aspect of public administration, military operations, or defense--for example,
   A. A military barracks
   B. A city or town hall
   C. A fall-out shelter
   D. A local fire house or police station
   E. A military, naval, or veterans' hospital

III. An object useful in carrying out some phase of public administration or military operations--for example,
   A. A vehicle used in public administration--e.g., a fire truck, a police car
   B. A military vehicle--e.g., a jeep, a tank
   C. A military vessel--e.g., an aircraft carrier
   D. A military weapon--e.g., a bayonet, a bomb

PROCESS

1. How to reduce absenteeism in (local, state, federal) government
2. How to reduce accidents in government--generally; locally
3. How civilians may be protected during an air raid
4. How animals are (cared for, used) in the armed forces
5. How to improve the administration of our armed forces
6. How to improve basic training--generally; in a particular Service
7. How to improve the President's Cabinet
8. How to improve the administration of camps in our armed forces--generally; locally, at Camp ______
9. How to improve the administration of our city governments --generally; specifically in the city of ______
10. How to (improve, promote) civil defense--generally; locally
11. How to improve the administration of (local, state, federal) civil service
12. How to mobilize civilian manpower in time of war
13. How to improve the U.S. Coast Guard
14. How to (reduce, eliminate) corruption in (local, state, federal) public services
15. How to improve county government--generally; locally
16. How to improve discipline in our armed forces
17. How to improve the draft
18. (How, How not) to entertain servicemen
19. How to reduce expenditures in (local, state, national) government
20. How to be a Frogman
21. How to get a government contract
22. How to buy surplus government property
23. How to improve our (military, naval, veterans') hospitals --generally; locally
24. How to make international forces (such as those under the auspices of the United Nations) effective
25. How the jeep originated
26. How to improve the administration of a specific branch or service of local government--e.g., the civil service
27. How to improve the Marine Corps
28. How to improve the merchant marine
29. How to determine the merit of a (local, state, federal) public (official, servant)
30. How to improve the National Guard
31. How to (improve, simplify) public administration on the (local, state, federal) level
32. How to promote public safety
33. How to improve the administration of public welfare-- generally; locally
34. How public officials may be removed from office
35. How to improve our (military, naval) reserves
36. How to improve the Secret Service

37. How to (build, stock, stay alive in) (an air raid, a fall-out) shelter
38. How to improve our State Department
39. How to set up a target range
40. How to (set up, strike) a tent
41. How to (improve, promote) the training of veterans for civilian life
42. How to (improve, standardize) uniforms in the armed forces
43. How to improve the administration of public welfare--generally; locally

ARGUMENTATION

PROPOSITIONS OF FACT

1. Is (local, state, federal) government administration (effective, ineffective; honest, dishonest)?
2. Are aircraft carriers "sitting ducks" in modern war?
3. Are our aircraft detection methods (satisfactory, unsatisfactory) under civil defense?
4. Are U.S. armed forces (adequate, inadequate)--at home; abroad?
5. Are large armies (necessary, obsolete) in modern war?
6. Are U.S. (air, military, naval) bases on foreign soil (necessary, unnecessary; wise, unwise)--generally; in the country of ______?
7. Is (Air Force, Army, Marine, Navy) basic training (adequate, inadequate; effective, ineffective; fair, unfair)?
8. Is the battleship obsolete?
9. Do our veterans receive (deserved, undeserved; too many, too few) benefits?
10. Is the President's Cabinet (effective, ineffective; necessary, unnecessary)?
11. Is the office of chaplain incongruous in warfare?
12. Is the government of our city (efficient, inefficient; honest, dishonest)?
13. Do civil service examinations accomplish their purpose?
14. Is a civilian Commander-in-Chief of the Army and Navy (i.e., the President of the United States) suited to the task?
15. Is compulsory (military, naval) service (democratic, undemocratic; effective, ineffective; fair, unfair)?
16. Do conscientious objectors have (a, no) case?
17. Is conscription (of manpower, of wealth) in wartime (just, unjust; justified, unjustified)?
18. Is the government of ______ county (efficent, inefficient; honest, dishonest)?
19. Are our disabled veterans (adequately, inadequately) cared for?
20. Do veterans with non-service-connected disabilities deserve hospital care at government expense?

21. Do we exempt (the right, the wrong) people from military service?
22. Does civil service keep (the best, the worst) federal employees?
23. Is our local (fire, police) department (adequate, inadequate)?
24. Are U.S. firearms (inferior, superior) to those of other countries?
25. Do we have (too many, too few) government employees-- locally; in the state; in Washington, D.C.?
26. Is Governor __________ of the (Commonwealth, State) of ________ effective, ineffective; a cheap politician, an unselfish statesman)?
27. Do (local, state, federal) government workers have (too many, too few) holidays?
28. Is the H-Bomb (a legal, an immoral) weapon of war?
29. Is our (local, state, federal) highway department (efficient, inefficient)?
30. Are our (military, naval, veterans') hospitals (adequate, inadequate; effective, ineffective)?
31. Is the infantry obsolete in modern warfare?
32. Can (a Department, a Secretary) of Labor be unbiased?
33. Are leaders (born, made)?
34. Are loyalty oaths for government employees (justified, unjustified)?
35. Does the Marine Corps (make, break) men?
36. Does the merit system for (local, state, federal) government workers work?
37. Does military (life, training) (benefit, harm) the civilian?
38. Is our (local, state) National Guard (effective, ineffective; prepared, unprepared)?
39. Does nepotism (help, hurt) government?
40. Is nuclear warfare (avoidable, unavoidable; moral, immoral)?
41. Is blind obedience to military authority (essential, unwise)?
42. Is our (county, city) ordinance pertaining to ________ (reasonable, unreasonable; legal, illegal)?
43. Is the (local, federal) Post Office Department (efficient, inefficient; adequate, inadequate)?
44. Is press censorship by (local, state, national) government (desirable, undesirable; wise, unwise; avoidable, unavoidable)?
45. Is public administration needlessly complex?
46. Does the public respect public property?
47. Is rank but the guinea's stamp?
48. Do religious services in the armed forces violate the Constitution?
49. Does the salute indicate (respect, disrespect; inferiority, superiority, equality)?
50. Are government-financed (air raid, fall-out) shelters (necessary, unnecessary)?
51. Is a limited term of office for (state governors, the

President) (desirable, undesirable)?

52. Are distinctive uniforms for our armed forces (desirable, undesirable; necessary, unnecessary)?
53. Does society owe its veterans a living?
54. Is the custom of "veterans' preference" (regardless of ability) in selecting government personnel (wise, unwise)?
55. Do women belong in the armed forces?

PROPOSITIONS OF POLICY

1. Should the United States (build, keep, abandon) air bases on foreign soil?
2. Should (individuals, our state, the federal government) build (air raid, fall-out) shelters?
3. Should the Navy scrap its (aircraft carriers, battleships)?
4. Should the United States have dropped the A-bomb in World War II?
5. Should __________ (an enemy country) be blockaded by the United States?
6. Should our (city, town) change its form of government?
7. Should civil service examinations be required of applicants for all (local, state, federal) government jobs?
8. Should civilians replace military personnel behind the lines--e.g., in clerical jobs?
9. Should the clothing of our women (military, naval) personnel be (fashionable, utilitarian)?
10. Should a civilian be Commander-in-Chief of the Army and Navy?
11. Should all personnel in (local, state, federal) public service take competitive examinations?
12. Should service in the armed forces be (compulsory, voluntary)?
13. Should conscientious objectors be (fined, given medals, jailed, shot)?
14. Should womanpower be conscripted in wartime?
15. Should (property, wealth) be conscripted in time of war?
16. Should the term of a state governor be limited?
17. Should (servicemen, veterans) with non-service-connected disabilities be hospitalized at government expense?
18. Should labor unions be (outlawed, permitted) in (local, state, federal) functions vital to the national interest?
19. Should all personnel in (local, state, federal) government be required to take loyalty oaths?
20. Should the Merchant Marine be (nationalized, subsidized)?
21. Should military service be (required, voluntary) for all able-bodied (men, women) in time of (peace, war)?
22. Should Utopia make military training (voluntary, compulsory)?
23. Should nepotism in public office be outlawed?
24. Should patronage in (local, state, national) government be dispensed solely on the basis of merit?

25. Should <u>pensions</u> be paid to the dependents of all veterans (with, without) service-connected disabilities or deaths?
26. Should all <u>policemen</u> be required to have at least high school educations?
27. Should the <u>President's</u> term of office be limited?
28. Should (military, naval) personnel be <u>promoted</u> on the basis of (merit, seniority)?
29. Should all veterans, regardless of the nature of their service, have equal <u>rights</u>?
30. Should the armed <u>services</u> be unified?
31. Should the Joint Chiefs of <u>Staff</u> be (abolished, continued)?
32. Should all veterans be <u>trained</u> at government expense?
33. Should all armed forces have identical <u>uniforms</u>?
34. Should Congress set up a Department of <u>Urban</u> <u>Affairs</u>?
35. Should all <u>veterans</u> receive government medical care regardless of (the nature of their disabilities, their ability to pay)?
36. Should <u>veterans</u> have preference in civil service jobs?
37. Should <u>women</u> be drafted into the armed forces?

EVALUATION

OBJECTS

I. <u>Facilities</u> of an agency or organization of (a local, a state, the federal) government devoted to public administration--for example,
   A. Facilities of an air, military, or naval base or camp
   B. Facilities of a local fire or police department
   C. Facilities of a local jail
   D. Facilities of the local branch of the Post Office (or other) Department

II. An <u>object</u> useful to an agency or organization of (a local, a state, the federal) government devoted to some phase of public administration--for example,
   A. A military or naval aircraft--e.g., the X-15, a helicopter
   B. A military vessel--e.g., a battleship
   C. An article of clothing used by or distributed to members of our armed forces
   D. A pen, or other article, supplied for public use by the Post Office Department
   E. A piece of equipment used by our armed services to promote safety--e.g., a parachute
   F. A weapon used by our armed forces--e.g., a rifle

POLICIES

Evaluation of a policy in effect or proposed, of an individual or by an agency of (a local, a state, the federal) government relating to public administration--for example,

A. A policy of a state governor or of the President of the United States--e.g., a policy embodied in an executive order
B. A policy of one of the departments of the federal governments--e.g., a policy of the Department of Agriculture relating to crop production, price supports, etc.
C. A policy of the Marine Corps--e.g., a policy having to do with enlistment, training, promotion retirement, etc.
D. A policy of one of the Service Academies--e.g., a policy relating to cheating, discipline, marriage, etc.
E. A policy of the Secret Service--e.g., a policy having to do with the protection of the President

SOCIAL WELFARE 360-369.99

Thought Starters for ANALYSIS

What about:

1. Abortion: criminal
2. Accident and health insurance
3. Adultery: criminology
4. Aged: welfare services
5. Agencies, welfare
6. American Legion
7. Asylums, mental
8. Asylums, orphan
9. Backward children: welfare services
10. Bank deposit insurance
11. Benevolence: welfare services
12. Blue Cross and Blue Shield insurance
13. Boy and Girl Scouts
14. Business insurance
15. CARE
16. Camp Fire Girls
17. Casualty insurance
18. Chain gangs: prison labor
19. Charities
20. Child guidance clinics
21. Child welfare services
22. Civil War Societies, U.S.
23. Colonial Societies, U.S.
24. Community chest
25. Compulsory insurance
26. Convicts
27. Correctional courts
28. Correctional institutions
29. Crime
30. Crime, causes of
31. Crime detection
32. Crime prevention
33. Criminal anthropology
34. Criminal classes
35. Criminal identification
36. Criminal investigation
37. Criminal psychology
38. Criminals
39. Criminals, juvenile
40. Criminology
41. Crop insurance
42. Daughters of the American Revolution
43. Delinquency, causes of
44. Deposit insurance
45. Disability insurance
46. Disabled, welfare services for
47. Disaster insurance
48. Disaster relief
49. Discharged convicts and delinquents
50. Discipline, prison
51. Domestic relations courts
52. Earthquakes: disaster relief
53. Economic factors in crime
54. Environmental factors in crime
55. Espionage: criminology
56. Family casework
57. Family welfare services
58. Fingerprints: criminal investigation
59. Fire insurance
60. Flood relief
61. Forgery
62. Fraternal associations, orders, and organizations
63. Freemasons
64. Fund raising: social welfare
65. Gangs: juvenile delinquency
66. Government welfare services
67. Group insurance
68. Handicapped: welfare services

NOTE: See also PSYCHOLOGY (130-139.99 and 150-159.99), SOCIOLOGY (301-309.99), LAW (340-349.99), and others

69. Health insurance: industrial and voluntary
70. Hereditary societies
71. Hospitalization insurance
72. Hospitals for specific diseases
73. Identification of criminals
74. Illiteracy: factor in crime
75. Immigration control: crime prevention
76. Imprisonment
77. Incorrigibility: juvenile delinquency
78. Insane, welfare services for
79. Insurance
80. Interviewing: social casework
81. Jails
82. Junior republics: welfare services
83. Juvenile courts
84. Juvenile delinquency
85. Ku Klux Klan
86. Law enforcement
87. Legal aid: welfare services
88. Liability insurance
89. Lie detection: criminal investigation
90. Life insurance
91. Lynching
92. Medical care insurance
93. Mental factors in crime
94. Mental hospitals: welfare services
95. Military societies
96. Mobs: criminology
97. Mothers, welfare services for
98. Motion pictures: factors in crime
99. NSLI: war risk life insurance
100. Numbers game: criminology
101. Nursing homes
102. Obscenity: criminology
103. Occupational factors in crime
104. Old age assistance
105. Pardon: criminology
106. Parole: criminology
107. Patriotic societies
108. Penal institutions
109. Penology
110. Pensions: social security
111. Physical factors: causes of crime
112. Police: crime prevention
113. Political societies
114. Poor, welfare services for
115. Population control: crime prevention
116. Prison labor: penology
117. Prison systems: penology
118. Prisons: penology
119. Prostitution: criminology
120. Public opinion: crime prevention
121. Public welfare: social services
122. Punishment, criminal: penology
123. Rates, insurance
124. Red Cross
125. Reformatories: criminology
126. Reformatory courts
127. Retarded children: welfare services
128. Riots: criminology
129. Rotary International
130. Sanitariums: welfare services
131. Secret orders and societies
132. Service clubs, servicemen's
133. Social clubs
134. Social factors: causes of crime
135. Social security insurance
136. Sterilization, human: crime prevention
137. Subversive activities: criminology
138. Suicide: criminology

139. Summer camps: welfare services
140. Temperament: criminal psychology
141. Theft: criminology
142. Transportation insurance
143. Unemployment: factors in crime
144. Veterans' hospitals
145. Voluntary accident and health insurance
146. Workmen's compensation insurance
147. World War I Societies
148. World War II Societies
149. Young people's societies
150. Youth welfare services

CAUSE and EFFECT

1. (Major) Causes of criminal abortion
2. (Major) Causes of adultery--among men; among women
3. (Major) Effects of age on crime
4. (Major) Effects of the automobile on crime
5. Why I believe in (compulsory, voluntary) automobile insurance
6. (Major) Causes of backwardness in children
7. (Major) Effects of (birth control, overpopulation) on crime--national; in a foreign country
8. Why I (approve of, disapprove of) the aims of the Black Muslims
9. Why I consider CORE (beneficial, detrimental) to the cause of racial equality in America
10. (Major) Effects of the church on crime--generally; locally; a particular church
11. (Major) Causes of class hatreds--in America; elsewhere (e.g., in classless Russia)
12. (Major) Effects of climate on crime
13. (Major) Effects of comic books on crime
14. (Major) Causes of crime--locally; regionally; nationally; in a foreign country
15. Why crime (pays, does not pay)
16. (Major) Effects of cultural factors--e.g., art, literature, motion pictures, radio, television, the theater--on crime
17. (Major) Effects of darkness on crime
18. (Major) Causes of (adult, juvenile) delinquency
19. (Major) Effects of (education, lack of education) on crime
20. (Major) Effects of environment on crime--in rural areas; in urban communities, etc.
21. Why no two fingerprints are alike
22. Why juveniles (join, do not join) gangs
23. Why geniuses turn to crime
24. Why it (pays, does not pay) to hire the handicapped
25. (Major) Effects of heredity on crime
26. Why everyone needs hospitalization insurance
27. Why I consider our houses of correction (capable, incapable) of correction
28. (Major) Effects of immigration on crime

29. (Major) Effects of <u>imprisonment</u> on the criminal
30. Why <u>insurance</u> is (a bargain, a waste of money; a luxury, a necessity)
31. (Major) Effects of (too much, too little) <u>insurance</u>
32. Why I (approve of, disapprove of) the aims of the <u>John Birch Society</u>
33. (Major) Effects of <u>leisure</u> on crime
34. Why I (consider, do not consider) the <u>lie detector</u> a potential liar
35. Why the cost of <u>medical care</u> goes up
36. Why <u>Medicare</u> (makes sense, makes nonsense)
37. Why I consider the <u>NAACP</u> (beneficial, detrimental) to the cause of colored people in America
38. Why <u>population control</u> is (necessary, unnecessary) in crime prevention
39. (Major) Causes of <u>poverty</u>--generally; regionally; locally; at home; abroad
40. (Major) Effects of the <u>press</u> on crime--nationally; locally
41. (Major) Causes of <u>prostitution</u>
42. Why I consider (automobile, burglar, fire, health, life, etc.) insurance <u>rates</u> (reasonable, unreasonable)
43. (Major) Effects of <u>science</u> on crime
44. (Major) Effects of the <u>seasons</u> on crime
45. (Major) Effects of <u>sports</u> on crime
46. Why I consider our local <u>veterans' hospital</u> (satisfactory, unsatisfactory; superior, inferior)
47. (Major) Effects of <u>war</u> on crime
48. Why I consider <u>wiretapping</u> (a legal, an illegal) weapon in criminal investigation

CLASSIFICATION

Kinds/Types of:

1. Aid provided by welfare
2. Charities/charity
3. Correctional institutions
4. Corrective methods
5. Do-gooders
6. Evidence in criminal investigation
7. Fraternal organizations
8. Insurance
9. Methods in crime detection
10. Penal institutions
11. Relief
12. Social welfare
13. Welfare services

COMPARISON and CONTRAST

1. <u>AA</u> and WCTU
2. <u>American Legion</u> and French Foreign Legion
3. <u>Asylums</u>: here and there; yesterday and today--e.g., in the nineteenth century and in the twentieth century
4. <u>Beggar</u>, pauper and tramp
5. <u>Black Muslims</u> and White Citizens' Council
6. <u>Blue Cross</u> and Blue Shield

7. Boy Scouts and Girl Scouts
8. Bread and circuses: here and there; yesterday and today --e.g., in ancient Rome and in modern America
9. Camp Fire Girls and Girl Scouts
10. Charity: at home and abroad--e.g., in foreign aid
11. Correctional courts and punitive courts
12. Correctional methods: here and there; yesterday and today--e.g., in the Middle Ages and today
13. Crime and punishment: here and there; yesterday and today--e.g., in the U.S.A. and in the U.S.S.R.
14. Criminal investigation: here and there; yesterday and today; in fact and in fiction (e.g., on television)
15. Detectives: in fact and in fiction
16. FBI and Scotland Yard
17. Fingerprints and snowflakes
18. Heredity and environment as factors in crime
19. Home and house
20. Homes for the poor and homes for the rich
21. Impulse and premeditation: criminal psychology
22. Insane, treatment of: here and there; yesterday and today
23. Insurance: adequate and inadequate; compulsory and voluntary; government and private
24. Integration and segregation: factors in crime
25. Ku Klux Klan and Black Muslims
26. Lie detector and truth serum
27. Lie detector: here and there; yesterday and today--e.g., during the Massachusetts witch trials and today
28. Mafias: foreign and domestic
29. Manslaughter and murder
30. Murder: first, second, and third degree
31. Outlaws: here and there; yesterday and today; in fact and in fiction--e.g., Al Capone and Robin Hood
32. Parental control and parental indulgence: factors in crime
33. Patriotic societies and subversive societies
34. Patriotism and chauvinism
35. Police: in fact and in fiction
36. Pornography and art
37. The press: in crime prevention and in crime causation
38. Prisons: here and there; yesterday and today--e.g., in Dickens' England and in modern America
39. Private eye: in fiction and in fact
40. Probabilities and certainties: insurance
41. Problem children and problem adults
42. Reform schools, private schools, and public schools
43. Sports: in crime causation and in crime prevention
44. Suicide: in criminology; in law; in religion; in medicine

DEFINITION

1. Accident
2. Charity
3. Crime/criminal
4. Delinquency

5. Inferiority
6. Insanity
7. Liability
8. Literacy
9. Poverty
10. Privacy
11. Responsibility
12. Sanity
13. Self-reliance
14. Superiority
15. Welfare

DESCRIPTION

I. A building, or part thereof, devoted to some phase of social welfare--for example,
   A. An auditorium used by the American Legion
   B. An asylum devoted to the mentally ill or to orphans
   C. A boys' club
   D. Headquarters, local or national, of the FBI
   E. Headquarters of a fraternal or political organization --e.g., the Masons; the NAACP
   F. A jail, penitentiary, or reformatory
II. A camp used to promote, directly or indirectly, social welfare--for example,
   A. A Boy or Girl Scout camp
   B. An abandoned or reactivated CCC Camp
   C. A newly activated Job Corps Camp
   D. A prison or prisoner of war camp

PROCESS

1. How AA helps the alcoholic help himself
2. How to (apply for, secure) aid from a (private, public) welfare agency--generally; locally
3. How to become a (Boy Scout, Girl Scout, Camp Fire Girl)
4. How chemistry is used in criminal investigation
5. How our churches (can, do) help in crime prevention
6. How to commit the perfect crime
7. How to (collect, interpret) criminal evidence
8. How to secure a public defender
9. How deposit insurance works
10. How to become an FBI agent
11. How to lift fingerprints
12. How to conduct a successful fund raising campaign for social welfare
13. How to be (admitted to, discharged from) a (mental, penal) institution
14. How insurance originated
15. How to (buy, sell) insurance
16. How insurance companies "beat the odds"
17. How to conduct an interview in social casework
18. How the lie detector works
19. How to combat the sale of (pornographic, salacious, smutty) literature
20. How to secure medical aid from welfare services--generally; locally

21. How to be an Odd Fellow
22. How to secure (a pardon, a parole)
23. How to be (a wise, a foolish) philanthropist
24. How photography aids in criminal investigation
25. How to help our local police combat crime
26. How to (decrease, abolish) poverty--locally, regionally; nationally; throughout the world
27. How the press (combats, aggravates) crime--generally; locally
28. How to improve our prison systems
29. How to be a "private eye"
30. How to (control, curb, abolish) prostitution--generally; locally
31. How to curb abuses in public welfare
32. How insurance rates are determined
33. How to start a fire with two Boy Scouts
34. How seeing-eye dogs are trained
35. How to get a seeing-eye dog
36. How to apply for social security
37. How wires are tapped
38. How to improve our veterans' hospitals--generally; locally

ARGUMENTATION

PROPOSITIONS OF FACT

1. Are our laws governing abortion (just, unjust; up-to-date, old-fashioned?
2. Do (the right, the wrong) people receive welfare aid--generally; locally?
3. Are our asylums (for the mentally ill; for orphans) (satisfactory, unsatisfactory)--generally; locally?
4. Are automobile insurance rates (reasonable, unreasonable)--generally; in our state?
5. Do the Black Muslims (help, hurt) the cause of the American Negro?
6. Is (Blue Cross, Blue Shield) insurance a (bad, good) buy--generally; in this region?
7. Am I my brother's keeper?
8. Does CORE serve (a useful, a harmful) purpose?
9. Does charity begin (at home; away from home; abroad)?
10. Are our churches (effective, ineffective) in crime prevention--locally; nationally?
11. Is (economic, racial, religious, sexual, some other form of) discrimination by (private, public) social clubs (proper, improper; avoidable; unavoidable)?
12. Are comic books (underrated, overrated) as a cause of crime?
13. Is compulsory (automobile, etc.) insurance (lawful, unlawful; wise, unwise)?
14. Does confinement in prison reform the prisoner?
15. Is it (right, wrong; wise, unwise) to hire ex-convicts?

16. Do our correctional (courts, institutions) correct?
17. Does crime (ever, never) pay?
18. Does the American public condone crime?
19. Is the criminal (born, made)?
20. Is society (too harsh, too lenient) on juvenile criminals?
21. Are our day nurseries (adequate, inadequate)--generally; locally?
22. Are our juvenile and domestic relations courts (effective, ineffective)--generally; locally?
23. Are our family welfare services (adequate, inadequate); satisfactory, unsatisfactory)--generally; locally?
24. Is the female of the criminal species more deadly than the male?
25. Do habitual criminals (have, lack) freedom of will?
26. Is fund-raising under (public, private) social welfare (fairly, unfairly; honestly, dishonestly) administered --generally; locally?
27. Is government life insurance (a good, a bad) buy?
28. Do government welfare services (encourage, discourage) self-reliance?
29. Will a policy of unrestricted immigration (reduce, increase, have no effect on) crime in the United States?
30. Does imprisonment accomplish its purpose?
31. Are the initiations undertaken by fraternal and secret associations (necessary, unnecessary; sensible, silly)?
32. Are Americans (under-, over-) insured?
33. Are our jails (adequate, inadequate; satisfactory, unsatisfactory)--generally; locally?
34. Is the John Birch Society a power (for good, for ill) in America today?
35. Are Ku Klux Klansmen (saints, sinners)?
36. Is the law enforcement in our community (adequate, inadequate; satisfactory, unsatisfactory)?
37. Is legal aid available to the needy in our community (adequate, inadequate; satisfactory, unsatisfactory)?
38. Is life insurance (a luxury, a necessity)?
39. Do our local welfare services provide (adequate, inadequate; satisfactory, unsatisfactory) medical aid to the needy?
40. Does the nation need Medicare?
41. Are the mental hospitals in our community (adequate, inadequate; satisfactory, unsatisfactory)?
42. Do motion pictures (encourage, discourage) crime?
43. Does the NAACP (advance, retard) the lot of the American Negro--generally; locally?
44. Do we pardon (the right, the wrong) criminals?
45. Does crime result from (too much, too little) parental control?
46. Do we parole (the right, the wrong) criminals?
47. Are our patriotic societies--e.g., the American Legion --(chauvinistic, sincerely patriotic)?
48. Do our penal institutions (penalize, reform) the criminal?

49. Is there an adequate substitute for penitentiaries?
50. Is poverty a crime?
51. Does the press glamorize (crime, the criminal)?
52. Does the press (overemphasize, underemphasize) crime?
53. Do stone walls make a prison (or iron bars a cage)?
54. Are private charities enough?
55. Are our laws governing prostitution (just, unjust; realistic, unrealistic)?
56. Does public opinion in America (encourage, discourage) crime?
57. Does public welfare (help, injure) the recipients thereof?
58. Is organized religion (ill equipped, well equipped) to combat crime?
59. Was Robin Hood (a rugged patriot, a socialist, a communist)?
60. Does the Salvation Army save?
61. Are our sanitariums (adequate, inadequate)--generally, locally?
62. Do our laws (encourage, discourage) sex crimes?
63. Is social security a delusion?
64. Does television (exalt, debase) crime?
65. Are our veterans' hospitals (adequate, inadequate; satisfactory, unsatisfactory)?
66. Is there (too much, too little) social welfare--locally; regionally; in our state; in the nation; given to foreign countries?
67. Is wiretapping (a legitimate, an illegal) method of securing information in criminal investigation?
68. Are our youth (strengthened, weakened) by (public, private) welfare services?

PROPOSITIONS OF POLICY

1. Should accident and health insurance be (compulsory, voluntary)?
2. Should accident and health insurance be financed through Social Security?
3. Should the chief responsibility for the care of the aged rest (with the aged themselves; with their families; with society)?
4. Should persons without automobile liability insurance be allowed to operate automobiles on our highways?
5. Should automobile licenses be made by prison labor?
6. Should the chain gang be abolished?
7. Should comic books which make (crime, immorality) attractive be banned from our newsstands?
8. Should criminals be identified by race in the press?
9. Should the names of juvenile criminals be made public--e.g., in the press?
10. Should habitual criminals be sterilized in the interest of crime prevention?
11. Should habitual juvenile delinquents be exposed to public displeasure--e.g., placed in cages, stocks, etc.?

12. Should the parents of habitual juvenile delinquents be held liable for the misdeeds of their children?
13. Should employers be liable for the accidents of their employees?
14. Should habitual unmarried fathers be sterilized by the state?
15. Should all U.S. citizens be fingerprinted at birth by the federal government?
16. Should our community have a new hospital?
17. Should our hospitals refuse to admit those unable to pay?
18. Should the Federal Government finance hospitalization insurance by means of social insurance?
19. Should (our state, the federal government) legalize houses of prostitution?
20. Should the known parents of illegitimate children be compelled to contribute to the support of their offspring?
21. Should known illiterates be compelled to attend school at government expense?
22. Should the federal government institute a policy of free --i.e., unrestricted--immigration?
23. Should a ceiling (of, say, thirty years) be placed on so-called life imprisonment?
24. Should life insurance be financed through Social Security?
25. Should habitual unmarried mothers be sterilized?
26. Should motion pictures be censored in the interest of crime prevention?
27. Should provocative advertisements of motion pictures be banned from our newspapers?
28. Should membership lists of the NAACP be (made public, kept secret)?
29. Should our community (expand, curtail) its welfare services for needy persons?
30. Should old age pensions be financed (privately, publicly)?
31. Should certain illegal organizations--e.g., the American Communist party, the IWW, etc.--be legalized (in order to bring them out into the open)?
32. Should all policemen be required to have at least a high school education?
33. Should the poor be paid (by the state, by the federal government) to (go to, remain in) school?
34. Should the press (play up, play down) crime news?
35. Should prostitution be legalized (in our state, by Act of Congress)?
36. Should (our community, our locality, our county, our town, our city, our state, the federal government) engage in (less, more) public welfare?
37. Should the punishment fit the crime?
38. Should (public, private) social clubs be allowed to discriminate?
39. Should our chronically unemployed be sent to (conservation, rehabilitation) camps?

40. Should (our county, our town, our city, our state, the federal government) (curtail, expand) its welfare program?
41. Should our (delinquent, unemployed) young people be sent to youth camps?

EVALUATION

OBJECTS

I. Facilities of an agency, institution, or organization--local, state, or federal; public or private--devoted to some aspect of social welfare--for example,
   A. Facilities of a local day nursery
   B. Facilities of a fraternal lodge
   C. Facilities of a local (public, private) hospital
   D. Facilities of a local nursing home
   E. Facilities of a local orphanage
   F. Facilities of an area service club for servicemen
   G. Facilities of a local summer camp

II. An object used by an individual or an organization to promote social welfare--for example,
   A. A drunkometer
   B. A fire extinguisher
   C. A pair of handcuffs
   D. A lie detector
   E. A two-way radio used in police work

POLICIES

A policy in effect or proposed by an agency, organization, or institution--local, state, or federal; public or private--devoted to the promotion of social welfare, public or private--for example,

A. A policy of the (local, regional) Blue Cross/Blue Shield Association--e.g., policy on coverage
B. A policy of CARE--e.g., policy relating to eligibility of recipients of CARE packages
C. A policy of (CORE, the NAACP) relating to civil disobedience
D. A policy of a fraternal organization--e.g., membership policy of the Elks
E. A policy of a local hospital--e.g., visiting hours
F. A policy of an insurance company--e.g., a policy regarding teen-age drivers

EDUCATION 370-379.99

Thought Starters for ANALYSIS

What about:

1. Acceleration in schools and colleges
2. Accreditation
3. Administration
4. Admission standards
5. Adult education
6. Alumni
7. Athletics: intercollegiate and intramural
8. Attendance
9. Audio-visual instruction
10. Behavior, student
11. Career, choice of
12. Certification of teachers
13. Church and state in education
14. Coeducation
15. Colleges and universities
16. Compulsory education
17. Consolidated schools
18. Core curriculum
19. Curriculum
20. Customs, student
21. Degrees, earned and honorary
22. Denominational schools
23. Discipline
24. Dormitories
25. Educational measurements
26. Educational methods
27. Educational systems
28. Educational television
29. Educational tests
30. Educators
31. Elementary education
32. Entrance requirements
33. Examinations
34. Extension courses
35. Extracurricular activities
36. Faculties
37. Federal aid
38. Fellowships and scholarships
39. Fraternities and sororities
40. Freedom, academic
41. Girls' education
42. Grades: school credits
43. Grades: school organization
44. Graduate education
45. Grouping, student
46. Handicapped, education of
47. High schools
48. Homework
49. Honor systems
50. Housing, student
51. Integration and segregation
52. Intelligence tests
53. International education
54. Interscholastic athletics
55. Journalism, school
56. Junior colleges
57. Juvenile delinquency
58. Laws and regulations
59. Liberal education
60. Literacy and public education
61. Loyalty oaths
62. Manual training
63. Orientation courses
64. Parent-teacher associations
65. Parochial schools
66. Physical education
67. Placement services
68. Practice teaching
69. Primary schools
70. Private schools and colleges

NOTE: See also PSYCHOLOGY (130-139.99 and 150-159.99), SOCIOLOGY (301-309.99), SOCIAL WELFARE (360-369.99), and others.

71. Problem children
72. Progressive education
73. Promotion, student
74. Public education
75. Rating teachers
76. Remedial education
77. Requirements, educational
78. School buses
79. School meals
80. School systems
81. Schools
82. Secondary education
83. Secret societies
84. Self-education
85. Sex education
86. Sports
87. Standards, academic
88. State aid
89. State control
90. Student aid
91. Student government
92. Student life
93. Student morale
94. Student morality
95. Study
96. Subsidies, school
97. Superior children
98. Teachers' colleges
99. Teaching aids
100. Teaching methods
101. Technical education
102. Textbooks
103. Trade schools
104. Truancy
105. Tuition
106. Uniforms, academic
107. Vacations, school
108. Vocation, choice of
109. Vocational education
110. Vocational guidance
111. Vocational rehabilitation
112. Women, education of
113. Women's colleges

CAUSE and EFFECT

1. (Major) Effects of the (overemphasis, underemphasis) of athletics--generally; at Utopia
2. (Major) Effects of a policy of (compulsory, voluntary) attendance--generally; at Utopia
3. (Major) Effects of the possession of automobiles by students--generally; at Utopia
4. Why I (approve, disapprove) of compulsory chapel attendance
5. (Major) Causes of student cheating--generally; at Utopia
6. (Major) Effects of (small, large) classes on education--generally, at Utopia
7. (Major) Effects of coeducation--generally; at Utopia (Effects on students; on education)
8. Why I (approve, disapprove) of compulsory attendance laws
9. Why school dances are (proper, improper)
10. (Major) Causes of delinquency in schools--generally; at Utopia
11. (Major) Effects of delinquency in schools
12. Why discipline breaks down in schools--generally; at Utopia
13. Why students drink--generally; at Utopia
14. Why driver training is (a proper, an improper) function of our public schools
15. Why students drop out of school--generally; at Utopia
16. Why education is (a privilege for the few; a right for the many)

17. Why "education courses" are (valuable, worthless) to would-be public-school teachers
18. Why higher education for women is (beneficial, harmful)
19. Why the exemption of private educational institutions from taxation is (necessary, unnecessary; proper, improper; wise, unwise)
20. Why federal aid to (public, private) education is (beneficial, essential, dangerous)
21. Why fraternities are (beneficial, harmful) to the (high school, college) student
22. Why grades are (important, overrated)
23. Why the high schools in our (community, state) are (adequate, inadequate; satisfactory, unsatisfactory; superior, inferior)
24. Why the goal of higher education for all in America is (a realizable, an unrealizable) ideal
25. Why I (approve, disapprove) of homework--generally; at Utopia
26. Why our community (needs, does not need) a junior college
27. Why kindergarten is (useful, useless)
28. Why a liberal education is (necessary, outmoded) in a modern technological age
29. Why free lunches (should, should not) be provided for (some, all) students in public schools
30. Why practice teaching is (a necessary, an expendable) part of teacher training
31. Why private schools are (desirable, undesirable) on the (primary, secondary, higher) level of education
32. Why problem children (are, have) problems in our schools
33. Why I have (great, little) faith in Progressive Education
34. Why religious education is (beneficial, harmful) in our (public, private) schools
35. Why remedial courses in basic subjects are (necessary, unnecessary; wise, unwise) on the collegiate level of education
36. Why I (need, deserve) a scholarship
37. Why the year-round school session is (necessary, unnecessary)
38. Why the censorship of schoolbooks is (necessary, unnecessary; wise, unwise)
39. Why I (like, dislike) school
40. Why our schools (are a, are no) bargain--generally; locally
41. Why segregation by sex in our (public, private) schools is (desirable, undesirable; wise, unwise)
42. Why a program of sex education in our (public, private) schools is (necessary, unnecessary; wise, unwise)
43. (Major) Causes of student failure--generally; at Utopia
44. Why student grouping is (fair, unfair; effective, ineffective)--generally; at Utopia
45. Why superior children (should, should not) have special consideration in our (public, private) schools
46. Why teachers' colleges are (worth while, worthless)
47. Why teachers quit

48. Why I (would, would not) like to be a teacher
49. Why our community (needs, does not need) educational television
50. (Good, Bad) Effects of television on education

CLASSIFICATION

Kinds/Types of:

1. ability
2. colleges
3. education
4. educational tests
5. housemothers
6. professors
7. schools
8. state aid
9. student aid
10. students
11. teachers

COMPARISON and CONTRAST

1. Academic freedom and academic slavery
2. Boarding and living at home
3. Campus: in brochure and in fact
4. College degree and union card
5. Curriculum in public schools: for the college-bound student and for the terminal student
6. Degrees: academic and honorary
7. Education: for a trade and for a profession
8. Education: in a convent and in a secular school
9. Education: liberal and technical
10. Education: progressive and (traditional, classical)
11. Education: for followers and for leaders
12. Education: for the many and for the few
13. Education: for the subnormal; for the normal; for the superior
14. Education: in the one-room schoolhouse and in the big-city high school
15. Education: in a small college and in a large university
16. Education: for a livelihood and for living
17. Education: for a career and for marriage
18. Failure: of the student and of the teacher
19. Federal aid and federal hindrance to education
20. Fraternities: high school and college
21. Freedom of teaching: in school, college, and university
22. Games: in kindergarten and in college
23. High schools and prep schools
24. Holidays: for students and for teachers
25. Homework: in school and in college
26. Homework and housework
27. Homework in public school and in private school
28. Homework: by student and by business or professional man or woman.
29. Journalism: school, college, and professional
30. Knowledge and wisdom
31. Learning from books and learning from experience
32. Liberal arts college and technical institute

33. Orientation to school and orientation to life
34. Preparation for life: in public and in private schools
35. Rating teachers: by merit and by length of service
36. Rating teachers: in school and in college
37. Religious education: in public and in private (schools, colleges)
38. Scholar and teacher
39. Scholarships: for athletes and scholarships for scholars
40. School textbooks: sophisticated and puerile
41. School transportation: in public and in private schools
42. Sex education: via the street; via the family; via the school; via the doctor; via the church
43. Songs: in kindergarten and in college
44. Student life: in private and in public school
45. Student morale: in a coeducational school and in an all (boys', girls') school; in a racially integrated school and in a racially segregated school
46. Student morality: in a public school and in a private school; in a parochial school and in a tax-supported school; in a coeducational school and in an all (boys', girls') school; in high school and in college
47. Student mortality: in a public and a private (school, college)
48. Study: before and after the coming of (radio, television)
49. Teachers: in fact and in fiction--e.g., on television
50. Teachers: male and female
51. Teachers: married and unmarried
52. Teachers: with and without children
53. Teachers: in public and in private schools
54. Teachers: in all-male and in all-female schools
55. Teachers: in school and in college
56. Teaching, freedom of: in a church-related (school, college) and in a tax-supported (school, college)
57. Teaching methods: progressive and traditional
58. Television: as an aid and as a hindrance to education
59. Textbooks: objective and slanted
60. Ungraded and graded classes

DEFINITION

1. Ability
2. Censorship
3. Curriculum
4. Education/educator
5. Egghead
6. Equality
7. Freedom
8. Grade
9. Indoctrination
10. Intelligence
11. Ivory tower
12. Knowledge
13. Mediocrity
14. Moonlighting
15. Motivation
16. Plagiarism
17. Privacy/private
18. Research
19. Scholarship
20. Sportsmanship
21. Wisdom

DESCRIPTION

I. A building, or part thereof, of an agency, institution, or organization--local, state, or federal; public or private--devoted to some aspect of education--for example,
   A. A building on Utopia's campus:
      1. Utopia's chapel
      2. Utopia's gymnasium
      3. Utopia's library
   B. A room at Utopia:
      1. A dormitory room
      2. A professor's office
      3. Utopia's rathskeller
      4. The student lounge

II. Facilities used by an agency, institution, or organization devoted to some phase of education--for example,
   A. Utopia's athletic facilities
   B. Utopia's library facilities
   C. Facilities of a particular academic department at Utopia--e.g., the Chemistry Department, the Fine Arts Department

III. An object used in some phase of education--for example,
   A. An academic hood
   B. A piece of audio-visual equipment
   C. A student's desk

PROCESS

1. How to prevent accidents in school
2. How to adjust to (school, college)
3. How to gain admittance to the (school, college) of one's choice
4. How to improve athletics at Utopia
5. How to improve Utopia's campus
6. How to choose a career
7. How to (prepare for, select) a college
8. How to finance a college education
9. How state control of education (helps, hinders) the cause of education (in school, college)
10. How to choose a course of study in college
11. How to reduce the number of drop-outs from (school, college)
12. How to improve the education of our teachers
13. How to improve our elementary schools
14. How to (prepare for, take) an examination
15. How to get a (college, university) fellowship
16. How to prepare for a field trip
17. How to select (a fraternity, a sorority) in (high school, college)
18. How to circumvent the fraternity system in (high school, college)
19. How to stay healthy--in school; in college

20. How to use a library--and spare the librarian
21. How to apply for and get a (school, college) loan
22. How to mix marriage and school
23. How to judge a teacher's merit
24. How the PTA (helps, hurts) education
25. How to (choose, prepare for) a profession
26. How to apple-polish a professor (with, without) an apple
27. How to improve public education--generally; in our state; in our community
28. How to improve the public status of our teachers
29. How to rate a teacher
30. How religion (promotes, retards) education
31. How to educate oneself
32. How the state (aids, frustrates) education
33. How to secure student employment
34. How to raise student morale--generally; at Utopia
35. How to study
36. How to read a textbook
37. (How, How not) to educate women
38. How to work your way through college

ARGUMENTATION

PROPOSITIONS OF FACT

1. Is ability grouping fair to the students so grouped?
2. Do (teachers, professors) in our (schools, colleges) have academic freedom?
3. Are the admission standards in our (schools, colleges) (arbitrary, flexible; reasonable, unreasonable)--generally; at Utopia?
4. Are all-year sessions for our (schools, colleges) (advisable, inadvisable; necessary, unnecessary)?
5. Is the Associate in Arts (A.A.) degree (meaningful, meaningless)?
6. Does Utopia place (too much, too little) emphasis on athletics?
7. Does our state need (compulsory, voluntary) attendance laws for school children?
8. Are (high school, prep school) teachers glorified baby-sitters?
9. Is (compulsory, voluntary) Bible study in our (public, private) schools (constitutional, unconstitutional; desirable, undesirable)?
10. Is our (local, state) board of education (effective, ineffective; satisfactory, unsatisfactory)?
11. Are the cap and gown (desirable, undesirable) on the (primary, secondary, higher) level of education?
12. Is centralization of our public schools (desirable, undesirable; practicable, impracticable)?
13. Is the certification of our (public, private) school teachers (meaningful, meaningless)?
14. Is compulsory chapel (fair, unfair; effective, ineffective)--generally; at Utopia?

15. Can one receive a proper education (with, without) the Christian church?
16. Is a college degree little more than (an "insurance policy," a "union card")?
17. Is a college education wasted on (men, women)?
18. Can (anyone, everyone) benefit from a college education?
19. Do our (colleges, universities) adequately prepare our youth (for life, for living)?
20. Are there (too many, too few) (colleges, universities) in the United States today?
21. Are compulsory school attendance laws (necessary, unnecessary; legal, illegal)?
22. Is state control of public school textbooks (desirable, undesirable; necessary, unnecessary; wise, unwise)?
23. Does (cosmetology, driver-training) belong in the curriculum of our public schools?
24. Is Utopia's curriculum (adequate, inadequate; inferior, superior)?
25. Do our (colleges, universities) grant (too many, too few) (academic, honorary) degree?
26. Is Utopia's policy regarding drinking (effective, ineffective; fair, unfair; realistic, unrealistic)?
27. Is education (a right, a privilege)?
28. (Will, Can) education save the world?
29. Does the (secondary, higher) education provided for women in America (adequately, inadequately) prepare them (for earning a living, for living, for home-making)?
30. Does educational television educate?
31. Do our elementary schools (adequately, inadequately) prepare students for secondary school--generally; at Utopia?
32. Is Utopia's English (or other) program (effective, ineffective; satisfactory, unsatisfactory)?
33. Are Utopia's entrance requirements (reasonable, unreasonable)?
34. Is Utopia's faculty (competent, incompetent; inspired uninspired)?
35. Is federal aid to education (necessary, unnecessary; beneficial, harmful)--generally; at Utopia?
36. Is the four-quarter system for (colleges, universities) (advisable, inadvisable; wise, unwise)?
37. Do (high school, college) fraternities serve (a, no) useful purpose?
38. Does Utopia (encourage, discourage) freedom of teaching?
39. Is the education of gifted children in our (public, private) schools (adequate, inadequate; satisfactory, unsatisfactory)?
40. Do (educators, students, parents) place (too much, too little) emphasis on grades?
41. Do our high schools (adequately, inadequately) prepare their graduates (for business; for college; for making a living; for living; for making a home)?
42. Do our high schools do (too much, too little) for our children?

43. Does coeducation in our high schools (contribute to, detract from) serious study?
44. Is higher education in the United States (progressive, medieval)?
45. Is homework (beneficial, harmful) on the (primary, secondary, higher) level of education?
46. Is the Honor System obsolete in our (schools, colleges, universities)?
47. Is Utopia Junior College (adequate, inadequate)?
48. Does kindergarten have a (beneficial, harmful) influence on the education of children?
49. Is a liberal education (necessary, superfluous) in today's world?
50. Is Utopia's library (adequate, inadequate; satisfactory, unsatisfactory)?
51. Is the loyalty oath for (school, college, university) personnel (necessary, unnecessary; wise, unwise)?
52. (Can, Do) school and marriage mix?
53. Is the Master's Degree (meaningful, meaningless) in education?
54. Do our (schools, colleges, universities) (stress, neglect) moral education?
55. Does our community need a night school?
56. Are parochial (schools, colleges) (beneficial, harmful) in American education?
57. Is Utopia's physical education program (adequate, inadequate; satisfactory, unsatisfactory)?
58. Do our preparatory schools prepare?
59. Do the primers (books) used in our primary schools (bore, challenge, insult, interest) the children reading them?
60. Do private schools produce (good citizens, snobs)?
61. Do college professors understand undergraduates (too little, too well, not at all)?
62. Does progressive education educate?
63. Do our public schools (adequately, inadequately) prepare children (for living; for loafing)?
64. Do our public schools spend (too much, too little) time and money on (academic, non-academic) aspects of education?
65. Do courses in remedial (English, reading, mathematics) belong in higher education--generally; at Utopia?
66. Are our state requirements for teachers (reasonable, unreasonable; satisfactory, unsatisfactory)?
67. Are the school teachers in our (public, private) schools allowed to teach?
68. Is the present (school term, school year) (satisfactory, unsatisfactory) in (primary, secondary, higher) education?
69. Is a crash program in science education (necessary, unnecessary; wise, unwise)--generally; at Utopia?
70. Does segregation (by ability, by race, by sex) in our (public, private)(schools, colleges) (help, hurt) those segregated?

71. Is self-education the only true education?
72. Is the sex education of the young the proper function of (the home; our schools; the church)?
73. Does Utopia place (too much, too little) emphasis on sports?
74. Are Utopia's standards for (admission, graduation) (reasonable, unreasonable; too high, too low)?
75. Are our state colleges and universities monopolies?
76. Does Utopia need a summer school?
77. Can anyone teach?
78. Do teachers' colleges serve (a worth-while, a worthless) purpose?
79. Are teaching machines overrated?
80. Is television (a blessing, a curse) in American education today?
81. Do the writers of (school, college, university) textbooks seek to (inform, indoctrinate) students?
82. Is the trimester system (advisable, inadvisable; effective, ineffective)--generally; at Utopia
83. Do ungraded classes (properly, improperly) serve the cause of education?
84. Are (students, teachers) in our schools given (too many, too few) vacations?
85. Is Utopia's program of vocational education (adequate, inadequate; effective, ineffective)?
86. Are women (discriminated against, given preferential treatment) in American (colleges, universities)?
87. Do our (schools, colleges, universities) adequately prepare women (for life, for living, for making a home, for business, for marriage)?
88. Does education (save, ruin) women?
89. Are there (too many, too few) women teachers in our (public, private) (schools, colleges)?
90. Are women's colleges (necessary, unnecessary; obsolete) in modern America?

PROPOSITIONS OF POLICY

1. Should students be grouped according to (ability, race, religion, sex)?
2. Should colleges and universities grant academic degrees posthumously even though all the requirements for the degrees may not have been met?
3. Should academic degrees be granted for work done solely in correspondence schools?
4. Should academic freedom be (absolute, qualified)--generally; at Utopia?
5. Should Utopia (hire, fire) an avowed (agnostic, atheist, non-Christian)?
6. Should our (schools, colleges, universities) (abandon, initiate) all-year sessions?
7. Should Utopia (abolish, offer) the Associate in Arts (A.A.) degree?

8. Should athletes be given (special consideration, no special consideration) in our (schools, colleges, universities)?
9. Should participation in (interscholastic, intercollegiate) athletics at Utopia be restricted to weekends?
10. Should Bible study in our (public, private) (schools, colleges, universities) be (initiated, continued, outlawed)?
11. Should school books be censored?
12. Should all students attending (public, private) schools be given free bus transportation?
13. Should all students at Utopia be required to live on campus?
14. Should the cap and gown be (instituted, abolished) in our (schools, colleges, universities)--generally; at Utopia?
15. Should chapel attendance at Utopia be (compulsory, voluntary)?
16. Should (school, college) chaperones be paid for their services?
17. Should children begin school a year (earlier, later) than they do?
18. Should class attendance at Utopia be (compulsory, optional)?
19. Should Utopia (abolish, institute) Saturday classes?
20. Should Utopia (abolish, institute) ungraded classes?
21. Should Utopia (institute, abolish) coeducation?
22. Should Utopia (institute, abandon) coeducational dormitories?
23. Should Utopia require for graduation a course in communism?
24. Should the public schools in our community be consolidated?
25. Should students in (high school, prep school, college) be allowed to select their own courses?
26. Should chronic delinquents be kept in school until, say, the age of sixteen?
27. Should denominational (schools, colleges, universities) receive financial aid from (state, federal) government?
28. Should students be disciplined by (their parents or guardians; their teachers, their fellow students)?
29. Should young men and women be taught at home how to drink alcoholic beverages (i.e., before they go to college)?
30. Should driver-training in our public schools be given (under private auspices, at public expense)?
31. Should teen-age drop-outs in our schools be placed in (state, federal) work camps?
32. Should every qualified person in the United States be given an education at (state, federal) expense?
33. Should our future teachers major in education?
34. Should superior students be exempt from final examinations--generally; at Utopia?

35. Should examinations be (proctored, held under an Honor System)--generally; at Utopia?
36. Should Utopia (abandon, offer) extension courses?
37. Should the members of a (school, college, university) faculty fraternize with students?
38. Should a (school, college, university) faculty be permitted to strike?
39. Should the faculty at Utopia (establish, join) a union?
40. Should faculty promotions be made on the basis of (merit, length of service)?
41. Should (school, college, university) faculties be granted (complete, limited) academic freedom?
42. Should federal aid be (given, denied) (private, parochial) (schools, colleges, universities)?
43. Should students attending private (schools, colleges) be granted tuition fees by the (state, federal) government?
44. Should Utopia (institute, scrap) a foreign study program?
45. Should Utopia (adopt, abandon) the four-quarter system?
46. Should Utopia (abolish, institute) fraternities?
47. Should freshmen at Utopia be permitted to join (fraternities, sororities)?
48. Should(teachers, professors) be granted (restricted, unrestricted) freedom of teaching?
49. Should gifted students be educated (separately, with other students)?
50. Should girls be educated (separately, with boys)--generally; at Utopia?
51. Should the formal study of English grammar be (revived, continued, dropped) in our (schools, colleges, universities)?
52. Should Utopia offer health education courses in (mixed, segregated) classes?
53. Should teachers take homework home?
54. Should homework be abolished in our (primary, secondary) schools?
55. Should Utopia (institute, continue, scrap) the honor system?
56. Should Utopia (continue, drop, institute) the practice of granting honorary degrees?
57. Should Utopia be (integrated, segregated) by (race, religion, sex)?
58. Should (the United States, the United Nations) establish a university specifically devoted to international education?
59. Should interscholastic sports and games (be limited to, extend beyond) the boundaries of a state?
60. Should our community establish a junior college?
61. Should qualified "lay readers" be employed in our (schools, colleges) to grade papers?
62. Should Utopia award letters to its scholars (as well as to its athletes)?
63. Should our (schools, colleges, universities) make the loyalty oath a condition for (hiring, firing, tenure)?

64. Should Utopia (permit, prohibit) student marriages?
65. Should a (girl, woman) delay college until after she has married and has children able to take care of themselves?
66. Should married high-school students be barred from participation in extra-curricular activities?
67. Should the thesis be (continued, dropped) as a requirement for the Master's Degree--generally; at Utopia?
68. Should Utopia (institute, discontinue) a (military, naval, air force, space) training program?
69. Should the moral education of youth be the responsibility of (the family, the school, the church)?
70. Should the parents of promising students in our (schools, colleges, universities) be allowed (state, federal) tax exemptions?
71. Should Utopia make (one, two, three, four) years of physical education (compulsory, voluntary) for graduation?
72. Should private (schools, colleges, universities) be tax-exempt?
73. Should chronic problem children in our public schools (be compelled to attend school until the age of sixteen; be sent to state or federal labor camps)?
74. Should (college, university) professors "publish or perish"?
75. Should Utopia promote students regardless of achievement?
76. Should public education be restricted to those unable to pay for private schooling?
77. Should Utopia (abandon, build) a rathskeller?
78. Should Utopia require for graduation a course in religion?
79. Should religious education be outlawed in our public schools?
80. Should religious education in our (public, private) schools be (compulsory, voluntary)?
81. Should Utopia (College, University) offer remedial instruction in basic subjects--e.g., English, mathematics, reading?
82. Should report cards be abolished?
83. Should scholarships be awarded on the basis of (merit, need)?
84. Should school teachers be exempt from non-teaching duties?
85. Should school teachers receive (no) extra compensation for (extracurricular, nonteaching) duties?
86. Should school teachers be allowed to (drink, smoke, use make-up, dance, marry)?
87. Should (semesters, terms) in the (school, college, university) year be (lengthened, shortened)?
88. Should Utopia offer a course in sex education?
89. Should sex education be the primary responsibility of (the home, the school, the church, the family doctor)?

90. Should specialized (i.e., technical) education be begun in the freshman year at college?
91. Should Utopia limit its sports competition to within the state?
92. Should the states adopt uniform standards for (public, private) instruction in our (schools, colleges, universities)?
93. Should Utopia's male students be required to wear coats and ties?
94. Should students be grouped according to (ability, race, sex, religion, background, other)--generally; at Utopia?
95. Should (school, college) textbooks be censored?
96. Should (our school, our state) (abandon, institute) the Tuition Grant Plan (whereby students electing to attend public schools outside their districts or private, non-sectarian schools will be given tuition grants by the state)?
97. Should Utopia (adopt, abandon) ungraded classes?
98. Should a wife work her husband's way through (college, professional school)?
99. Should women be educated (with, without) men?
100. Should women go to college?
101. Should women be taught by (men, women)?
102. Should men be taught by (men, women)?
103. Should women's colleges be (continued, abolished)?
104. Should one work one's way through college?

EVALUATION

OBJECTS

I. Facilities of an agency, institution, or organization devoted to some phase of education--for example,
   A. Facilities of Utopia's athletic department
   B. Facilities of Utopia's cafeteria or dining-hall
   C. Facilities of Utopia's infirmary
   D. Facilities of Utopia's library
   E. Facilities of Utopia's manual arts department
II. A piece of equipment useful in education--for example,
   A. A piece of equipment used in audio-visual education--e.g., a motion-picture projector; a tape-recorder
   B. A piece of equipment used in Utopia's driver-training program--e.g., an automobile
   C. A piece of equipment used in instruction--e.g., a blackboard; a piece of chalk; an eraser
   D. A piece of equipment used in Utopia's Physical Education Department--e.g., a tackling dummy

POLICIES

A policy in effect or proposed by an agency, institution, or organization--local, state, or federal; public or private--devoted, directly or indirectly, to education--for example,

A. A policy of an accrediting association
B. A policy of Utopia* relating to admission or graduation
C. A policy of Utopia relating to class attendance
D. A policy of Utopia relating to discipline
E. A policy of a State Board of Education relating to teacher certification
F. A policy of the federal Department of Health, Education, and Welfare relating to federal aid to education
G. A policy of Utopia relating to the hiring and firing of faculty members

*The student is advised to consult official publications put out by Utopia--e.g., brochures, catalogues, and so forth.

COMMERCE 380-389.99

Thought Starters for ANALYSIS

What about:

1. Air routes
2. Airplanes
3. Automobile transportation
4. Balance of trade: international commerce
5. Bridges: vehicular transportation
6. Broadcasts; radio and TV
7. Buses
8. Channels, television
9. Clipper ships
10. Collecting stamps
11. Colonial trade
12. Commerce
13. Commerce, domestic
14. Commerce, international
15. Communication
16. Communication services
17. Control: public utilities
18. Counterfeit stamps
19. Dial telephones
20. Dining car service
21. Export trade
22. Facilities: air transportation
23. Facilities: automobile transportation
24. Facilities: public utilities and services
25. Facilities: radio communication
26. Facilities: railroad transportation
27. Facilities: telephonic communication
28. Facilities: television communication
29. Facilities: ocean transportation
30. Fares, air
31. Fares, maritime
32. Fares, railroad
33. Federal Communications Commission
34. Franking privileges
35. Freight rates
36. Freight services
37. Government ownership and control: communication
38. Government ownership and control: transportation
39. Harbors: inland waterways and ocean
40. Helicopters
41. Highway traffic control
42. Highways
43. Import trade
44. International highways
45. Interstate commerce
46. Interstate Commerce Commission
47. Lake transportation
48. Land grants: railroads
49. Landing fields
50. Laws and regulations: public utilities
51. Laws and regulations: communication
52. Laws and regulations: transportation
53. Mail delivery
54. Maritime transport
55. Mass communication
56. Medieval ships
57. Merchant marine
58. Merchant ships
59. Metric system
60. Metrology
61. Monorails
62. Motor vehicles: transportation
63. Nationalization: railroad transportation
64. Networks: radio and TV
65. Newscasts: radio and TV
66. Ocean transportation
67. Ownership: public utilities
68. Panama Canal

NOTE: See also such fields as ECONOMICS (330-339.99), LAW (340-349.99), PUBLIC ADMINISTRATION (350-359.99), and others

69. Parking areas
70. Passenger fares: transportation
71. Passenger services: transportation
72. Philately
73. Pipelines
74. Pneumatic dispatch: postal services
75. Ports: inland and ocean
76. Postage stamps
77. Postal communication
78. Postal rates
79. Postal services
80. Postmarks
81. Primitive crafts
82. Private postal systems
83. Public services
84. Public utilities
85. Radio communication services
86. Railroads
87. Rapid transit systems
88. Rates: public utilities and services
89. Ratings, program: radio and TV
90. Regulations: public utilities
91. River transportation
92. Roads
93. Seaports
94. Ships
95. Signals and signaling
96. Stamp collecting
97. Standardization: weights and measures
98. Steamships
99. Stock tickers
100. Subways
101. Suez Canal
102. Superhighways
103. Taxation: public utilities and services
104. Taxicabs
105. Telecasts
106. Telegrams
107. Telephones
108. Television communication
109. Telstar
110. Tolls: transportation charges
111. Trade
112. Trade, domestic
113. Trade, foreign
114. Trade, world
115. Traffic engineering
116. Traffic regulations
117. Trains
118. Transoceanic flights
119. Transoceanic voyages
120. Transportation
121. Trolley buses and cars
122. Trucking
123. Tunnels
124. Underground railways
125. Urban transportation
126. Vehicular transportation
127. Water transportation
128. Watermarks: stamps
129. Weights and measures: metrology
130. World trade
131. ZIP codes

CAUSE and EFFECT

1. Why I support the (public, private) administration of (radio, telephonic, telegraphic, television) communication --generally; locally
2. Why I believe in the (private, public) administration of (air, automobile, ocean, railroad) transportation
3. Why I support the (private, public) administration of utilities
4. (Major) Causes of airplane accidents--generally; locally
5. (Major) Causes of automobile accidents--generally; locally
6. (Major) Reasons for the (origin, disappearance) of clipper ships
7. (Major) Effects of clipper ships on colonization; on world trade

8. Why I (believe in, do not believe in) encouraging commerce between Communist countries--e.g., Red China--and those of the Free World
9. (Major) Effects of (private, public) control of communication services--in the United States; abroad
10. Why I believe in the (public, private) control of utilities--generally; locally
11. (Major) Causes of the (rise, fall) of the dirigible
12. (Major) Causes of (the rise, the fall) of the DC-3
13. Why export trade is (essential, non-essential) to our economy--generally; specifically (with reference to local economy, a local business, etc.)
14. Why we have the Federal Communications Commission
15. Why I (approve of, disapprove of) the Federal Trade Commission as a regulatory agency
16. Why I (support, do not support) government ownership and control of (air, automobile, ocean, railroad) transportation
17. Why (local, intrastate, interstate) highways are (adequate, inadequate; superior, inferior)
18. (Major) Causes of highway accidents--generally; in our state; in our locality
19. (Major) Causes of highway congestion--generally; in our community
20. Why I believe in (encouraging, discouraging) international commerce--between the United States and friendly countries; between the United States and hostile countries
21. Why I (approve, disapprove) of the Interstate Commerce Commission as a regulatory agency
22. Why our local transit system is (satisfactory, unsatisfactory; superior, inferior)
23. Why dogs (like, dislike) mailmen
24. (Major) Effects of mass communications (What forms of mass communication? Kinds of effects? Effects on what or whom?)
25. Why government (support, ownership) of our merchant marine is (desirable, undesirable; necessary, unnecessary)
26. Why I consider our metric system (effective, ineffective; sound, unsound)
27. Why I (approve of, disapprove of) the nationalization of (radio, telegraphic, telephonic, television) communications in the United States
28. Why the nationalization of public utilities in the United States is (desirable, undesirable)
29. Why the nationalization of (air, automobile, ocean, railroad) transportation in the United States is (necessary, unnecessary)
30. Why I consider passenger services provided by our (commercial airplanes, buses, ocean liners, railroads, taxis) (satisfactory, unsatisfactory)--generally; locally
31. Why the services provided by our railroads (are, are not) satisfactory--generally; with reference to a specific Line
32. Why I have (a high, a low) opinion of ratings for radio and/or television programs--generally; locally

33. Why reforms in our metric system are (necessary, unnecessary)
34. Why our (local, state, federal) roads are (inferior, superior)
35. (Major) Effects of (good, poor) roads--generally; in our state
36. (Major) Causes of the (rise, fall) of the streetcar
37. (Major) Causes of the (rise, fall) of the subway
38. Why the (nationalization, internationalization) of the Suez Canal is (necessary, unnecessary; wise, unwise)
39. (Major) Effects of superhighways--generally; in our region
40. (Major) Effects of telstar--nationally; internationally
41. (Major) Effects of the tourist trade--generally; in our state; locally
42. Why I (support, do not support) efforts to construct tunnels in the interest of international communication and trade (e.g., under the Bering Sea; under the English Channel)
43. Why world trade is necessary to world peace
44. Why I am (enthusiastic, less than enthusiastic) about ZIP codes

CLASSIFICATION

Kinds/Types of:

1. Airplanes in transportation
2. Airports
3. Ancient ships
4. Bridges, vehicular
5. Communication
6. Communication services
7. Control of public utilities
8. Freight services
9. Highways
10. Mail delivery
11. Medieval ships
12. Merchant ships
13. Motor vehicles
14. Postal services
15. Postmarks
16. Primitive crafts
17. Public utilities
18. Railroads
19. Roads
20. Ships
21. Signals and signaling
22. Stamps
23. Taxation of public utilities and services
24. Television stations
25. Telegrams
26. Telephones
27. Trade
28. Transportation
29. Watermarks

COMPARISON and CONTRAST

1. Air mail and regular mail
2. Baggage services: on bus; on plane; on train
3. Balloon and helicopter
4. British system and metric system: metrology
5. Bus, streetcar, and taxi
6. Clipper ships and steam ships
7. Collecting: stamps and (coins, match covers, etc.)

8. Commuting: by bus; by car; by train
9. Counterfeit stamps and genuine stamps
10. Dial telephones and manually operated telephones
11. Dining car service and airline meal service
12. Fares: air, bus, train, ship
13. Featherbedding: on planes; on ships; on trains
14. Ferry and bridge
15. First-, second-, third-, and fourth-class mail
16. Helicopters and autogyros
17. Highways and byways
18. Insured mail and registered mail
19. Long distance calls: here and there; yesterday and today
20. Panama Canal and Suez Canal
21. Passenger services in air; in automobile; in ship; in railroad transportation
22. Public utilities and private utilities
23. Roads: ancient and modern
24. Ships: ancient, medieval, and modern
25. Stamp collecting: for pleasure and for profit
26. Telegrams, day letters and night letters
27. Telephones: yesterday, today, and tommorrow
28. Telstar and cable
29. Trains: here and there; yesterday, today, and tommorrow
30. Transoceanic flights: yesterday, today, and tommorrow
31. Transportation: air, land, and sea
32. Viking ships and space ships
33. World trade: at the time of Marco Polo and today

DEFINITION

1. Colonialism
2. Commerce
3. Dimension
4. Eminent domain
5. Featherbedding
6. Franchise
7. Frequency
8. Mass
9. Omnibus
10. Salvage
11. Star route
12. Three-mile limit

DESCRIPTION

I. A building or other structure, or part thereof, devoted to public services and public utilities--for example,
   A. An airplane hangar
   B. A railroad station, or part thereof
   C. A telephone booth
II. Facilities of an agency or organization--local, state, or federal; public or private--devoted to public services and public utilities--for example,
   A. Facilities of a public utility company
   B. Facilities of a firm engaged in (air, bus, railroad, taxi) transportation
III. An object used to promote public services and public utilities--for example,

A. A commercial aircraft--e.g., an airliner; a helicopter
B. A vehicular bridge
C. A railroad dining car
D. An ocean liner, or part thereof
E. A riverboat

PROCESS

1. How to become an air line hostess
2. How to improve (local, regional) air service
3. How to improve (radio, television) broadcasting--generally; locally
4. How to improve bus service--generally; locally
5. How clipper ships originated
6. How to improve (domestic; international) commerce
7. How public utilities are controlled
8. How to improve our highways--locally; in our state; in the nation
9. A letter: from mail box to post office to mail box
10. How to improve our local transit system
11. How to improve our merchant marine
12. How to prepare for an ocean voyage
13. How the Panama Canal was built
14. How to improve postal services--generally; locally
15. How to improve the Post Office--generally; locally
16. How to collect stamps (for pleasure; for profit)
17. How stamps are made
18. How the stock ticker works
19. How to survive on the subway
20. How the Suez Canal was built
21. How to send a telegram
22. How to (make a telephone call; answer the telephone)
23. How the telephone works
24. How to be (a good, a bad) tourist
25. How traffic is regulated
26. How to prepare for a (bus, car, plane, train) trip
27. How tunnels are built
28. How to live (with, without) ZIP codes

ARGUMENTATION

PROPOSITIONS OF FACT

1. Are (local, state, federal) air routes (effective, ineffective; satisfactory, unsatisfactory)?
2. Are our (local, national) airports (adequate, inadequate; satisfactory, unsatisfactory)?
3. Is (local, intrastate, interstate, international) air transportation (efficient, inefficient; safe, unsafe)?
4. Is the baggage service provided by our (air lines; buses; trains) (satisfactory, unsatisfactory)?

5. Do our (local, intrastate, interstate, school) buses provide (satisfactory, unsatisfactory) service?
6. Is commerce a form of cheating?
7. Are the facilities provided for (air, automobile, maritime, railroad) transportation (adequate, inadequate; satisfactory, unsatisfactory)--generally; locally?
8. Are our (radio, telegraph, telephone, television) communication facilities (adequate, inadequate; satisfactory, unsatisfactory)--generally; in our state; locally?
9. Are (air, automobile, maritime railroad) fares (reasonable, unreasonable)?
10. Is the Federal Communications Commission (the friend, the enemy) of (the American people; the communications industry)?
11. Does the Federal Trade Commission (promote, restrain) honest trade in the United States?
12. Is featherbedding necessary?
13. Do government officials (and others) with the franking privilege (use wisely, abuse) the privilege?
14. Are freight rates (reasonable, unreasonable)?
15. Is government (ownership, control) of transportation (wise, unwise; necessary, unnecessary)?
16. Is government (ownership, control) of communications (necessary, unnecessary; wise, unwise)?
17. Are our harbors (adequate, inadequate)--generally; regionally; locally?
18. Are our (local, intrastate, interstate, super-) highways (adequate, inadequate)?
19. Is the Interstate Commerce Commission the (friend, enemy) of (the public, businesses engaged in such commerce)?
20. Is lake transportation (adequate, inadequate; satisfactory, unsatisfactory)--generally; locally?
21. Are (local, state, federal) laws and regulations governing public utilities (effective, ineffective; fair, unfair)?
22. Are (local, state, federal) laws and regulations governing (radio, telegraph, telephone, television) communication (discriminatory, nondiscriminatory; fair, unfair)?
23. Are (local, state, federal) laws and regulations governing (air, automobile, maritime, railroad) transportation (fair, unfair)?
24. Is our local transit system (efficient, inefficient; adequate, inadequate)?
25. Are our (local, state, federal) mail services (efficient, inefficient; up-to-date, out-of-date)?
26. Is our merchant marine (efficient, inefficient; adequate, inadequate)?
27. Is the metric system (satisfactory, unsatisfactory)?
28. Is nationalization of (communications, transportation) in the United States (necessary, unnecessary; wise, unwise)?
29. Is the Panama Canal obsolete?
30. Are postal rates (reasonable, excessive)?

31. Is a private postal system the answer?
32. Are our railroads (efficient, inefficient)?
33. Are program ratings for (radio, TV) (meaningful, meaningless)?
34. Is metrology in need of reform?
35. Are our (local, state) roads (a credit, a discredit) to (the locality, the state)?
36. Are our public utilities taxed (fairly, unfairly)?
37. Is the telephone (a blessing, a curse)?
38. Does television (inform, indoctrinate, brainwash) the American people?
39. Are trucks on our highways (a blessing, a curse)?
40. Do ZIP codes accomplish their purpose?

PROPOSITIONS OF POLICY

1. Should U.S. airlines be nationalized?
2. Should billboards be banned from interstate highways?
3. Should toll be charged on _______ Bridge?
4. Should the United States join the Common Market?
5. Should our (radio, telegraph, telephone, television) communication services be nationalized?
6. Should the _______ Railroad (institute, continue, discontinue) dining car service?
7. Should the _______ (Airlines, Bus Company, Railroad, Steamship Line) (expand, curtail) its facilities and/or services?
8. Should the _______ Utility Company (expand, curtail) its facilities and/or services?
9. Should the _______ (Telegraph, Telephone) Company (expand, curtail) its facilities and/or services?
10. Should the _______ (Radio, Television) Network (expand, curtail) its facilities and/or services?
11. Should the _______ (Airlines, Bus Company, Steamship Company, Railroad) (raise, lower) its fares?
12. Should the United States (promote, discourage) foreign trade with communist countries?
13. Should the franking privilege be (expanded, discontinued)?
14. Should freight rates on our public carriers be (raised, lowered)?
15. Should the federal government own and control public (communications, transportation, utilities)?
16. Should our merchant marine be nationalized?
17. Should the United States adopt the metric system?
18. Should our railroads be nationalized?
19. Should our radio and/or television networks be nationalized?
20. Should the American people rely on private postal systems?
21. Should private firms engaged in public service--e.g., air mail, merchant marine--be subsidized by the Federal Government?
22. Should the Suez Canal be internationalized?

23. Should world television--e.g., via telstar--be internationalized?
24. Should the three-mile limit be extended?
25. Should the United States (promote, oppose) free trade?
26. Should a tunnel link (France and England; Alaska and Siberia)?
27. Should the use of ZIP codes be (continued, discontinued)?

EVALUATION

OBJECTS

I. Facilities of an agency or firm--local, state, or federal; public or private--devoted to public services and public utilities--for example,
   A. Facilities of an airline
   B. Facilities of a local transit (bus or subway) system
   C. Facilities of a radio/TV station
   D. Facilities of a railroad
   E. Facilities of a telephone/telegraph company
II. An object used to promote public services and public utilities--for example,
   A. A bus
   B. A highway, road, or street
   C. A mailbox
   D. A local parking area
   E. A taxicab
   F. A telephone

POLICIES

A policy, in effect or proposed, of an agency, firm, or organization--local, state, or federal; public or private--devoted to public services and public utilities--for example,

A. A policy of a local gas or electric company--e.g., in relation to the reading of meters
B. A policy of the Federal Communications Commission--e.g., in relation to the licensing of television stations
C. A policy of the Federal Trade Commission--e.g., in relation to false advertising
D. A policy of the Interstate Commerce Commission--e.g., in relation to the shipment of weapons across state lines
E. A policy of the Post Office--e.g., in relation to the number of mail deliveries per day
F. A policy of a local radio or television station or of a national radio or television network--e.g., in relation to the acceptance of liquor advertisements
G. A policy of a telephone or telegraph company--e.g., in relation to the delivery of telegrams

CUSTOMS AND FOLKLORE 390-399.99

Thought Starters for ANALYSIS

What about:

1. Animals: folklore
2. Armor: war customs
3. Arthur, King: legends
4. Barbering
5. Bathing
6. Battle cries
7. Beards
8. Behavior codes: etiquette
9. Beliefs, traditional
10. Bigamy
11. Birth
12. Birthdays
13. Blunders
14. Bridal customs
15. Brownies: folklore
16. Burial customs
17. Buried treasure: legends
18. Carnivals
19. Celebrations, public
20. Cemeteries
21. Chapbooks
22. Charms: folklore
23. Christening
24. Christmas celebration
25. Circumcision
26. Clothing
27. Conventions, traditional
28. Costume and costume accessories
29. Courting customs
30. Cremation
31. Cries, popular
32. Cures: folklore
33. Curses: folklore
34. Customs: folklore
35. Dances, social and war
36. Dating etiquette
37. Dead: disposal and treatment
38. Death customs
39. Dowry
40. Dreams: folklore
41. Dress
42. Dress reform movements
43. Drinking: social customs
44. Dueling
45. Dwarfs: folklore
46. Easter celebration
47. Eating
48. Emancipation: women
49. Embalming
50. Engagement
51. Engagement: etiquette
52. Entertaining: etiquette
53. Etiquette: social customs
54. Evil spirits
55. Fairies
56. Fairs: social customs
57. Family customs
58. Fashion customs
59. Fashion movements
60. Feminism: sociology
61. Festivals, public
62. Fire: folklore
63. Folkways: customs
64. Funeral customs
65. Ghosts
66. Giants
67. Goblins
68. Good Friday observation
69. Grail legends
70. Graves: burial customs
71. Gremlins
72. Gypsies
73. Habits: customs
74. Hairdressing customs
75. Hara-kiri suicide customs
76. Haunted places
77. Heroes and heroines: legends
78. Holidays: celebration
79. Home life customs
80. Honeymoon customs

NOTE: See also such related fields as ETHICS (170-179.99), RELIGION (200-299.99), and SOCIOLOGY (300-309.99).

81. Hospitality: etiquette
82. Kissing customs
83. Legal status of women
84. Legendary characters: folklore
85. Legends: folklore
86. Local customs: folklore
87. Love letters: etiquette
88. Magic: folklore
89. Mardi gras: celebration
90. Marriage customs
91. Marriage: etiquette
92. Medical superstitions: folklore
93. Men: costumes
94. Mermaids: folklore
95. Mother Goose: folklore
96. Mothers: customs
97. Mourning customs
98. Mourning: etiquette
99. Mummies: customs
100. Mythology, geographical
101. Numbers: folklore
102. Official ceremonies: social customs
103. Parades: social customs
104. Perfumes: customs
105. Personal appearance: customs
106. Poltergeists: folklore
107. Polyandry: sex customs
108. Polygamy: marriage customs
109. Prophecies: folklore
110. Proverbs: folklore
111. Puberty: sex customs
112. Rhymes: folklore and nursery
113. Riddles: folklore
114. Rings, costume
115. Round Table legends
116. Sea serpents
117. Sex customs
118. Shaving customs
119. Shoes: costume accessories
120. Showers: wedding etiquette
121. Social conduct: etiquette
122. Social customs
123. Suicide customs
124. Supernatural beings
125. Superstitions
126. Symbolism: folklore
127. Table manners
128. Tales: folklore
129. Talismans
130. Tall tales
131. Tattooing: customs
132. Tobacco: social customs
133. Toilet: customs
134. Torture: war customs
135. Tournaments: social customs
136. Traditions: etiquette and folklore
137. Travel etiquette
138. Underwear: costume accessories
139. Vampires
140. Wakes: mourning customs
141. War customs
142. Weapons: war customs
143. Wedding customs
144. Wedding etiquette
145. Werewolves: folklore
146. Wigs
147. Woman
148. Women, careers for
149. Women's rights

CAUSE and EFFECT

1. Why men (wore, wear) beards--generally; at a particular time and place
2. Why we (behave, misbehave) like human beings
3. Why (men, women) in (civilized, primitive) societies, practice bigamy
4. Why the bride is "given away"
5. (Major) Causes of the (rise, decline) of the practice of bundling
6. Why I consider our burial customs (civilized, barbaric)

7. Why cannibals eat human flesh
8. Why chivalry is (dead, still alive) in the modern world
9. Why I (welcome, dread) the celebration of Christmas in modern America
10. Why (men, women, children) wear clothes
11. Why I (approve, disapprove) of the clothes worn by (men, women, children)
12. (Major) Effects of clothes--on morality; on morale; on health; on economics, etc.
13. Why (men, women, children) (wear, wore) corsets
14. Why (men, women) (use, used) cosmetics
15. Why courtesy pays
16. Why men show courtesy to women--and vice versa
17. Why our courting customs are (still vital, old-fashioned)
18. Why (men, women, children) dance
19. Why I consider our death customs (civilized, barbaric)
20. Why the giving of a dowry is (a sensible, a foolish) custom
21. Why I consider dress reform (necessary, unnecessary) in the United States
22. Why (men, women) drink
23. Why the emancipation of women is (desirable, undesirable; wise, unwise; necessary, unnecessary; possible, impossible)--e.g., in America; in Russia
24. Why I believe in (long, short) engagements
25. Why I believe in evil spirits
26. Why I believe in fairies
27. Why family customs (live, die)--generally; in my family
28. Why fashion is fickle
29. Why American women are (mad, sensible) about fashion
30. (Major) Effects of fashion--on economics; on health; on morale; on morality
31. (Major) Effects of feminism--on women; on men; on children
32. Why people worshiped fire
33. Why I consider our funeral customs (civilized, barbaric)
34. Why (men, women) wear hats
35. Why head-hunters hunt heads
36. (Major) Effects of home on woman
37. Why I consider honeymoon customs (vital, old-fashioned)
38. Why the custom of "ladies first" is (still vital, old-fashioned)
39. Why I consider our local custom of ________ (wise, foolish)
40. (Major) Causes of the decline of manners in America today
41. (Major) Effects of the decline of manners in modern America
42. Why our marriage customs are (vital, old-fashioned)
43. Why I (believe in, do not believe in) the institution of marriage
44. Why I consider men's clothes (sensible, ridiculous)

45. Why I consider our mourning customs (civilized, barbaric)
46. Why people (were, are) mummified--e.g., in ancient Egypt
47. Why women wear perfume
48. Why I consider Americans (too much, too little) concerned with personal appearance
49. Why (men, women, adolescents, children) (are, are not) polite to each other
50. Why I consider the practice of polyandry (proper, improper)
51. Why I consider the practice of polygamy (proper, improper)
52. Why religion (has, has not) gone out of our religious holidays
53. Why people shake hands
54. Why (men, women, adolescents, children) (do, do not) wear shoes
55. Why I consider wedding showers (a fine, a cynical) custom
56. Why people use snuff
57. Why people are superstitious
58. Why table manners are (important, overrated)
59. Why (men, women) get tattooed
60. Why (men, women, adolescents) use tobacco
61. Why people (adhere to, flout) tradition(s)
62. Why women wear veils--e.g., in America; in the Middle East
63. Why women (go, do not go) to war
64. Why I consider our wedding customs (vital, old-fashioned)
65. Why (men, women) wear wigs
66. Why women kiss (men, other women)
67. Why I fight (for, against) women's rights

CLASSIFICATION

Kinds/Types of:

1. Accessories, costume
2. Amazons
3. Beards
4. Bridal customs
5. Burial customs
6. Cannibalism
7. Clothes/clothing
8. Clothes horses
9. Dating customs/etiquette
10. Drinking customs
11. Earth burial customs
12. Emancipation for women
13. Engagement customs
14. Family customs
15. Fashion
16. Feminists
17. Funeral customs
18. Headdress
19. Honeymoon customs
20. Hospitality
21. Marriage customs
22. Mourning customs
23. Sex customs
24. Shoes/slippers
25. Showers, wedding
26. Suicide customs
27. Superstitions
28. Torture in war
29. War customs
30. War dances
31. Wedding customs

1. Amazons: ancient and modern
2. Apparitions: in folklore and in psychiatry
3. Armies, customs of: ancient, medieval, and modern
4. Banqueting customs: here and there; yesterday and today --e.g., in ancient Rome and in Elizabethan England
5. Bathing customs: here and there; yesterday and today-- e.g., in America and in Japan
6. Battle cries: primitive and civilized
7. Birth customs: here and there; yesterday--and today e.g., in ancient Sparta and in modern America
8. Burial customs: here and there; yesterday and today-- e.g., in pagan Rome and in modern America
9. Celebrations, public: here and there; yesterday and today--e.g., for a Roman Emperor and for an American President
10. Chivalry: here and there; yesterday and today--e.g., in the days of King Arthur and in the ante-bellum South
11. Christmas celebration: here and there; yesterday and today--e.g., at the birth of Christ and in modern America
12. Christmas celebration: in the church and in the market-place
13. Clothing customs: among men and among women
14. Cosmetics: here and there; yesterday and today--e.g., in ancient Egypt and in modern America
15. Courtesy: with and without breeding
16. Courting customs: here and there; yesterday and today-- e.g., in the Age of chivalry and today
17. Dress: here and there; yesterdav and today--e.g., in France before and after the Revolution
18. Eating and drinking customs: here and there; yesterday and today--e.g., in ancient, medieval, and modern times
19. Emancipation of women: here and there; yesterday and today--e.g., in France and in Russia after their Revolutions
20. Fairs: ancient, medieval, and modern
21. Fashion: here and there; yesterday and today--e.g., during the Restoration and today
22. Feminists: here and there; yesterday and today--e.g., in the United States and in the Soviet Union
23. Hospitality: Northern, Southern, Eastern, Western
24. Marriage customs: here and there; yesterday and today-- e.g., among Quakers, Jews, and Catholics
25. Outlaws: in legend and in fact
26. Patriotic holidays: as they should be and as they are
27. Religious holidays: in theory and in fact
28. Social drinker and alcoholic
29. Suicide customs: here and there; yesterday and today-- e.g., in ancient Rome and in modern Japan
30. Torture: physical and mental (e.g., brainwashing)
31. War customs: here and there; yesterday and today--e.g., in ancient, medieval, and modern times

32. Weapons: here and there; yesterday and today--e.g., in ancient, medieval, and modern times
33. Wigs: here and there; yesterday and today--e.g., in 18th century (England, France) and in modern America
34. Woman's place: here and there; yesterday and today--e.g., in the Latin American countries and in the United States
35. Women in war: here and there; yesterday and today--e.g., in the United States and in the Soviet Union during World War II
36. Women's costumes: here and there; yesterday and today--e.g., in ancient, medieval, and modern times

DEFINITION

1. Accessory
2. Amazon
3. Apparition
4. Bogy
5. Bundling
6. Chivalry
7. Conundrum
8. Courtesy
9. Elf
10. Fable
11. Fashion
12. Fete
13. Gnome
14. Harem
15. Incantation
16. Joust
17. Leprechaun
18. Lingerie
19. Lullaby
20. Maypole
21. Myth
22. Omen
23. Poltergeist
24. Primitivism
25. Saga
26. Seppuku
27. Totem pole

DESCRIPTION

I. A building or other structure (or part thereof) devoted to some aspect of custom or folklore, including etiquette, fashion, personal appearance--for example,
   A. A barber shop or beauty salon
   B. A funeral parlor
   C. A haunted house, or part thereof
   D. A honeymoon cottage

II. An article of clothing or ornamentation formerly or presently worn as part of custom, etiquette, fashion, or personal appearance, etc.--for example,
   A. A suit of armor
   B. A charm bracelet
   C. An engagement ring
   D. A wig

III. An object associated with custom, etiquette, fashion, or personal appearance--for example,
   A. A coffin
   B. A fan
   C. A hara-kiri knife
   D. A May or Totem pole

PROCESS

1. How the Amazons originated
2. How the barber pole came about
3. How battle cries--e.g., the "Rebel Yell"--came about
4. How to grow a beard
5. How a certain birthday custom originated--e.g., blowing out candles
6. How a particular bridal custom came about--e.g., tossing the bridal bouquet
7. How a particular burial custom originated--e.g., sprinkling dirt on the coffin
8. How to be chivalrous today
9. (How, How not) to celebrate Christmas
10. How a particular custom associated with the celebration of Christmas originated--e.g., gift-giving
11. How clothes originated
12. How a particular article of clothing originated--e.g., the veil
13. How a particular courting custom originated--e.g., giving a corsage
14. How the dowry originated
15. How a particular custom associated with eating and drinking originated--e.g., the official taster; the drinking of toasts, etc.
16. How a custom associated with engagement originated--e.g., the engagement ring
17. How a particular family custom originated
18. How the Faust legends originated
19. How to be a feminine feminist
20. How the feminist movement originated
21. How a particular funeral custom originated--e.g., the riderless horse in a State Funeral
22. How the Grail Legends originated
23. (How, How not) to celebrate a holiday
24. How a custom associated with the honeymoon originated--e.g., the shivaree
25. How to (kiss, be kissed)
26. How the Mardi Gras originated
27. How the custom known as May Day originated
28. How the Mother Goose legends arose
29. How a particular mourning custom originated--e.g., the wearing of black
30. How a custom associated with a national holiday originated--e.g., shooting firecrackers on July 4
31. How to improve one's personal appearance
32. How polyandry originated
33. How polygamy originated
34. How a custom associated with a religious holiday originated--e.g., the Christmas tree
35. How the legends of Robin Hood originated
36. How the military salute originated
37. How the custom of scalping originated
38. How to catch a sea serpent

39. How a particular sex custom originated--e.g., concubinage
40. How to give a (wedding) shower
41. How the practice of using snuff originated
42. How to commit suicide
43. How table manners originated
44. How tipping originated
45. How a particular custom associated with a wedding originated--e.g., the practice of throwing rice
46. How to forget that a woman is a woman

ARGUMENTATION

PROPOSITIONS OF FACT

1. Is the adage ___________ (sound, silly)? (E.g., "Two heads are better than one.")
2. Do beards signify (affectation, distinction)?
3. Is bigamy (natural, unnatural; moral, immoral)?
4. Are our bridal customs (sensible, silly)?
5. Are our burial customs (barbaric, civilized)?
6. Is there buried treasure (nearby, somewhere)?
7. Can cannibalism be justified?
8. Is our local cemetery (adequate, inadequate)?
9. Is chivalry dead in modern America?
10. Is christening (a meaningful, a meaningless) rite?
11. Do Americans celebrate Christmas (properly, improperly)?
12. Is a civil marriage enough?
13. Do clothes make (the man, the woman)?
14. Are our clothing customs (sensible, silly)?
15. Is courtesy dead?
16. Are our courting customs (sensible, silly)?
17. Is the practice of cremation (civilized, barbaric)?
18. Are our dating customs (sensible, silly)?
19. Is the dowry (justified, unjustified)?
20. Is embalming (a civilized, a barbaric) practice?
21. Are our engagement customs (sensible, senseless)?
22. Do evil spirits exist?
23. Do fairies exist?
24. Is fashion (sensible, fickle)?
25. Are feminists (smart, foolish)?
26. Are our funeral customs (civilized, barbaric)?
27. Do ghosts exist?
28. Is the harem (a natural, an unnatural; a moral, an immoral) institution?
29. Do Americans have (too many, too few) holidays?
30. Are our honeymoon customs obsolete?
31. Is (Northern, Southern, Eastern, Western) hospitality a myth?
32. Is ours (a man's, a woman's) world?
33. Are good manners (acquired, instinctive)?
34. Are our marriage customs obsolete?
35. Is the celebration of May Day (civilized, barbaric)?

36. Can any of our medical superstitions be justified?
37. Do men dress for women or for themselves?
38. Do we pay (too much, too little) attention to personal appearance?
39. Is polyandry (a moral, an immoral; a natural, an unnatural) state?
40. Is (man, woman) naturally (monogamous, polygamous)?
41. Do we celebrate our religious holidays in (a holy, an unholy) way?
42. Was Robin Hood (a Communist, a Socialist)?
43. Do sea serpents exist?
44. Are wedding showers legalized extortion?
45. Do supernatural beings exist?
46. Is tipping a form of legalized extortion?
47. Is "tradition" a dirty word?
48. Are our wedding customs obsolete?
49. Are wigs (a legitmate, an illegitimate) form of deception?
50. Does a man chase a woman until she catches him?
51. Is woman's place (in the home; in business; in the professions)?
52. Do women belong to the weaker sex?
53. Are women (superior, inferior) to men?
54. Are women emancipated?
55. Do women dress (for other women, for men)?
56. Do women want to be placed on a pedestal?

PROPOSITIONS OF POLICY

1. Should one judge a person on the basis of (his, her) personal appearance?
2. Should people be (given numbers, fingerprinted) at birth?
3. Should adults over the age of ____ celebrate birthdays?
4. Should one be (buried, cremated, entombed)?
5. Should women court men (obviously)?
6. Should our courting customs be revised?
7. Should a girl ask a boy for a date?
8. Should a dating couple "go dutch"?
9. Should the dowry be (encouraged, discouraged)?
10. Should dress be reformed?
11. Should the family be abolished?
12. Should flowers be omitted at funerals?
13. Should honeymooners "go dutch"?
14. Should we have trial marriages?
15. Should we (encourage, discourage) (polyandry, polygamy)?
16. Should the wedding shower be discontinued?
17. Should teen-agers give up bus seats to adults?
18. Should tipping be (encouraged, discouraged)?
19. Should one (adhere to, ignore) tradition?
20. Should women actively fight in war?
21. Should a woman be president of the United States?
22. Should women be placed on pedestals?
23. Should women and children "be first"?

24. Should young people be taught at home how to drink alcoholic beverages?

EVALUATION

OBJECTS

A useful object associated with custom, etiquette, or tradition--for example,

A. An article of clothing--e.g., a girdle; a pair of shoes
B. A coffin
C. A costume accessory--e.g., a handbag
D. A gravestone
E. A razor
F. A wedding gown

POLICIES

A policy of an agency, firm, organization, or institution--local, state, or federal; public or private--associated with some aspect of custom or folklore, including etiquette, fashion, or personal appearance--for example,

A. A policy implied in an adage or proverb--e.g., "Neither a borrower nor a lender be"
B. A policy of a church relating to (birth, marriage, death)
C. A policy of funeral parlor
D. A policy of a local cemetery
E. A policy of a business establishment regarding tipping
F. A policy of a firm relating to the dress of employees

ASTRONOMY AND ALLIED SCIENCES 520-529.99

Thought Starters for ANALYSIS

What about:

1. Aerial surveying
2. Analysis: spectrum
3. Ancient astronomy
4. Ancient calendars
5. Astrology
6. Astronomers
7. Astronomical geography
8. Astronomical horology
9. Astronomical photography
10. Astrophysics
11. Boundary surveying
12. Calendars: chronology
13. Celestial bodies
14. Celestial navigation
15. Christian calendars
16. Chronology
17. Church chronology
18. Clocks
19. Comets
20. Constellations
21. Coordinates
22. Copernican theory
23. Cosmic chemistry
24. Cosmic time
25. Cosmology
26. Craters, lunar
27. Days
28. Destruction: universe
29. Dimensions: celestial bodies
30. Distances: celestial bodies
31. Earth
32. Eclipses: lunar and solar
33. Energy, solar
34. Equator
35. Equinoxes
36. Expanding universe
37. Extragalactic systems
38. Falling stars
39. Galactic system
40. Geocentric theory
41. Geodesy
42. Glacial cosmogony
43. Greenwich time
44. Gregorian calendar
45. Halley's comet
46. Heat: lunar, solar, and terrestrial
47. Heliocentric theory
48. Hydrographic surveying
49. Intervals of time
50. Julian calendar
51. Jupiter
52. Kepler's laws
53. Light: lunar, solar, and terrestrial
54. Lunar astronomy
55. Lunar climatology
56. Lunar spectroscopy
57. Lunar tides
58. Maps: cartography
59. Maritime surveying
60. Mars
61. Mathematical geography
62. Medieval astronomy
63. Mercator projection: cartography
64. Mercury
65. Meteorites and meteors
66. Milky Way
67. Months
68. Moon
69. Motion in space
70. Mountains: lunar topography
71. Natural astrology
72. Nautical almanacs
73. Nautical astronomy
74. Nautical surveying
75. Nebular hypothesis
76. Nebulae
77. Neptune
78. Non-Christian calendars
79. Observational techniques
80. Observatories
81. Orbits: celestial bodies

NOTE: See also PHYSICS (530-539.99), EARTH SCIENCES (550-559.99), and others

82. Orreries
83. Outer space
84. Photographic surveying
85. Physical astronomy
86. Plane surveying
87. Planetariums
88. Planets
89. Plurality of worlds
90. Pluto
91. Popular astronomy
92. Ptolemaic theory
93. Radiation: celestial bodies
94. Radio astronomy
95. Reform, calendar
96. Relativity
97. Rotation: celestial bodies
98. Satellites
99. Saturn
100. Seasons: earth astronomy
101. Selenography
102. Shooting stars
103. Solar astronomy
104. Solar system
105. Space
106. Spectroscopy: celestial bodies
107. Star names: descriptive astronomy
108. Stars
109. Stellar astronomy
110. Structure: universe
111. Sun
112. Sun rising and setting
113. Sundials
114. Sunspots
115. Surveying, geographic
116. Telescopes
117. Terrestrial astronomy
118. Tides: lunar, solar, and terrestrial
119. Time
120. Topography, lunar and terrestrial
121. Transits: descriptive astronomy
122. Triangulation: surveying
123. UFO's
124. Universal gravitation
125. Universe
126. Uranography
127. Uranus
128. Venus
129. Watches
130. Weeks
131. World astronomy
132. World calendars
133. Years
134. Zodiac

CAUSE and EFFECT

1. Why the earth's axis is tilted
2. Why we have different calendars
3. Why celestial bodies (move; remain in their orbits; fall)
4. Why the moon has (craters, mountains)
5. Why (days, nights) vary in length
6. Why distances from the earth (to the moon; to the planets) vary
7. Why the earth was created
8. Why the earth has (seasons; tides)
9. (Major) Effects of (the moon, the sun) on the earth
10. (Major) Causes of (lunar, solar) eclipses
11. (Major) Effects of (lunar, solar) eclipses on the earth
12. (Major) Effects of gravity on the earth
13. Why chronologists employ Greenwich Time
14. Why we have the International Date Line
15. Why we see a man in the moon
16. Why the moon sometimes has a ring around it
17. Why the moon rises at different times of the day
18. Why the moon appears to change its shape

19. Why the moon shines
20. Why we see only one side of the moon
21. Why one weighs less on the moon than on the earth
22. (Major) Effects of the moon on the earth
23. Why planets travel in elliptical paths
24. Why planets have moons
25. Why our seasons change
26. Why the sky seems blue
27. Why stars (shine, twinkle)
28. Probable effects of a marked (increase, decrease) of the sun's temperature on the earth
29. (Beneficial, Harmful) Effects of the sun on the earth
30. Why telescopes employ (lenses, mirrors)
31. (Major) Causes of (lunar, solar) tides
32. (Major) Effects of (lunar, solar) tides on the earth
33. Why we have different time zones
34. Why Venus has clouds

CLASSIFICATION

Kinds/Types of:

1. Astronomers/astronomy
2. Astronomical instruments
3. Calendars
4. Celestial bodies
5. Clocks
6. Eclipses
7. Energy
8. Equinoxes
9. Light
10. Maps
11. Moons
12. Motion in space
13. Satellites
14. Stars
15. Surveying
16. Telescopes
17. Tides
18. Time
19. Timepieces
20. Time systems
21. Watches

COMPARISON and CONTRAST

1. Aerial surveying and plane surveying
2. Astrolabe and sextant
3. Astrology and astronomy
4. Astronomer's camera and box camera
5. Astronomy: here and there; yesterday and today--e.g., in ancient, medieval, and modern times
6. Calendars: here and there; yesterday and today--e.g., in ancient, medieval, and modern times
7. Celestial navigation: here and there; yesterday and today--e.g., before and after the Age of Columbus
8. Christian calendars and non-Christian (e.g., Oriental) calendars
9. Chronology: here and there; yesterday and today--e.g., in the Bible and in modern times
10. Clock and watch
11. Clocks: here and there; yesterday and today
12. Copernican theory and Ptolemaic theory
13. Craters: lunar and terrestrial

14. Dawn and dusk
15. Day and night
16. Destruction of the universe and origin of the universe
17. Earth and Mars (or one of the other planets)
18. Eclipses: lunar and solar
19. Equinoxes: autumnal and vernal
20. Falling stars and fixed stars
21. Flat map and globe
22. Geocentric theory and heliocentric theory
23. Gregorian calendar and Julian calendar
24. High tide and low tide
25. Light: lunar and solar
26. Lunar year and solar year
27. Maps and map-making: here and there; yesterday and today--e.g., in the time of Marco Polo and today
28. Motion: planets, stars, and sun
29. Observational techniques in astronomy: here and there; yesterday and today--e.g., at the time of the birth of Christ and today
30. Observatory, planetarium, and solarium
31. Orbits: comet, moon, and planet
32. Planet and star
33. Satellites: man-made and natural
34. Seasons: on earth and on another planet(s)
35. Selenography and topography
36. Space and time
37. Star-gazing: in astrology and in astronomy
38. Sun and moon
39. Sunrise and sunset
40. Sundial and (clock, watch)
41. Surveying: here and there; yesterday and today--e.g., in the time of George Washington and today
42. Telescopes: here and there; yesterday and today--e.g., in the Age of Galileo and today
43. Tides: lunar and solar
44. Time-telling: here and there; yesterday and today--e.g., in a primitive society and in a modern society
45. World's end: in science and in the Bible

DEFINITION

1. Almanac
2. Asteroid
3. Atmosphere
4. Cartography
5. Climate
6. Corona
7. Cosmos
8. Distance
9. First Cause
10. Gravity
11. Horizon
12. Horology
13. Horoscope
14. Hour
15. International date line
16. Light year
17. Lunacy
18. Moon-struck
19. Music of the spheres
20. Perturbations
21. Sky
22. Star catalogue
23. Star-cross'd
24. Sunspot
25. Temperature
26. Time belt/zone

DESCRIPTION

1. An astronomer's (laboratory, observatory, office, etc.), or part thereof
2. A bench mark
3. Big Ben
4. A globe of the world
5. An hourglass
6. The man in the moon
7. A map (general details)
8. The moon
9. An orrery
10. A planet
11. A planetarium, or part thereof
12. A quadrant
13. A solarium, or part thereof
14. A spectroscope
15. The sun
16. A sundial
17. A telescope
18. A timepiece
19. A transit

PROCESS

1. How astrologers "read" the stars
2. How boundaries are determined in surveying
3. How to improve (reform) our calendar
4. How celestial bodies move
5. How celestial bodies are (charted, photographed)
6. How astronomers secure evidence concerning celestial bodies and phenomena
7. How clocks tell time
8. How distance is determined in astronomy--e.g., from earth to the moon or from earth to one of the other planets
9. How the age of the earth is determined (cf. GEOLOGY)
10. How the earth (began, may end)
11. How (the size, the shape, the weight) of the earth is determined
12. How to look at (a lunar, a solar) eclipse
13. How (lunar, solar) eclipses take place
14. How (lunar, solar) eclipses are predicted
15. How gravity is (determined, defied)
16. How the heavens are mapped
17. How to make an hourglass
18. How to read a map
19. How maps are made
20. How the moon originated
21. How pictures of the moon are taken
22. How the moon controls tides
23. How to moon-watch
24. How to put a man on the moon

25. How to navigate celestially
26. How to build a home observatory
27. How the pendulum works
28. How to construct a perpetual motion machine
29. How photography is used (in astronomy, in surveying)
30. How planets (move, maintain equilibrium and motion)
31. How the planets in our solar system originated
32. How to determine one's position by means of celestial bodies
33. How radar is used in astronomy
34. How (radio, television) is used in astronomy
35. How the earth's seasons change
36. How the spectroscope works
37. How to star-gaze
38. How stars are located in the heavens
39. How the sun manufactures heat
40. How the sun originated
41. How the temperature of the sun is determined
42. How to (make, set up) a sundial
43. How property is surveyed
44. How to survey a piece of property
45. How to build a telescope
46. How the Mount Palomar telescope was made
47. How the telescope works
48. How the earth's tides (rise, fall)
49. How to tell time (with, without) a man-made timepiece
50. How to make a tripod
51. How to use a transit
52. How the universe (evolved, will end)
53. How to buy a watch

ARGUMENTATION

PROPOSITIONS OF FACT

1. Is the study of astrology (useful, useless)?
2. Is Utopia's Astronomy Department (adequate, inadequate)?
3. Are our astronomical instruments (satisfactory, unsatisfactory)?
4. Is calendar reform (desirable, necessary, possible)?
5. Will the earth collide with the head of a comet?
6. Does daylight saving time save (daylight, time)?
7. Is the destruction of the (world, universe) inevitable?
8. Is the earth doomed to destruction?
9. Is the earth shaped like (a ball, a pear)?
10. Are there other (galaxies, solar systems, worlds, universes)?
11. Does life (in any form, as we know it) exist on other planets?
12. Are our maps (of the earth, of the heavens) (accurate, inaccurate)?
13. Are there canals on Mars?
14. Is the moon dead?

15. Is there erosion on the moon's surface?
16. Does God intend man to go to (the moon, one of the planets)?
17. Will the moon be pulled into the earth?
18. Is the ________ Observatory (adequate, inadequate)?
19. Is Einstein's theory of relativity (sound, unsound)?
20. Is our solar system (expanding, shrinking)?
21. Is space (finite, infinite)?
22. Is the sun burning up?
23. Do sunspots have (any, a beneficial, a harmful) effect on the earth's inhabitants?
24. Does time stand still (e.g., in outer space)?
25. Is perfect time (i.e., time-telling) possible?
26. Are there other (universes, worlds)?
27. Does Venus always keep the same side to the sun?
28. Is a world calendar (desirable, necessary, possible)?

PROPOSITIONS OF POLICY

1. Should Utopia (offer courses in, expand its offerings in) astronomy?
2. Should our (Christian, non-Christian) calendars be reformed (i.e., made uniform)?
3. Should our (region, State) adopt (daylight-saving, standard, some other) time?
4. Should Greenwich Time be abandoned?
5. Should the United States strive to put men (on the moon, on Mars, etc.)?
6. Should the moon be placed under international control (as through the UN)?
7. Should our community have (an observatory, a planetarium)?
8. Should the United States adopt the thirteen-month calendar?
9. Should a new topographic survey be made (locally, regionally, nationally, internationally)?

EVALUATION

OBJECTS

1. A piece of equipment used in astronomical photography--e.g., a camera
2. A piece of equipment useful in astronomy--e.g., a telescope
3. A piece of equipment useful in surveying boundaries--e.g., a surveyer's transit
4. Facilities of an observatory or planetarium
5. A sextant or other piece of equipment useful in nautical navigation
6. A piece of equipment useful in (plane, aerial) surveying
7. A telescope
8. A timepiece--e.g., a sundial, a clock, a watch

POLICIES

1. A policy, in effect or proposed, of Utopia's Astronomy Department
2. A policy of a clock or watch manufacturer
3. A policy of a map-making establishment
4. A policy of an observatory or planetarium--e.g., the Naval Observatory or the Franklin Planetarium
5. A policy of a firm engaged in surveying
6. A policy of a manufacturer of telescopes or other astronomical instruments
7. An area or regional time system--e.g., daylight, standard, etc.

PHYSICS 530-539.99

Thought Starters for ANALYSIS

What about:

1. Acoustics
2. Aerodynamics
3. Aeromechanics
4. Aerostatics
5. Archimedes' principle: liquids
6. Atmosphere
7. Atomic energy
8. Atomic physics
9. Buoyancy
10. Capillarity, liquids
11. Cathode-ray tubes
12. Centrifugal forces
13. Centripetel forces
14. Color
15. Compression
16. Condensation
17. Conservation, principles of
18. Cosmic rays: nuclear physics
19. Cyclotrons
20. Dynamics
21. Earth magnetism
22. Echoes
23. Einstein, Albert: theory
24. Elasticity: gases, liquids, solids
25. Electric currents: geomagnetism and physics
26. Electricity: geomagnetism and physics
27. Electrodynamics
28. Electromagnetism
29. Electronics
30. Electrostatics
31. Energy
32. Equilibrium: air, gases, liquids
33. Evaporation
34. Explosions
35. Falling bodies
36. Floating bodies
37. Flow of liquids
38. Fluids
39. Fluorescence
40. Force transmission
41. Fourth dimension
42. Freezing
43. Friction
44. Gamma rays
45. Gases
46. Geiger-Muller counters
47. Geomagnetism
48. Gravity
49. Gyroscopes
50. Heat
51. Heat transfer
52. High temperature: production and measurement
53. Hydraulics
54. Hydrodynamics
55. Hydromechanics
56. Hydrometry
57. Hydrostatics
58. Impact
59. Incandescence
60. Inertia
61. Infrared spectroscopy
62. Ionosphere
63. Kinematics
64. Kinetic theory of gases: of heat; of liquids
65. Light
66. Liquids
67. Lodestones
68. Logic of physics
69. Low temperature
70. Luminescence
71. Machines
72. Magnetic field: geomagnetism
73. Magnetism
74. Magnets
75. Mass: gases, liquids, and solids
76. Matter
77. Mechanics of gases; of liquids; of solids

NOTE: See also CHEMISTRY (540-549.99), ENGINEERING (620-629.99), and others

78. Melting
79. Microwaves
80. Mirages
81. Modern physics
82. Molecular physics
83. Motion
84. Newton's laws of motion
85. Noise
86. Nuclear fission and fusion
87. Nuclear physics
88. Nuclear reactions
89. Optics
90. Pendulum motion
91. Perpetual motion
92. Philosophy of physics
93. Phosphorescence
94. Photoelectric cells
95. Physicists
96. Polarized light
97. Quantum physics
98. Radiation: nuclear physics
99. Radioactivity: nuclear physics
100. Relativity
101. Rotation
102. Solids: mechanics
103. Solids: properties
104. Sound
105. Space-time
106. Spectroscopy
107. Static electricity
108. Statics
109. Sunspots: geomagnetism
110. Temperature
111. Thermodynamics
112. Thermoelectricity
113. Thermometry
114. Thermonuclear fusion
115. Trajectories
116. Tubes, electronic
117. Tuning forks: sound generation
118. Vacuum
119. Vaporization
120. Velocity: liquid flow
121. Vibration
122. Viscosity: gases; liquids; solids
123. Wave mechanics
124. Wave motions
125. Wheels
126. X-rays

CAUSE and EFFECT

1. (Major) Effects of (age, time) on matter--e.g., metal, plastic, rubber, wood, etc.
2. Why a rubber ball bounces
3. Why sounds "bounce"
4. Why there are different colors in nature
5. Why a compass points north
6. Why moisture condenses--as in a damp basement or in a refrigerator
7. (Major) Effects of cosmic rays
8. (Major) Causes of echoes
9. Why birds sitting on a high-tension wire are not electrocuted
10. (Major) Causes of evaporation of liquids--e.g., water
11. Why bodies--e.g., a pendulum; a projectile; a freely falling object--fall
12. Why floating bodies float
13. (Causes, Effects) of friction between two bodies--e.g., a tire and a road
14. (Causes, Effects) of gravity
15. Why (a gyroscope, a spinning top) spins
16. (Major) Effects of (heat, cold) on matter--e.g., metal; plastic; rubber; wood
17. Why (gases, liquids, solids) become (hot, cold)

18. (Major) Effects of impact on (moving, stationary) bodies --as in the collision of two moving vehicles; as of a bullet striking an object, etc.
19. Why lenses are called "the eyes of science"
20. (Major) Causes of (lightning, thunder)
21. (Major) Effects of (low, freezing) temperature on (animate, inanimate) matter--e.g., human tissue; metals
22. (Major) Causes of mirages
23. Why bodies move
24. (Causes, Effects) of noise
25. (Major) Causes of optical illusions
26. Why a pendulum moves
27. Why a perpetual motion machine is (possible, impossible)
28. (Major) Effects of radioactivity on (animate, inanimate) matter
29. Why rainbows appear
30. Why people receive shocks
31. Why the sky appears blue (instead of, say, green)
32. (Major) Causes of sound waves
33. (Major) Effects of stress and strain on elastic bodies
34. Why rubber stretches
35. (Major) Effects of sunspots on the earth and its inhabitants
36. Why a liquid vortex goes (clockwise, counterclockwise)--as in a kitchen sink
37. Why water pipes burst in cold weather
38. (Major) Causes of motion in an ocean wave
39. Why wheels on a stage coach in a movie appear to be going backward
40. (Major) Causes of weightlessness

CLASSIFICATION

Kinds/Types of:

1. Current(s)
2. Energy
3. Explosions
4. Flow
5. Forces
6. Heat
7. Levers
8. Light
9. Machines
10. Magnets
11. Motion
12. Radiation
13. Radioactivity
14. Rays
15. Spectra
16. Tension
17. Thermometers
18. Vacuums
19. Waves

COMPARISON and CONTRAST

1. A.C. and D.C.
2. A.M. and F.M.
3. An airplane and a bird
4. Ampere, volt, and watt
5. Atomic or hydrogen bomb and conventional (TNT) bomb

6. Atomic energy: in peace and in war
7. Batteries: automobile and flashlight
8. Black and white
9. A brick and a feather
10. Brains: human and electronic
11. Camera and eye
12. Candle, kerosene lamp, and electric light
13. Centigrade and Fahrenheit
14. Centrifugal force and centripetal force
15. Contact lenses and conventional spectacles
16. Currents: air, electric, and water
17. Dry cell and wet cell
18. Ear and mechanical recorder
19. Electric light and firefly
20. Electricity as the servant of man and man as the slave of electricity
21. Fission and fusion
22. Friction: beneficial and harmful
23. Fuse plug and penny
24. Gunpowder and the hydrogen bomb
25. Gyroscopes: for work and play; in peace and war
26. Immortality of the soul and indestructibility of matter
27. Incubators: for babies and for chickens
28. Larynx and phonograph
29. Law, opinion, principle, and theory
30. Long wave and short wave
31. Light bulbs: incandescent and fluorescent
32. Machines: friend and enemy of man
33. Matches: kitchen and safety
34. Matter: in physics and in metaphysics
35. Microscope and telescope
36. Music and noise
37. Physics: ancient, medieval, and modern
38. Power: in physics and in religion
39. Power plants: conventional and nuclear
40. Pump and heart
41. Radios: crystal and transistor
42. Sun and sunlamp
43. Transistor and vacuum tube
44. Truth: in physics and in (religion, philosophy)
45. Tubes: radio and television
46. Turbine and water wheel
47. Weight: on earth and on the moon

DEFINITION

1. Acceleration
2. Air
3. BTU
4. Chain reaction
5. Charge
6. Combustion
7. Decibel
8. Density
9. Fulcrum
10. Generation
11. Induction
12. Isotope
13. Neutron
14. Ohm
15. Oscillation
16. Osmosis

17. Pitch
18. Pneumatics
19. Porosity
20. Pressure
21. Propagation
22. Proton
23. Radar
24. Reflection
25. Refraction
26. Speed
27. Sublimation
28. Tension
29. UHF
30. Work

DESCRIPTION

I. A piece of equipment or apparatus useful in the fields of physics and/or electronics--for example,
   A. An anemometer
   B. An antenna for radio or televsion
   C. An atom smasher
   D. A cyclotron
   E. An electron tube
   F. An electron microscope
   G. A galvanometer
   H. A Geiger counter
   I. A generator
   J. A gyroscope
   K. A nuclear power plant
   L. A radio or television tube
   M. A thermocouple
   N. A tuning fork
   O. A wheel
   P. An X-ray machine

II. A building, or part thereof, devoted to study or research in the field of physics--for example,
   A. An observatory
   B. A physics laboratory
   C. A physicist's office or study

PROCESS

1. How an airplane flies
2. How the atom bomb was born
3. How atomic energy is converted to produce electricity
4. How a clock uses energy
5. How the condenser works
6. How a dam produces electricity
7. How the human ear hears
8. How echoes are (produced; absorbed)
9. How a home electrical appliance--e.g., a clothes washer or dryer; a percolator; a refrigerator, etc.--works
10. How the "electric eye" works
11. How the electron microscope works
12. How the human eye (sees; perceives color)
13. How frequency modulation eliminates static
14. How fluorescent lights work
15. How the Geiger-counter works

16. How the generator generates
17. How gravity works
18. How the gyroscope works
19. How the hearing aid helps
20. How heat is (conducted, generated, measured, produced, transferred; transmitted)--in gases; in liquids; in solids
21. How an ice cream freezer freezes
22. How the larynx produces sound
23. How light is bent
24. How a light bulb lights
25. How the lightning bug does it
26. How liquids (boil, evaporate, expand and contract, flow, freeze, melt)
27. How a magnet works
28. How mirages form
29. How mirrors reflect
30. How science combats noise
31. How a nuclear power plant generates power
32. How to construct a perpetual motion machine
33. How to understand physics
34. How to improve Utopia's Physics Department
35. How the piano works
36. How the Polaroid camera takes and develops a picture
37. How the pressure cooker cooks
38. How the pump works
39. How radar works
40. How (radio, television) (transmits, receives)
41. How rainbows are formed
42. How the spectroscope works
43. How the speed (of light, of sound) is determined
44. How the steam (engine, turbine) works
45. How (the telegraph, the telephone) works
46. How to make a toy telephone that works
47. How temperature is measured
48. How the thermometer works
49. How the transformer transforms
50. How (air, sound, water) waves move
51. How windmills work
52. How sound travels over (telephone, telegraph) wires
53. How the X-ray machine takes a picture

ARGUMENTATION

PROPOSITIONS OF FACT

1. Can "the bomb" be banned?
2. Where do cosmic rays come from?
3. Is the earth losing more energy than it gains?
4. Can nuclear explosions (destroy the earth; throw the planet off its orbit)?
5. Is a frictionless machine (possible, impossible)?
6. Are courses in general science (worth while, worthless)?

7. Is the jargon of physics necessary?
8. Are the laws and principles of physics (absolute, relative; sound, unsound)?
9. Do machines (make, eliminate) work?
10. Is matter indestructible?
11. Is nature (indifferent, kind, ruthless, malevolent)?
12. Is a perpetual motion machine (likely, unlikely)?
13. Is Utopia's Physics Department (adequate, inadequate; effective, ineffective)?
14. Can anyone learn physics?
15. Are the inhabitants of the earth (in great, in little) danger from radioactive fall-out
16. Are scientists morally responsible for the consequences of their discoveries?
17. Is seeing believing?
18. Is (space, time) infinite?
19. Do sunspots affect earth-dwellers (physically, psychologically, mentally)?
20. Does nature abhor a vacuum?
21. Are X rays (beneficial, harmful) to man?

PROPOSITIONS OF POLICY

1. Should our community establish an anti-noise ordinance?
2. Should the United States (continue, discontinue) nuclear testing?
3. Should Utopia require a course in physics for graduation?
4. Should scientists be held morally responsible for the results of their discoveries?
5. Should the Federal Government adopt a uniform method of measuring temperature?
6. Should periodic X rays be (encouraged, discouraged)?

EVALUATION

OBJECTS

I. A piece of equipment useful in the fields of physics or electronics--for example,
   A. A cyclotron
   B. An electron microscope
   C. A Geiger counter
II. Facilities of an organization or institution devoted to the fields of physics or electronics--for example,
   A. The library of a private or public concern
   B. Facilities of Utopia's Physics Department

POLICIES

1. A policy, in effect or proposed, of a (private, public) agency or organization engaged in physical research
2. A policy, in effect or proposed, of Utopia's Physics Department

CHEMISTRY AND ALLIED SCIENCES 540-549.99 and CHEMICAL TECHNOLOGY AND METALLURGY 660-669.99

Thought Starters for ANALYSIS

What about:

1. Additives, petroleum
2. Aerosols: organic and physical chemistry
3. Alchemy
4. Alcoholic beverages: manufacture
5. Alcohols: industrial mfg.
6. Alicyclic compounds: organic chemistry
7. Aliphatic compounds and terpenes: organic chemistry
8. Alkaloids: organic chemistry
9. Alloys
10. Analytic chemistry
11. Antibiotics
12. Applied chemistry
13. Aromatic compounds
14. Artificial structural products
15. Atomic chemistry
16. Baking: food technology
17. Beverages: mfg.
18. Bottling beverages
19. Bricks: mfg.
20. Caffeine: organic chemistry
21. Canning beverages and food
22. Cellulose plastics
23. Ceramic industries
24. Cereals: processing
25. Chain reactions: organic and physical chemistry
26. Chemical analysis: cosmetics and perfumes
27. Chemical analysis: food and drink
28. Chemical analysis: minerals
29. Chemical apparatus and equipment
30. Chemical engineering
31. Chemical laboratories
32. Chemical preservation: food technology
33. Chemical reactions: physical chemistry
34. Chemical technology
35. Chemical weed killers: mfg.
36. Chemicals: mfg.
37. Chemists
38. Chemurgy
39. Chinaware manufacture
40. Chlorination: organic chemistry
41. Cinder blocks: mfg.
42. Coal technology
43. Coal-tar chemistry
44. Coffee processing
45. Condiments: mfg. and refining
46. Crystallography
47. DDT manufacture
48. Dairy products: chemical analysis
49. Dehydrated food technology
50. Detergents: manufacture
51. Diamonds: crystallography and mineralogy
52. Diamonds, synthetic: mfg.
53. Diesel fuels: mfg.
54. Distillation: liquor mfg.
55. Distillation: petroleum technology
56. Dyes: organic chemistry
57. Early chemical theories
58. Economic chemistry
59. Elasto-plastics: organic chemistry

NOTE: See also MEDICINE (610-619.99), HOME ECONOMICS (640-649.99), and others

60. Electrochemistry
61. Electrolysis: chemical technology
62. Elixir of life: alchemy
63. Enzymes
64. Explosives: mfg.
65. Fats: chemical technology
66. Fats, edible: mfg. and refining
67. Ferro-alloying metals: metallography and metallurgy
68. Fertilizers: mfg.
69. Fireworks: mfg.
70. Fissionable metals: metallography and metallurgy
71. Flavoring aids: mfg. and refining
72. Flour milling
73. Fluoridation
74. Food manufacture: technology
75. Food technology
76. Frozen foods: technology
77. Fruit processing and preservation: technology
78. Fuel technology
79. Fungicides: chemical analysis and mfg.
80. Gas analysis and technology
81. Gasolines: mfg. and refining
82. Gems: mineralogy
83. Glass mfg. and technology
84. Gravimetric analysis
85. Halides
86. Heat: organic and physical chemistry
87. Heat transfer: chemical technology
88. Heavy chemicals: manufacture
89. Heavy hydrogen
90. Heavy metals: metallography and metallurgy
91. Heavy oxygen
92. Heavy water
93. Herbicides: chemical analysis and mfg.
94. Heterocyclic compounds and terpenes: organic chemistry
95. Industrial chemicals
96. Industrial chemistry
97. Ink: manufacture
98. Inorganic chemistry
99. Insecticides: chemical analysis and mfg.
100. Iron: metallography and metallurgy
101. Isomers: physical chemistry
102. Jam and jelly making: food technology
103. Laboratory techniques: chemistry
104. Laundering, commercial
105. Light metals: metallography and metallurgy
106. Lubricants: chemical technology
107. Machinery: chemical technology
108. Manufactures
109. Margarine: mfg. and refining
110. Masonry adhesives: mfg.
111. Matches: mfg.
112. Medieval theories: chemistry
113. Metallography
114. Metallurgy
115. Metals: inorganic chemistry
116. Metals: mineralogy
117. Metals: production
118. Mineralogy
119. Molecular chemistry
120. Motor fuels: mfg.
121. Natural gas: technology
122. Neon: inorganic chemistry
123. Nicotine: organic chemistry
124. Nitrates
125. Nonalcoholic beverages: mfg.
126. Nonferrous metals: metallography and metallurgy

127. Nonmetals
128. Nylon
129. Octane: organic chemistry
130. Oils: chemical technology
131. Ores: chemical analysis and mineralogy
132. Organic chemistry
133. Oxides
134. Paints: mfg.
135. Pesticides: chemical analysis and mfg.
136. Petroleum chemistry
137. Petroleum technology
138. Philosopher's stone: alchemy
139. Photosynthesis, artificial: organic and physical chemistry
140. Physical chemistry
141. Pipelines: gas technology
142. Pipelines: petroleum technology
143. Plastics: organic chemistry and mfg.
144. Poisons: chemical analysis
145. Precious metals: metallography and metallurgy
146. Proteins: organic chemistry
147. Qualitative analysis
148. Quantitative analysis
149. Quantum chemistry
150. Radiation chemistry
151. Radioactive isotopes: organic and physical chemistry
152. Radioactive metals: metallurgy
153. Radiocarbon dating
154. Radiochemistry
155. Radium: inorganic chemistry
156. Rare-earth elements: inorganic chemistry
157. Refrigeration: food technology
158. Rocket propellants: mfg.
159. Rocks: chemical analysis
160. Rodenticides: chemical analysis and mfg.
161. Rubber: organic chemistry
162. Salt: chemistry
163. Salts: chemistry and mfg.
164. Scientists
165. Sea food processing and preservation: technology
166. Sex hormones: organic chemistry
167. Silicone plastics: chemistry and mfg.
168. Soap: mfg.
169. Soft drinks: mfg.
170. Space chemistry
171. Spectrochemical analysis
172. Spontaneous combustion: physical chemistry
173. Steel: metallography and metallurgy
174. Steel production: technology
175. Strontium: inorganic chemistry
176. Sugar: organic chemistry and mfg.
177. Sulfa drugs
178. Sulfides
179. Synthetic dyes: mfg.
180. Synthetic fibers: organic chemistry
181. Synthetic gasolines: mfg.
182. Synthetic petroleum: mfg.
183. Synthetic resins: organic chemistry
184. Synthetic rubber: organic chemistry
185. Synthetic textiles: dyeing and printing
186. Synthetics: organic chemistry
187. Tea processing
188. Thalidomide: organic chemistry
189. Thermochemistry: organic chemistry
190. Thermodynamics, chemical

191. Toxicants: chemical analysis
192. Transmutation of metals: alchemy
193. Uranium: inorganic chemistry
194. Vegetable processing and preservation
195. Vermicides: mfg.
196. Vitamins: organic chemistry
197. Volumetric analysis
198. Water: inorganic chemistry
199. Wine manufacture

CAUSE and EFFECT

1. Why acids are sour
2. Why additives (are, are not) added to (gasoline, motor oils)
3. Why adhesives stick
4. (Major) Effects of alkaloids on the human body
5. Why alloys are added to metals
6. Why antibiotics are so named
7. (Beneficial, Harmful) Effects of antibiotics on the human body
8. (Major) Effects of caffeine on the human body
9. Why the body needs (calcium, carbohydrates, etc.)
10. (Major) Effects of carbon on an automobile engine
11. (Major) Causes of chemical change(s)--in gases; in liquids; in solids; in animals; in vegetables; in minerals
12. (Major) Effects of chemical weed killers on soil
13. Why the study of chemistry is important--e.g., in and around the home; in agriculture; in industry; in medicine, etc.
14. (Major) Effects of chlorination of drinking water--on the water; on the drinker
15. (Major) Effects of condiments on health
16. Why cream sours
17. Why food decays
18. (Major) Effects of dehydration on food
19. (Major) Effects of (household, commercial) detergents--on fabrics; on water; on the housewife
20. (Major) Effects of a filter on a cigarette
21. (Major) Effects of fluoridated drinking water--on the water; on the drinker
22. (Major) Effects of (chemical preservatives; freezing) on processed food
23. Why grass is green
24. Why iron rusts
25. Why lead is added to gasolines
26. Why molecules move
27. (Major) Effects of nicotine on health
28. Why the body needs (nitrogen, oxygen)
29. (Major) Chemical effects of over-indulgence in (food, drink)
30. (Major) Effects of pesticides on (animals; human beings; vegetable matter)

31. Why quicksilver is so called
32. (Major) Effects of (radiation, radium) on the human body
33. Why our bodies need salt
34. Why silver tarnishes
35. (Major) Effects of soft drinks on health--e.g., on complexion; on teeth
36. (Major) Effects of space travel--e.g., a state of weightlessness--on body chemistry
37. Why Strontium 90 is so named
38. Why sugar is sweet
39. (Major) Effects of sunlight on chlorophyll
40. (Major) Effects of extremes in temperature on (metals, plastics, rubber)
41. Why the body needs (vitamins, minerals)

CLASSIFICATION

Kinds/Types of:

1. Acids
2. Alcohols
3. Alloys
4. Chemistry/chemists
5. Compounds
6. Cosmetics
7. Detergents
8. Dyes
9. Explosives
10. Fertilizers
11. Food preservation/preservatives
12. Fuels
13. Gas/gases
14. Gasoline(s)
15. Inorganic chemicals
16. Lubricants
17. Oil(s)
18. Ore(s)
19. Organic chemicals
20. Paint(s)
21. Pesticides
22. Petroleum
23. Plastics
24. Poisons
25. Propellants
26. Radiation
27. Rocket fuels
28. Rocks
29. Rubber
30. Salt(s)
31. Solvents
32. Steel
33. Waxes

COMPARISON and CONTRAST

1. Acids and bases
2. Alchemy and chemistry
3. Alcohol: denatured, ethyl, methyl, and isopropyl
4. Alloys and hybrids
5. Amalgam filling and (gold, silver) filling
6. Aspirin and some other pain reliever
7. Atomic weight and molecular weight
8. Atoms and ions
9. Baking powder, baking soda, cream of tartar, and yeast
10. Beet sugar and cane sugar
11. Bath-tub gin and commercially manufactured gin
12. Benzene, toluene, and naphthalene
13. Beverages: bottled, canned, and fresh
14. Brewery and distillery

15. Brick-making: here and there; yesterday and today--e.g., in 1800 and today
16. Butter and oleomargarine
17. Brown sugar and white sugar
18. Caffeine and nicotine
19. Candle-making: here and there; yesterday and today--e.g., in colonial America and in modern America
20. Canned, dehydrated, fresh, and frozen food
21. Carriage lamp and modern automobile headlight
22. Cellophane, celluloid, and waxed paper
23. Celluloid and ivory
24. Ceramics: here and there; yesterday and today
25. Charcoal, coal, and coke
26. Chemistry and physics
27. China-making: here and there; yesterday and today--e.g., in the Orient and in the West
28. Chlorinated water and fluoridated water
29. Chloroform and ether
30. Cigarette lighter and match
31. Coal and coal tar
32. Coffee: brewed and instant
33. Corn syrup and maple syrup
34. Cream: fresh and powdered
35. Crystal, metal, and mineral
36. Detergent and soap
37. Diamond and zircon
38. Dimes, dollars, nickels, pennies, quarters
39. Distillation: alcohol and petroleum
40. Drugs: ancient, medieval, and modern
41. Dye and ink
42. Dyes: natural and synthetic
43. Eighteen-carat gold and sterling silver
44. Fat, oil, and wax
45. Fermentation and distillation
46. Fibers: animal and plant; natural and synthetic
47. Fire-making: here and there; yesterday and today
48. Fireworks: here and there; yesterday and today--e.g., in ancient China and in modern America
49. Flavorings: imitation and natural (e.g., vanilla)
50. Fool's gold and real gold
51. Fresh (dairy products, fruits, meats, vegetables) and processed (dehydrated, frozen, etc.) dairy products, etc.
52. Fuel technology: here and there; yesterday and today--e.g., c. 1900 and today
53. Fuels: bagasse, briquettes, sawdust, and wood
54. Fungicides, insecticides, and pesticides
55. Gas: bottled and natural
56. Gelatin and glue
57. German silver and sterling silver
58. Gin and vodka
59. Glass, isinglass, and obsidian
60. Glass-making: here and there; yesterday and today
61. Glue and paste
62. Graphite and lead

63. Gunpowder and A-bomb
64. Hard water and soft water
65. Heating agents: coal, electricity, gas, oil, wood
66. Helium and hydrogen
67. High explosives and low explosives
68. High octane and low octane
69. Immortality of the soul and indestructibility of (the atom, matter)
70. Ink: permanent and washable; visible and invisible
71. Iodine and mercurochrome
72. Iron and steel
73. Lacquer and polish
74. Matches: kitchen and safety
75. Meat packing: in 1900 and today
76. Metallography and metallurgy
77. Milk: condensed, evaporated, fresh, and powdered
78. Miracle drugs: in alchemy and in chemistry
79. Mustard and mustard gas
80. Neon light and incandescent light
81. Oil refinery and sugar refinery
82. Olive oil and turpentine
83. Paraffin, oil, and tallow
84. Pearls: natural, cultured, and artificial
85. Perfumes: natural and synthetic
86. Petroleum: natural and synthetic
87. Pipe: copper, lead, and plastic
88. Plastic, glass, metal, paper, and wood (as, for example, containers)
89. Rocket fuels: liquid and solid
90. Rubber: natural and synthetic
91. Saccharine and sugar
92. Steel: American and foreign (e.g., Japanese)
93. Structural products: natural (e.g., marble) and artificial (e.g., steel)
94. Wine-making: here and there; yesterday and today--e.g., in ancient Italy and in modern California

DEFINITION

1. Affinity
2. Antiseptic
3. Bath
4. Change
5. Combustion
6. Compression
7. Cosmetology
8. Cracking
9. Crucible
10. Density
11. Emulsion
12. Fermentation
13. Flask
14. Fool's gold
15. Gel
16. Iatrochemistry
17. Ionization
18. Kiln
19. Lastex
20. Leavening
21. Liquefaction
22. Mass
23. Matter
24. Mold
25. Oil
26. Oxidation
27. Paraffin
28. Pigment

29. Polyunsaturated
30. Reagent
31. Resin
32. Shortening
33. Solvent
34. Spirit(s)
35. Sulfur
36. Synthesis
37. Table
38. Technology
39. Terra cotta
40. Theory
41. Valence
42. Viscosity
43. Weight

DESCRIPTION

1. An alchemist's laboratory
2. A cannery, or part thereof
3. A chemistry laboratory, or part thereof
4. A cleaning-and-dyeing plant, or part thereof
5. A commercial bakery
6. A distillery
7. A piece of equipment used in the manufacture or processing of:
   a. cosmetics
   b. glassware
   c. fireworks and/or explosives
   d. industrial chemicals
   e. paint
   f. perfume
   g. rubber products
   h. soap and/or detergents
   i. soft drinks
   j. steel
8. An oil refinery

PROCESS

1. How an <u>acetylene</u> <u>torch</u> works
2. How an <u>aerosol</u> "<u>bomb</u>" works
3. How we <u>age</u>
4. How <u>alchemy</u> (originated, died out)
5. How (<u>alcoholic</u>, non-alcoholic) <u>beverages</u> are manufactured
6. How <u>aluminum</u> is refined
7. How <u>antibiotics</u> are manufactured
8. How <u>antiseptics</u> (destroy, arrest) the growth of germs
9. How <u>artificial</u> <u>gems</u> are made
10. How <u>artificial</u> <u>structural</u> <u>products</u>--e.g., cinder blocks--are manufactured
11. How <u>bakery</u> <u>products</u>--breads, cakes, etc.--are made commercially
12. How <u>blast</u> <u>furnaces</u> work
13. How <u>breakfast</u> <u>cereals</u> are manufactured
14. How <u>bricks</u> are made
15. How substances <u>burn</u>
16. How (<u>cake</u>, pancake, waffle) <u>mixes</u> are made
17. How <u>candy</u> is made commercially

18. How <u>carbon</u> <u>monoxide</u> kills
19. How <u>cellophane</u> is manufactured
20. How to succeed in freshman <u>chemistry</u> without really trying
21. How to (construct, equip) a home <u>chemistry</u> <u>laboratory</u>
22. How to "play it safe" in a <u>chemistry</u> <u>laboratory</u>
23. How <u>coal</u> burns
24. How <u>coal</u> is formed
25. How caffeine is removed from <u>coffee</u>
26. How <u>coins</u> are made
27. How <u>colors</u> fade
28. How <u>concrete</u> hardens
29. How <u>cosmetics</u> are manufactured
30. How foods--e.g., orange juice, milk--are <u>dehydrated</u>
31. How <u>detergents</u> are made
32. How artificial <u>diamonds</u> are manufactured
33. How to insure a balanced <u>diet</u>
34. How the body <u>digests</u> <u>food</u>
35. How <u>drugs</u> are (manufactured, tested)
36. How <u>dyes</u> are made commercially
37. How chemical <u>elements</u> are discovered
38. How <u>explosions</u> explode
39. How <u>fire</u> <u>extinguishers</u> work
40. How <u>food</u> is converted into energy
41. How <u>food</u> is preserved commercially
42. How <u>frozen</u> <u>foods</u>--juices, meats, vegetables, etc.--are processed
43. How <u>fruit</u> rots
44. How (<u>fungicides</u>, insecticides, pesticides) are (made, tested)
45. How (<u>furs</u>, leathers, textiles) are dry-cleaned commercially
46. How <u>gasoline</u> is (manufactured, refined, graded)
47. How <u>glass</u> is manufactured commercially
48. How <u>green</u> <u>plants</u> manufacture oxygen
49. How <u>hot</u> <u>dogs</u> are made
50. How <u>instant</u> <u>foods</u>--coffee, potatoes, etc.--are made commercially
51. How <u>iron</u> rusts
52. How <u>lead</u> <u>pencils</u> are manufactured
53. How <u>manufactured</u> <u>gas</u> is (produced, stored, transported)
54. How <u>maple</u> <u>syrup</u> is made
55. How <u>matches</u> ignite
56. How <u>meat</u> is (processed, preserved) commercially
57. How <u>metals</u> are (produced, removed) from ores
58. How to set up a <u>microscope</u>
59. How cows make <u>milk</u>
60. How <u>milk</u> sours
61. How <u>milk</u> is (homogenized, tested)
62. How to determine <u>molecular</u> <u>weights</u>
63. How <u>molecules</u> move
64. How <u>moth</u> <u>balls</u> are made
65. How <u>natural</u> <u>gas</u> is (processed, stored, transported)
66. How <u>natural</u> <u>rubber</u> is processed
67. How <u>nicotine</u> is removed from tobacco

68. How paints are made
69. How perfumes are manufactured
70. How petroleum is (located, refined, stored, distributed)
71. How plants make food
72. How plastics are manufactured
73. How platinum blondes get that way
74. How to make an antidote for common household poisons
75. How rubber is vulcanized
76. How synthetic rubber is manufactured
77. How to prevent rust
78. How salt is extracted from water
79. How sea food is (processed, preserved) commercially
80. How silverware is manufactured
81. How to eliminate industrial smog--generally; in our area
82. How soap is made commercially
83. How steel is made
84. How to remove Strontium 90 from milk
85. How sugar is (manufactured, refined)
86. How synthetic (dyes, fibers, gasolines, resins, rubber products, textiles) are manufactured
87. How water (freezes, boils, evaporates)
88. How water is purified
89. How to (prevent, remove) industrial wastes from our streams and rivers--generally; locally
90. How wood rots

ARGUMENTATION

PROPOSITIONS OF FACT

1. Is the use of antibiotics abused in America today?
2. Are artificial structural products (e.g., solite blocks) a satisfactory substitute for natural structural products (such as brick)?
3. Can (the atom, the hydrogen) bomb be banned?
4. Is modern baker's bread nutritious?
5. Can "baser" metals be made into gold?
6. Is bread the staff of life?
7. Are carbonated beverages (beneficial, harmful) to health?
8. Are the health claims made for processed breakfast cereals exaggerated?
9. Is Utopia's Department of (Chemistry, Chemical Technology) (adequate, inadequate)?
10. Is chemistry an exact science?
11. Can chemistry make man immortal?
12. Is the coal industry dying?
13. Are the health-and-beauty claims for cosmetics exaggerated?
14. Is DDT an obsolete insecticide?
15. Are (home, industrial) detergents contaminating our water supplies--generally; locally?
16. Are diamonds a girl's best friend?
17. Was the explosion of A-bombs over Japan in World War II

(a crime against humanity, a military necessity)?
18. Is <u>fluoridation</u> of drinking water (beneficial, harmful) to health?
19. Can the United States supply enough <u>food</u> for the world's starving peoples?
20. Are <u>frozen foods</u> nutritious?
21. Are gasoline and petroleum <u>additives</u> (beneficial, harmful)?
22. Do all (<u>gasolines</u>, motor oils) come from the same tank-car?
23. Are our (<u>insecticides</u>, pesticides, etc.) (effective, ineffective; harmful to animal and plant life)?
24. Can <u>instant foods</u>--e.g., coffee, rice, etc.--pass the blindfold test?
25. Is the <u>language of chemistry</u> necessary?
26. Does commercial <u>laundering</u> (prolong, shorten) the life of clothes?
27. How did <u>life</u> begin?
28. Can <u>margarine</u> pass the blindfold test?
29. Is <u>matter</u> (destructible, indestructible)?
30. Is <u>milk</u> nature's most perfect food?
31. Is <u>nature</u> (kind, ruthless, indifferent) to man?
32. Is the <u>nicotine</u> in tobacco harmful to health?
33. Are modern <u>processed foods</u> nutritious?
34. Is the world (in great, in little) danger from <u>radioactive fall-out</u>?
35. Is <u>science</u> "a sacred cow"?
36. Do <u>scientists</u> (forget, remember) God?
37. Are <u>scientists</u> morally responsible for the results of their discoveries?
38. Can industrial <u>smog</u> be (curbed, decreased, eliminated)--generally; in our community?
39. Are <u>soap and water</u> enough for cleanliness?
40. Are all commercial <u>soaps</u> alike?
41. Are <u>synthetic</u> (dyes, fibers, etc.) satisfactory substitutes for natural (dyes, fibers, etc.)?
42. Are <u>vitamin pills</u> (necessary, unnecessary)?

PROPOSITIONS OF POLICY

1. Should Utopia require <u>chemistry</u> for graduation?
2. Should the water used in (public, private) swimming pools be (<u>chlorinated</u>, filtered)?
3. Should artificial <u>coloring</u> be added to our foods (e.g., butter, fruits, meats, vegetables, etc.)?
4. Should the Federal Government purify ocean water through a program of <u>desalinization</u>?
5. Should one <u>dye</u> one's hair?
6. Should our community (welcome, outlaw) a depot for storing <u>explosives</u>?
7. Should our community (legalize, outlaw) <u>fireworks</u>?
8. Should our local water supply be <u>fluoridated</u>?
9. Should the United States (give, sell) <u>food</u> to needy peoples in (Communist, non-Communist, unaligned) nations?

10. Should the United States (discontinue, resume) nuclear testing?
11. Should scientists go on strike against further experimentation with bomb testing?
12. Should "thalidomide babies" be aborted?

EVALUATION

OBJECTS

I. A container used in chemistry or by a distributer or manufacturer in the field of chemical technology--for example,
   A. A test tube or some other container used in a chemistry laboratory
   B. A beer can or bottle
   C. A container used for corrosive products
   D. A milk carton or bottle
II. A piece of equipment used in chemistry or in chemical technology--for example,
   A. A blast furnace
   B. A bakery oven
III. Facilities of a chemical firm or laboratory, or of a firm engaged in chemical technology--for example,
   A. Facilities of Utopia's Chemistry Department
   B. Facilities of a firm engaged in the manufacture or processing of food products--e.g., a dairy, a meat-packing establishment
   C. Facilities of a firm engaged in a chemical manufacturing process--e.g., the manufacture of cosmetics, etc.

POLICIES

A policy, in effect or proposed, of (a local, a state, a national; a public, a private) agency, firm, or organization devoted to chemistry or to chemical technology--for example,
   A. A policy of Utopia's Chemistry Department
   B. A policy of a chemical firm--e.g., E. I. DuPont
   C. A policy of a local pharmacy or of a national drug firm--e.g., Eli Lily
   D. A policy of the Pure Food and Drug Administration
   E. A policy of the Federal Trade Commission relating to chemistry or chemical technology

EARTH SCIENCES 550-559.99

Thought Starters for ANALYSIS

What about:

1. Air and air currents: meteorology
2. Antarctic Ocean
3. Arctic Ocean
4. Atlantic Ocean
5. Atolls
6. Barometry: meteorology
7. Bays
8. Bering Sea
9. Blizzards: meteorology and climatology
10. Caribbean Sea
11. Caverns and caves
12. Climate and climatology
13. Clouds: meteorology
14. Coal: economic geology
15. Continental climates
16. Continental divide
17. Continental drift theory
18. Continental shelves
19. Continental winds: climatology and meteorology
20. Continents
21. Control, weather
22. Coral reefs
23. Craters, volcanic
24. Currents: oceanography
25. Cyclones: climatology and meteorology
26. Deserts
27. Dew: meteorology
28. Diamonds: economic geology
29. Drift: glaciology
30. Drought: meteorology
31. Dust storms: climatology and meteorology
32. Earth structure: geology
33. Earthquakes
34. Economic geology
35. Equatorial climates
36. Erosion: geology
37. Faulting: geology
38. Fissionable ores: economic geology
39. Floods: climatology and meteorology
40. Fogs: meteorology
41. Fronts: climatology and meteorology
42. Frost and frost lines: climatology and meteorology
43. Gas and gas deposits: geology
44. Gems: economic geology
45. Geochemistry
46. Geognosy
47. Geography, physical
48. Geological agents
49. Geological ages; epochs; eras; periods
50. Geologic time
51. Geologic work: water; waves; wind
52. Geological physics
53. Geologists
54. Geology
55. Geomorphology
56. Geysers
57. Glaciers and glaciology
58. Gold: economic geology
59. Gulf of Mexico: oceanography
60. Gulf Stream
61. Gulfs: oceanography
62. Hail: climatology and meteorology
63. Heat: geology and meteorology
64. Humidity: climatology and meteorology
65. Hurricanes: climatology and meteorology
66. Hydrography
67. Hydrology
68. Ice: geology
69. Icebergs: geology

NOTE: See also ECONOMICS (330-339.99), PHYSICS (530-539.99), and others

70. Islands
71. Isostasy
72. Lakes: geology
73. Landslides: geology
74. Lava: petrology and vulcanology
75. Lightning: meteorology
76. Limnology
77. Lithology
78. Lost Continent
79. Mediterranean Sea
80. Metals: economic geology
81. Meteorology
82. Minerals: economic geology
83. Mirages: meteorology
84. Mountains
85. Night skies: meteorology
86. Oases
87. Ocean floor: geology
88. Oceanography
89. Oil and gas: geology
90. Ore deposits: economic geology
91. Orology
92. Pacific Ocean
93. Petrography
94. Petroleum geology
95. Petrology
96. Physiography
97. Plutonic phenomena: geology
98. Precious metals and stones: economic geology
99. Pressure, atmospheric: meteorology
100. Radiation: meteorology
101. Rain-making: meteorology
102. Rain: climatology and meteorology
103. Rainbows: meteorology
104. Regional geology
105. Rivers: geology
106. Rocks: geology
107. Seas: oceanography
108. Seismography and seismology
109. Shore formation: geology
110. Silver: economic geology
111. Snow: climatology and meteorology
112. Snowstorms: climatology and meteorology
113. Soil erosion: geology
114. Soundings: oceanography
115. Speleology
116. Springs: geology
117. Storms: climatology and meteorology
118. Stratosphere: meteorology
119. Stratums: geology
120. Streams: geology
121. Strikes: geology
122. Structural geology
123. Submarine topography: oceanography
124. Synclines: geology
125. Temperature: climatology and meteorology
126. Thermodynamics: meteorology
127. Thermometry: meteorology
128. Thunder: meteorology
129. Tidal waves
130. Tides
131. Topography: physical geography
132. Tornadoes: climatology and meteorology
133. Trade winds: climatology and meteorology
134. Tropical climates
135. Typhoons: climatology and meteorology
136. Veins: geology
137. Volcanoes
138. Vulcanology
139. Water: geologic agent
140. Waves: oceanography
141. Weather belts: climatology
142. Weather: climatology
143. Weather forecasting
144. Weathering: geology
145. Wells: geology
146. Winds: climatology and meteorology

CAUSE and EFFECT

1. Why <u>air</u> is invisible
2. Why breathing is difficult at high <u>altitudes</u>

3. (Major) Causes of atmospheric optics--halos, mirages, rainbows, etc.
4. (Major) Causes of the "bends"
5. Why the Black Sea is so called
6. Why we have (hot, cold; dry, wet) climate
7. (Major) Effects of (hot, cold; wet, dry) climate on (health, personality, temperament, etc.)
8. Why we have clouds
9. (Major) Causes of earth craters
10. Why the Dead Sea is so called
11. Why Death Valley is so called
12. Why we have deserts
13. Why we have dew
14. (Major) Causes of droughts
15. Why the earth was created
16. (Major) Causes of earthquakes
17. (Major) Causes of erosion
18. (Major) Causes of floods--generally; regionally
19. Why we have frost
20. (Major) Causes of (glaciers, icebergs)
21. Why the Gulf Stream is warm
22. Why we have (hot springs, geysers)
23. Why we have hurricanes--generally; at certain times of the year
24. Why hurricanes are given feminine names
25. Why islands form
26. Why Benjamin Franklin conducted his kite experiment
27. (Major) Causes of (lightning, thunder)
28. Why mountains form
29. Why oceans are salty
30. Why Old Faithful is faithful
31. Why it rains
32. Why the Red Sea is so called
33. Why no two snowflakes are alike
34. (Major) Effects of (solar radiation, sunspots) on weather
35. (Major) Causes of tides
36. Why trade winds are so called
37. (Major) Causes of volcanoes
38. Why we have (weather, weather changes)
39. (Major) Effects of (atomic explosions, sunspots, volcanic eruptions) on weather

CLASSIFICATION

Kinds/Types of:

1. Barometers
2. Climate
3. Clouds
4. Coal
5. Craters
6. Deposits (in economic geology)
7. Earthquakes
8. Erosion
9. Geological faults
10. Gems and precious stones
11. Geological agents
12. Geologists
13. Hurricanes
14. Inland waters
15. Islands
16. Mountains

17. Optical illusions
18. Ores
19. Precipitation
20. Rocks and minerals
21. Storms
22. Tides
23. Weathering agents

COMPARISON and CONTRAST

1. Age of the earth: in geology and in theology
2. Anthracite and bituminous coal
3. Anticline and syncline
4. Antitrade winds and trade winds
5. Atoll and coral reef
6. Barometers: aneroid and mercury
7. Bathysphere and space capsule
8. Bridges: man-made and natural
9. Carlsbad Caverns and Disneyland
10. Cave, cavern, grotto, and karst hole
11. Climate and weather
12. Coal, coke, and peat
13. Continent and island
14. Craters: earth and moon
15. Cyclone, hurricane, tornado, and typhoon
16. Dark Continent and Lost Continent
17. Earthquake and volcano
18. Earthquakes: plutonic and volcanic
19. Fresh water and sea water
20. Geology and paleontology
21. Glacier and iceberg
22. Hail and sleet
23. Halo and rainbow
24. Hard water and soft water
25. Heat and humidity
26. High tide and low tide
27. Hurricanes and women
28. Icicles and stalactites
29. Lagoon, pond and lake
30. Mineral and rock
31. Natural gems and synthetic gems
32. Neap tide and spring tide
33. Ocean and sea
34. Planetary winds and terrestrial winds
35. Raindrops and snowflakes
36. Rain-making: by man and by nature
37. River and stream
38. Rivers: young, middle-aged, and old
39. Rocks: igneous, metamorphic, and sedimentary
40. Stalactites and stalagmites
41. Tropical belt and polar belt
42. Weather-forecasting: by sign and by science

DEFINITION

1. Artesian well
2. Atlantis
3. Atmosphere
4. Cloudburst
5. Cone
6. Delta
7. Doldrums
8. Dust bowl
9. Eruption
10. Fossil
11. Horse latitudes
12. Lithosphere
13. Monsoon
14. St. Elmo's fire
15. Seismograph
16. Thermocouple
17. Thunder-struck
18. Time

DESCRIPTION

1. A barometer
2. A bathometer
3. A bathysphere
4. A cave or cavern
5. A coal mine
6. A (cyclone, hurricane, tornado) shelter
7. A diving suit
8. A (city, town, etc.) following (an earthquake, flood, hurricane, tornado, etc.)
9. An iceberg
10. A lightning rod
11. A seismograph
12. A snowflake
13. A volcanic crater
14. A weather balloon
15. A weather bureau
16. A weather map
17. A weather station, or part thereof
18. A weather vane

PROCESS

1. How the age of the earth is determined
2. How air currents move
3. How the barometer works
4. How to explore (a cave, a cavern)
5. How (caves, caverns) are formed
6. How climate controls man
7. How man controls climate
8. How clouds form
9. How to "read" clouds
10. How coal originated
11. How coal is located
12. How our continents originated
13. How craters are formed
14. How to construct a (cyclone, hurricane, tornado) shelter
15. How to deep-sea dive
16. How to (survive, live) in the desert

17. How to convert a *desert*--e.g., the Sahara, the Gobi--into a Garden of Eden
18. How *dust storms* may be abolished
19. How the *earth* came into being
20. How *earthquakes* occur
21. How to combat *erosion*--generally; regionally
22. How *fissionable ores* are located
23. How to (prevent, control) *floods*--generally; locally
24. How radar sees through *fog*
25. How to combat *frost*--in, for example, orchards
26. How *gas deposits* are located
27. How the *Geiger counter* helps the geologist
28. How *gems* are located
29. How *geological* (*ages*, epochs, eras, periods) are determined
30. How (*geysers*, hot springs) are formed
31. How *glaciers* (are formed, move)
32. How to (prepare for, survive) a *hurricane*
33. How *icebergs* are detected
34. How to (equip, live on) an *island retreat*
35. How *islands* are formed
36. How the legend of *Jack Frost* originated
37. How to make a small *lake* (for boating, for fishing, for swimming)
38. How to make a *lightning rod*
39. How the *Lost Continent* was lost
40. How useful *metals* are located
41. How to find (a diamond, a gold, a silver, a uranium) *mine*
42. How to search for *minerals*
43. How *Mount Everest* was conquered
44. How to climb a *mountain*
45. How *mountains* are formed
46. How *natural gas* is located
47. How to preserve our *natural resources*--generally; regionally
48. How *oases* are formed
49. How *ocean depths* are determined
50. How to purify *ocean water*
51. How to find an *oil well*
52. How *ore deposits* are located
53. How to make a fish *pond*
54. How to find (*precious metals*, precious stones)
55. How to make *rain*
56. How *rainfall* is measured
57. How *rivers* form
58. How (*rocks*, minerals) are identified
59. How to build a *sea wall*
60. How the *seismograph* works
61. How to combat *soil erosion*
62. How to take *soundings*
63. How to *spelunk*
64. How to find (a *spring*, a well)
65. How the *temperature* of the earth is determined
66. How geologists tell *time*

67. How <u>volcanoes</u> (form, erupt)
68. How to find fresh <u>water</u>
69. How to test (spring, well) <u>water</u>
70. How <u>water</u> originated on the earth
71. How man "does something" about the <u>weather</u>
72. How to forecast the <u>weather</u>
73. How (<u>weather balloons</u>, weather satellites) help the weatherman
74. How to improve <u>weather forecasting</u>
75. How <u>weather maps</u> are made
76. How to make a <u>weather vane</u>
77. How <u>wells</u> are dug
78. How to make a <u>windmill</u>

ARGUMENTATION

PROPOSITIONS OF FACT

1. Is <u>artificial rain-making</u> (desirable, undesirable; moral, immoral)?
2. Are our <u>continents</u> (rising, slipping into the sea)?
3. Can the world's <u>deserts</u> be turned into Gardens of Eden?
4. Can <u>dust storms</u> be eliminated in the United States?
5. How old is the <u>earth</u>?
6. Can <u>earthquakes</u> be predicted?
7. Can <u>erosion</u> be effectively controlled?
8. Is <u>flood control</u> the proper function of (local, state, federal) authorities?
9. Can <u>floods</u> in the United States be controlled?
10. Is <u>geology</u> an exact science?
11. Is the <u>groundhog</u> (a reliable, an unreliable) weather forecaster?
12. Who owns (the <u>land</u>, the oceans)?
13. Do <u>lightning rods</u> work?
14. Is the <u>Lost Continent</u> a myth?
15. Did the moon come out of the <u>Pacific Ocean</u>?
16. Is our <u>rain water</u> contaminated by radioactivity?
17. Do <u>sea monsters</u> exist?
18. Who owns our <u>tidelands resources</u> (minerals, oil, etc.)?
19. Can man do anything about the <u>weather</u>?
20. Is <u>weather forecasting</u> (an art, a science)?
21. Was the <u>world</u> created in 4004 B.C.?

PROPOSITIONS OF POLICY

1. Should (the <u>Arctic</u>, the Antarctic) be under international control?
2. Should the United States and the Soviet Union construct a tunnel under the <u>Bering Sea</u>?
3. Should (the United Nations, the United States) undertake to reclaim the world's <u>deserts</u>?
4. Should Utopia (expand, revise) its offerings in <u>geology</u>?
5. Should (private citizens, localities, states, the federal

government) bear the chief financial burden of disasters such as floods, hurricanes, etc.?
6. Should every home be equipped with a lightning rod?
7. Should the United States sell vital natural resources--e.g., coal--to foreign countries?
88. Should the federal government engage in a program to remove salt from seawater?
9. Should the seas be free?
10. Should the United States (contract, extend) the three-mile limit?
11. Should tidelands be under the control of (the states, the federal government)?
12. Should men try to control the weather (e.g., through artificial rain-making)?

EVALUATION

OBJECTS

Apparatus, equipment, and/or facilities useful in the earth sciences--for example,
A. A barometer
B. A piece of equipment used in mountain climbing
C. Facilities found at a weather bureau or station
D. A lightning rod

POLICIES

A policy, in effect or proposed, of an agency or organization --local, state, or federal; public or private--devoted to the earth sciences--for example,
A. A policy of the American Speleological Society
B. A policy of Utopia's Geology Department
C. A policy of the United States Weather Bureau
D. A policy of a local weather station

ANTHROPOLOGY AND BIOLOGY 570-579.99

Thought Starters for ANALYSIS

What about:

1. Abnormalities: teratology
2. Aborigines: anthropology
3. Acclimation: biology and physical anthropology
4. Acquired characteristics
5. Adaptations: general biology
6. Alternation of generations
7. Anatomy: anthropology and biology
8. Animals
9. Anomalies: biology
10. Antarctic and arctic biology
11. Anthropogeny
12. Anthropogeography
13. Anthropometry
14. Aquariums: biology
15. Aquatic biology
16. Archeology
17. Artifacts: archeology
18. Biochemistry
19. Bioclimatology
20. Biogeography
21. Biological communities
22. Biological physiology
23. Biological specimens: collection and preservation
24. Biological techniques
25. Biologists
26. Biometeorology
27. Bionomics
28. Breeding habits: general ecology
29. Buried cities, prehistoric
30. Cave men
31. Cells
32. Chromosomes
33. Circulation: general physiology
34. Climate: physical anthropology
35. Coloration: general ecology
36. Comparative anatomy
37. Comparative biology
38. Comparative cytology
39. Comparative physiology
40. Cultural anthropology
41. Cytology
42. Darwinian theory
43. Death: general biology
44. Degeneration: biology and cytology
45. Degeneration of species: genetics
46. Desert biology
47. Digestion
48. Diseases: general biology
49. Economic biology
50. Egg cells: gametogenesis and histogenesis
51. Embryology
52. Environment: physical anthropology and general ecology
53. Enzymes: general biochemistry
54. Evolution: anthropology and biology
55. Excavations, archeological
56. Excretion: biology cytology, and physiology
57. Fertility: general physiology
58. Fertilization: general physiology
59. Food assimilation

NOTE: See also such related fields as SOCIOLOGY (301-309.00), CHEMISTRY (540-549.99), BOTANY (580-589.99), ZOOLOGY (590-599.99), and MEDICINE (610-619.99)

60. Fresh water biology
61. Genes
62. Genetics
63. Germ theory: origin of life
64. Group behavior: general biology
65. Heredity
66. Histology
67. Hormones: general biochemistry
68. Human race: anthropology
69. Hybrids: genetics
70. Inbreeding: heredity
71. Insular biology
72. Lamarkian theory
73. Locomotion: general physiology
74. Malformations: biology
75. Man: anthropology
76. Marine biology
77. Mendel's theory
78. Metabolism: cytology and physiology
79. Microbiology
80. Microscopy
81. Migrations, human: anthropology
82. Mongrelization: heredity
83. Morphology: biology and cytology
84. Mutation theories: organic evolution
85. Natural history: biology and physical anthropology
86. Natural selection: organic evolution
87. Nutrition: cytology and physiology
88. Organisms: biology
89. Origin of life
90. Origin of man
91. Origin of species
92. Outbreeding: heredity
93. Pathology
94. Phylogeny: general and human
95. Physiology, general
96. Pigmentation: biochemistry and cytology
97. Plants
98. Prehistoric art
99. Prehistoric civilization and culture
100. Prehistoric industries
101. Prehistoric man
102. Prehistoric shelters and structures
103. Primitive civilization and culture
104. Primitive customs
105. Primitive man
106. Protective adaptation, general
107. Races, human
108. Radiation effects: heredity
109. Reflex actions: general physiology
110. Regeneration: general physiology
111. Reproduction
112. Respiration: cytology and physiology
113. Savages: anthropology
114. Secretion: biology and physiology
115. Sex: general biology
116. Sexes: organic evolution
117. Sexual reproduction: general physiology
118. Sexual selection: general biology
119. Social anthropology
120. Sterility: heredity
121. Stone Age
122. Survival of fittest: organic evolution
123. Taboos: anthropology and ethnology
124. Taxidermy
125. Temperate zones: biology
126. Teratology
127. Tissues: general histology
128. Tropical biology
129. Viruses: general biology
130. Vital force: biology
131. Vital functions
132. Vitamins: general biochemistry
133. X-ray effects: heredity
134. Zonal biology

CAUSE and EFFECT

1. Why albinos are white
2. Why an ape-man is (likely, unlikely; possible, impossible)
3. Why man has an appendix
4. Why the body (has, needs) blood
5. Why blood is red
6. Why bodies need bones
7. Why man has a brain
8. (Major) Effects of breeding closely related members of a species
9. Why cannibals eat people
10. Why cells are important to life
11. Why cells differ (in shape, in size)
12. (Major) Effects of (hot, cold; wet, dry) climate on living organisms
13. (Major) Causes of disease in living organisms
14. (Major) Effects of disease on (bones, cells, tissue, etc.)
15. (Major) Causes of (dwarfism, giantism)
16. Why people have (black, brown, etc.) (eyes, hair)
17. Why no two fingerprints are alike
18. (Major) Effects of form on function
19. Why the funny bone is so called
20. Why the body (has, needs) glands
21. Why people (have, do not have) hair
22. (Major) Effects of X-rays on heredity
23. Why the body (has, needs) hormones
24. Why incest is unwise
25. Why we (have, need) kidneys
26. Why living things (live, die)
27. Why the body (has, needs) lungs
28. Why metabolism is important to living organisms
29. Why people migrate
30. (Major) Causes of biological monstrosities
31. Why the body (has, needs) muscles
32. Why we (have, need) nerves
33. (Major) Effects of (use, disuse) of bodily organs
34. Why the study of pathology is important in biology
35. Why pygmies do not grow tall
36. Why there are different races
37. (Major) Effects of radiation on chromosomes and genes
38. (Major) Effects of radiation on heredity
39. Why there are, ordinarily, only two sexes
40. Why there are different shades of skin
41. (Major) Causes of sterility
42. Why people have (tonsils, adenoids)
43. Why vitamins are important to human life
44. (Major) Effects on the body of vitamin deficiencies

CLASSIFICATION

Kinds/Types of:

1. Abnormalities
2. Adaptation
3. Anomalies

4. Artifacts
5. Bacteria
6. Blood/blood vessels
7. Cells
8. Chromosomes
9. Enzymes
10. Fertilization
11. Genes
12. Glands
13. Hormones
14. Life
15. Microbes
16. Monstrosities
17. Mutations
18. Races
19. Reproduction
20. Respiration
21. Secretion
22. Sexual selection
23. Species
24. Taboos
25. Viruses
26. Vitamins

COMPARISON and CONTRAST

1. Aborigines: here and there; yesterday and today--e.g., in Africa; in Australia; in the Americas
2. Acquired characteristics and inherited characteristics
3. Adaptation to environment: here and there; yesterday and today--e.g., by American Negro and by American Indian
4. Animal hybrids and plant hybrids
5. Arteries, capillaries, and veins
6. Auricle and ventricle
7. Autecology and synecology
8. Aztecs, Egyptians, Incas, and Mayas (e.g., as builders)
9. Bacteria, protozoa, and viruses
10. Biological Darwinism and social Darwinism
11. Breeding habits: among animals and among human beings
12. Cannibalism: among animals and among human beings
13. Cells: animal and plant
14. Cells: living and dead
15. Circulation: in animal and in plant
16. Civilization and culture
17. Corpuscles: red and white
18. Cow and tree
19. Craniology, phrenology, and psychiatry
20. Death and life
21. Dwarf, midget, and giant
22. Egg and sperm
23. Electronic "brain" and human brain
24. Environment: in biology and in sociology
25. Eugenics: animal and plant
26. Eye and camera
27. Family life: here and there; yesterday and today--e.g., among animals and among human beings; among the Eskimos and in the Fiji Islands
28. Fertility and sterility
29. Fish and man
30. Form and function: in anthropology and in architecture
31. Genesis and genetics
32. Group behavior: in biology and in sociology
33. Healthy cell and unhealthy cell
34. Heart and pump

35. Inbreeding and outbreeding
36. Man and monkey
37. Man and superman
38. Man and trilobite
39. Nerves and telegraph wires
40. Nutrition: for animal and for plant
41. Ovary and testis
42. Prehistoric art and modern art
43. Prehistoric cliff dwellers and modern apartment dwellers
44. Prehistoric earth house and modern (bomb, fall-out) shelter
45. Primitive man: prehistoric and modern
46. Reproduction: of animals and of plants
47. Respiration: in animal and in plant
48. Sex in biology and sex in religion
49. Sexual selection: here and there; yesterday and today--e.g., among primitive peoples and among civilized peoples
50. Survival: according to Christ and according to Darwin
51. Taboos: here and there; yesterday and today--e.g., dietary taboos among ancient Hebrews and among modern inhabitants of Israel
52. Virgin birth: in biology and in Christianity

DEFINITION

1. Atrophy
2. Biopsy
3. Blue blood
4. Breed
5. Embryo
6. Ethnology
7. Eugenics
8. First Cause
9. Genetic code
10. Genotypes
11. Guinea pig
12. Habitat
13. Heredity
14. Hermaphroditism
15. Host
16. Immortality
17. "Kissin' cousins"
18. Mimicry
19. Mongrel
20. Monstrosity
21. Naturalism
22. Nature
23. Phrenology
24. Pituitary
25. Plasma
26. Primitivism
27. Protoplasm
28. Race
29. Social Darwinism
30. Species

DESCRIPTION

1. An aquarium
2. An archeological artifact--e.g., an urn; a weapon
3. A biological specimen--e.g., a frog ready for dissection
4. A biology laboratory, or part thereof
5. An embryo
6. A piece of equipment used in a biology laboratory
7. Facilities of an organization devoted to the study of archeology, anthropology, or biology--e.g., those of Utopia's Department of Biology

8. A microscopic cell
9. A mummy
10. A museum of natural history, or part thereof
11. An item of prehistoric art--e.g., a wall painting
12. A prehistoric dwelling--e.g., a cave or cliff dwelling
13. A skeleton
14. A stuffed animal

PROCESS

1. How the age of man is determined
2. How to distinguish an animal from a plant
3. How (animals, plants) adapt to (their environment; the seasons)
4. How to mount animals
5. How to stuff animals
6. How to make a home aquarium
7. How an archeological expedition is (planned, conducted)
8. How archeologists determine age
9. How artifacts are preserved
10. How to (collect, preserve) biological specimens
11. How the blood circulates
12. How the body extracts nourishment from food
13. How the body grows
14. How the body mends itself
15. How we breathe
16. How to skin a cat (or some other animal)
17. How cells (multiply, divide)
18. How (animals, plants) die
19. How (animals, plants) digest food
20. How the human body fights disease
21. How to dissect a frog (or some other animal)
22. How the human embryo develops
23. How fertility is (achieved, prevented)
24. How genes may be changed
25. How our glands function
26. How (animals, plants) grow
27. How the heart functions
28. How to tan a hide
29. How (animals, plants) inherit (color, shape, size, etc.)
30. How the kidneys function
31. How life began
32. How to prolong life
33. How our lungs work
34. How man has survived
35. How to select a mate scientifically
36. How to use a microscope
37. How to select a microscope
38. How (animals, human beings) move
39. How to improve on nature
40. How (animals, plants) (preserve, protect) themselves
41. How (races, sexes, species) evolved
42. How (animal, plant) reproduction takes place

43. How we (see, hear, speak)
44. How to predict the sex of a child
45. How sex cells are formed (in animals, in human beings)
46. How to prepare a slide
47. How species (degenerate, become extinct)
48. How animals handle waste matter

ARGUMENTATION

PROPOSITIONS OF FACT

1. (What's right, What's wrong) with Utopia's Department of (Anthropology, Archeology, Biology)?
2. Is the language of biology necessary?
3. Does climate have (great, little) influence on man's intelligence?
4. Do conditions for life exist on other planets?
5. Is disease (avoidable, inevitable)?
6. Is (environment, heredity) all-important in man's (development, progress)?
7. Are the Eskimos becoming extinct?
8. Is Darwin's theory of evolution (sound, unsound)?
9. Is the theory of evolution Godless?
10. Is the female of the (animal, human) species more deadly than the male?
11. Are two fingerprints ever alike?
12. Where was the Garden of Eden?
13. Are all human genes identical?
14. Is the scientific study of genetics being (encouraged, discouraged, muzzled) in America today?
15. Is the germ theory of disease (sound, unsound)?
16. Is the human race doomed?
17. Can certain (skills, talents) be inherited?
18. Is human intelligence (acquired, inherited)?
19. Is eternal life (desirable, undesirable; possible, impossible)?
20. Where did life begin?
21. How old is man?
22. Is man only an animal?
23. Is man (a rational, an irrational) animal?
24. Is man descended from apes?
25. Can man live forever?
26. Where did man originate?
27. Are all men created equal?
28. Does nature discriminate?
29. Is nature (amoral, immoral, moral)?
30. Is race merely skin-deep?
31. Is race a myth?
32. Are all races equal?
33. Is sex necessary?
34. Are the sexes equal?
35. Is cancer (or some other disease) caused by a virus?
36. Are women biologically (inferior, superior) to men?

PROPOSITIONS OF POLICY

1. Should biology be required for graduation from Utopia?
2. Should artificial methods of birth control be legal (in our state; in the United States)?
3. Should human beings be bred scientifically?
4. Should the theory of evolution be taught at Utopia?
5. Should opposites attract?
6. Should races intermarry?

EVALUATION

OBJECTS

I. Apparatus or equipment useful in the study of anthropology, archeology, or biology--e.g., a magnifying glass, a microscope, a spade or other useful tool

II. Facilities of an agency or organization--local, state, or federal; private or public--devoted to biology--e.g., facilities of the National Geographic Society or of the Smithsonian Institution devoted to organizing or maintaining an archeological expedition, or to collecting, restoring, or displaying anthropological or archeological artifacts.

POLICIES

1. A policy, in effect or proposed, of (a local, a state, a national) organization devoted to the study of anthropology, archeology, or biology--e.g., a policy of a private or government-sponsored expedition regarding disposition or ownership of buried treasure
2. A policy, in effect or proposed, of Utopia's Department of (Anthropology, Archeology, Biology)
3. A policy, in effect or proposed, of a museum of natural history--e.g., the Smithsonian Institution

BOTANICAL SCIENCES 580-589.99

Thought Starters for ANALYSIS

What about:

1. Abnormalities: plants
2. Absorption: plant physiology
3. Adaptations: plant ecology
4. Algae and algae-like fungi
5. Allergenic plants: economic botany
6. Alternation of generations: plant physiology and ecology
7. Amino acids, manufacture: plant physiology
8. Anatomy, plant and plant cell
9. Annual plants
10. Anomalies, plant
11. Aquatic plants
12. Artificial fertilization: plant physiology
13. Artificial mutations: plants
14. Artificial propagation: plants
15. Asexual reproduction: plant physiology
16. Assimilation: plant physiology
17. Bacteria
18. Bacterial diseases: plant pathology
19. Bacteriology
20. Behavior: plant physiology
21. Beneficial plants
22. Biochemistry, plant
23. Bionomics: plant physiology
24. Biophysics, plant
25. Biosynthesis, plant
26. Botanical communities: ecology
27. Botanical gardens
28. Bulbs: plant propagation
29. Bushes
30. Carnivorous plants
31. Cell division and growth: plant physiology
32. Cells: plant cytology
33. Chemical constitution: plant physiology
34. Chemosynthesis: plant physiology
35. Chlorophyll
36. Chromosomes: plant cytology
37. Circulation: plant physiology
38. Climatic adaptations: plants
39. Coloration: plant ecology
40. Communities: plant ecology
41. Comparative anatomy: plants
42. Conifers
43. Deficiency diseases, plant
44. Deformities, plant
45. Degeneration: plant cytology
46. Desert botany
47. Diatoms
48. Digestion: plant physiology
49. Diseases, plant
50. Drought
51. Economic botany
52. Edible plants: economic botany
53. Electricity: plant growth
54. Embryology, plant
55. Environment: plants
56. Enzymes: plant biochemistry
57. Erosion prevention
58. Evergreen trees

NOTE: See also such related fields as BIOLOGY (570-579.99), AGRICULTURE (630-639.99), and MEDICINE (610-619.99)

59. Everlasting flowers
60. Evolution of species: plants
61. Excretion: plant physiology
62. Fertility: plant physiology
63. Fission: plants
64. Flora
65. Flowering plants
66. Food assimilation: plant
67. Food manufacture: plant physiology
68. Fresh-water botany
69. Fungi
70. Genetics: botany
71. Geographic botany
72. Growth: plant physiology
73. Habitat, plant
74. Harmful plants
75. Herbariums
76. Heredity, plant
77. Histochemistry, plant
78. Histology, plant
79. Hormones: plant biochemistry
80. Hybrids, plant
81. Industrial botany
82. Insectivorous plants
83. Insular botany
84. Leaves
85. Malformations: plant teratology
86. Marine biology
87. Medicinal plants
88. Metabolism, plant
89. Metamorphoses, plant
90. Microscopic botany
91. Mildews
92. Molds
93. Morphology, plant
94. Mutations, plant
95. Nutrition, plant
96. Parasitism, plant
97. Pathology: botany
98. Photosynthesis
99. Physiology, plant
100. Plant cytology
101. Plant ecology
102. Plant histogenesis
103. Plant maturation
104. Plant propagation
105. Plant pollination
106. Protective coloration
107. Proteins: plant metabolism
108. Proteins: manufacture by plants
109. Protoplasm: plant cytology
110. Reproduction: plant physiology
111. Respiration, plant
112. Salt water botany
113. Secretion, plant
114. Seed plants
115. Seedless plants
116. Sense organs: plants
117. Sex organs: plants
118. Teratology, plant
119. Tissues: plant histology
120. Trees
121. Tropical botany
122. Vitamins: plant biochemistry
123. Zonal botany

CAUSE and EFFECT

1. Why algae are (brown, green, etc.)
2. (Major) Causes of atrophy in plants
3. Why bacteria are of different shapes
4. Why chlorophyll is (important, necessary) to life
5. (Major) Causes of (good, poor) circulation in plants
6. (Major) Effects of (hot, cold; wet, dry) climate on plants
7. (Major) Effects of climate on soil
8. Why crops need to be rotated
9. (Major) Effects of (proper, improper) crop rotation (on plants, on soil)
10. Why desert plants--e.g., cacti--need little water
11. (Major) Causes of (good, poor) digestion in plants

12. (Major) Causes of disease in plants--generally; regionally; locally
13. (Major) Effects of drought on plants
14. (Major) Causes of soil erosion--generally; locally
15. Why evergreens are ever green
16. Why (flowers, plants) are important to man
17. Why flowering plants--e.g., fruit trees--(bloom, do not bloom)
18. (Major) Causes of poor food assimilation in plants
19. Why fresh-water plants need fresh (as opposed to salt) water
20. Why grass is green
21. Why leaves are (brown, green, etc.)
22. (Major) Causes of malformations in plants
23. (Major) Effects of (proper, improper) nutrition in plants
24. (Major) Effects of parasites on plants
25. Why people are allergic to certain plants
26. Why plants (have, lose) leaves
27. Why certain plants are (annuals, biennials, perennials)
28. Why plants (have, do not have) flowers
29. Why certain plants (are, are not) green
30. Why certain plants (need, do not need) sunlight
31. (Major) Effects of pruning on (plants, shrubs, trees, etc.)
32. (Major) Effects of radiation on plants
33. Why salt-water plants need salt (rather than fresh) water
34. Why trees die
35. Why I (am, am not) a vegetarian

CLASSIFICATION

Kinds/Types of:

1. Allergenic plants
2. Botanical gardens
3. Botanists
4. Harmful plants
5. Leaves
6. Lichens
7. Medicinal plants
8. Plant abnormalities
9. Plant absorption
10. Plant algae
11. Plant assimilation
12. Plant bacteria
13. Plant cells
14. Plant colonies/ communities
15. Plant degeneration
16. Plant diseases
17. Plant excretion
18. Plant malformations
19. Plant molds
20. Plant nutrition
21. Plant parasites
22. Plant reproduction
23. Plant respiration
24. Plant sense organs

COMPARISON and CONTRAST

1. Algae and fungi
2. Anabolism and catabolism
3. Apple and rose
4. Artificial fertilization: in plants and in animals
5. Asexual reproduction: in animals and in plants
6. Banyan and fig

7. Botanical garden: in 1750 and in 1820
8. Boxwood: American and English
9. Cacti and cattails
10. Camouflage: by man and by nature
11. Carnivorous plants and carnivorous animals
12. Cells: animal and plant
13. Climatic adaptation: plant and animal
14. Coffee and tea
15. Dentist and tree surgeon
16. Dicots and monocots
17. Digestion: plant and animal
18. Egg and eggplant
19. Fern and flowering plant
20. Food assimilation: plant and animal
21. Fresh-water plants and salt-water plants
22. Fruit and vegetable
23. Fungus and parasite
24. Goldenrod and ragweed
25. Greenhouse and herbarium
26. Growth: plant and animal
27. Holly and mistletoe
28. Hybrids: plant and animal
29. Insectivorous plants and insectivorous animals
30. Ivy: American and English
31. Land plants and water plants
32. Leaf and wing
33. Medicinal herbs: here and there; yesterday and today--e.g., among the American Indians and in modern America
34. Metabolism: in plants and in animals
35. Mold and moss
36. Mushroom and orchid
37. Mushroom and toadstool
38. Mutation: plant and animal
39. Nutrition: in plants and in animals
40. Onion and yucca
41. Parasites and people
42. Plants and animals
43. Poison ivy and Virginia creeper
44. Reproduction: in plants and in animals
45. Seed plants and seedless plants
46. Sense organs: plant and animal
47. Sex: in plants and in animals
48. Sundew plant and spider
49. Tissues: plant and animal
50. Weed and wild flower

DEFINITION

1. Allergy
2. Behavior
3. Camouflage
4. Conservation
5. Decay
6. Family
7. Freak
8. Garden
9. Ginkgo
10. Ginseng

11. Green thumb
12. Kelp
13. Legume
14. Nectar
15. Nightshade
16. Plant food
17. Pollen
18. Sport
19. Weed

DESCRIPTION

1. A botanical garden, or part thereof
2. A botanical laboratory, or part thereof
3. A cotton boll
4. A cotton gin
5. A diatom
6. Equipment useful in the study of botany--e.g., a microscope
7. Facilities of an agency, institution, or organization--local, state, federal; public, private--devoted to the study of botany or to the raising of plants--e.g., the facilities of Utopia's Department of Botany
8. A fern
9. A florist's shop, or part thereof
10. A greenhouse
11. An herbarium
12. A leaf
13. Lichens
14. Plankton
15. Seaweed
16. A terrarium
17. A tree
18. A watering can

PROCESS

1. How to make a botanical garden at home
2. How to plant bulbs--e.g., iris
3. How to (plant, care for) bushes
4. How to raise cacti
5. How carnivorous plants get food
6. How to protect plants--e.g., citrus groves--from frost
7. How (coffee, tea) is grown
8. How to conserve our (forests, soil, etc.)--generally; regionally; locally
9. How to raise corn
10. How cotton is grown
11. How (garden, field) crops are rotated
12. How to make dandelion wine
13. How to grow (a flower, a vegetable) garden--for home consumption; for profit
14. How to (make, plant) a (formal, rock) garden
15. How to raise grapes
16. How to (raise, care for) fruit trees
17. How to combat fungus

18. How to (select, grow, cut) grass--for lawns; for grazing
19. How to build a home greenhouse
20. How to furnish a greenhouse
21. How to trim a hedge
22. How to make an herbarium
23. How to grow house plants
24. How industry makes use of botany
25. How to protect plants from insects
26. How jumping beans jump
27. How leaves make food for plants
28. How maple sugar is made
29. How to prevent mildew in plants
30. How to raise mushrooms
31. How to grow orchids
32. How to combat parasites
33. How perfume is made from flowers
34. How to control plant diseases
35. How plants eat animals
36. How plants breathe
37. How plants are bred
38. How plants manufacture chlorophyll
39. How plants adjust to (hot, cold; wet, dry) climates
40. How plants get their color
41. How plants (decay, die)
42. How plants digest food
43. How plants adjust to their environment--e.g., soil
44. How plants--e.g., trees--are grafted
45. How plants (grow, mature)
46. How plants (absorb, store) (food, moisture)
47. How plants get their names
48. How plants (propagate, reproduce)
49. How to detect poison (oak, ivy, sumac)
50. How pollination takes place
51. How to plant shrubs
52. How to rejuvenate soil
53. How plants make sugar
54. How to make a terrarium
55. How tobacco is grown
56. How to transplant (shrubs, trees, etc.)
57. How the age of a tree is determined
58. How to perform tree surgery
59. How to plant (flowers, shrubs, trees, etc.)
60. How trees are (pruned, trimmed, etc.)
61. How water circulates in plants
62. How to kill weeds
63. How wheat is grown
64. How wild flowers are tamed
65. How to make a window box for flowers
66. How wood becomes petrified

ARGUMENTATION

PROPOSITIONS OF FACT

1. Will an apple a day keep the doctor away?
2. Are bacteria immortal?
3. Is botany an exact science?
4. Are men like plants?
5. Are people parasites?
6. Are all plants equal?
7. Is the tomato (a fruit, a vegetable)?
8. Can man make a tree?
9. Are tree houses harmful to trees?

PROPOSITIONS OF POLICY

1. Should our community set up a botanical garden?
2. Should Utopia require a course in Botany for graduation?
3. Should our community (oppose, welcome) the establishment of a federal Conservation Corps (for the purpose of reforestation, etc.)?
4. Should the __________ be our (state, national) (flower, tree)?
5. Should flowers be (encouraged, omitted) at funerals?
6. Should our community (cut down, plant) trees--at a particular location; along a particular street, etc.?

EVALUATION

OBJECTS

I. A piece of apparatus or equipment useful in the cultivation of plants or in the study of botany--for example,
   A. A piece of equipment in Utopia's botany laboratory
   B. A plant or tree sprayer
   C. A tool used by a tree surgeon
II. Facilities of an organization, institution, or firm devoted to the study, growth, or sale of plants--for example,
   A. Facilities of Utopia's Botany Department
   B. Facilities of a florist shop or nursery

POLICIES

A policy, proposed or in effect, of an agency or organization --local, state, federal; public, private--devoted, directly or indirectly, to the study or promotion of Botany--for example,
   A. A policy of a botanical garden
   B. A policy of Utopia's Department of Botany
   C. A policy of a local florist shop
   D. A policy of a local garden club
   E. A policy of a local nursery
   F. A policy of (a municipal, a national, a state) park

ZOOLOGY 590-599.99

Thought Starters for ANALYSIS

What about:

1. The aardvark
2. Abnormalities: animal
3. Acclimation: animals
4. Adaptation: animals
5. Amoeba
6. Amphibians
7. Anatomy, animal
8. Animal cytology
9. Animal ecology
10. Animal histology
11. Animal physiology
12. Anomalies, animal
13. Anthropoidea
14. Aquatic animals
15. Anthropoda
16. Articulates
17. Assimilation: animal physiology
18. Autecology, animal
19. Behavior: animal ecology
20. Biochemistry, animal
21. Bionomics: animal
22. Biosynthesis, animal
23. Bugs
24. Canines
25. Carnivora
26. Cats
27. Cells: animal cytology
28. Chiroptera
29. Chordata
30. Circulation: animal physiology
31. Coloration: animal ecology
32. Communication, animal
33. Communities: animal ecology
34. Comparative anatomy: ecology
35. Conchology
36. Craniata
37. Crustaceans
38. Cyclostomes
39. Deformities, animal
40. Descriptive zoology
41. Digestion: animal physiology
42. Diseases, animal
43. Economic zoology
44. Embryology
45. Entomology
46. Enzymes: animal biochemistry
47. Equines
48. Estivation
49. Excretion: animal physiology
50. Fauna
51. Fertility: animal physiology
52. Food assimilation
53. Fowls
54. Fresh water zoology
55. Genetics
56. Geographic zoology
57. Group behavior: animals
58. Growth: animal physiology
59. Habitat: animals
60. Habits, animals
61. Heredity
62. Hemiptera
63. Hibernation
64. Homing instinct
65. Hormones: animal biochemistry
66. Hybrids
67. Ichthyology
68. Insects
69. Instinct
70. Insular zoology
71. Invertebrates
72. Locomotion: animal physiology
73. Malformations: animal teratology
74. Mammals
75. Man
76. Marine zoology

NOTE: See also such related fields as BIOLOGY AND ANTHROPOLOGY (570-579.99), BOTANY (580-589.99), and MEDICINE (610-619.99).

77. Maturation: animal physiology
78. Menageries
79. Metabolism: animal physiology
80. Microscopic zoology
81. Migration
82. Mimicry: animal ecology
83. Molluscoidea
84. Morphology, animal
85. Moss animals
86. Mutations
87. Nucleus: animal cytology
88. Nutrition: animal physiology
89. Oology
90. Ornithology
91. Osteology
92. Paramecium
93. Parasites, animal
94. Pathology, animal
95. Pisces
96. Primates
97. Propagation: animal physiology
98. Protein metabolism
99. Protoplasm: animal cytology
100. Protozoa
101. Rays
102. Reproduction: animal physiology
103. Reptiles
104. Respiration: animal physiology
105. Rodents
106. Ruminants
107. Salt water fish
108. Salt water zoology
109. Sea animals
110. Seasonal migration
111. Secretion: animal physiology
112. Sense organs, animal
113. Sexual reproduction: animals
114. Shells
115. Sponges
116. Sports: animal genetics
117. Sugar metabolism, animal
118. Symbiosis: animals
119. Temperature: animal biophysics
120. Tissues: animal histology
121. Tropical zoology
122. Unicellular animals
123. Vertebrates
124. Vitamins: animal biochemistry
125. Zonal zoology
126. Zoogeography
127. Zoological gardens
128. Zoophysiology

CAUSE and EFFECT

1. Why some animals eat their young
2. Why certain animals--e.g., birds--estivate
3. Why animal species--e.g., dinosaurs--become extinct
4. Why animals--e.g., bears--hibernate
5. Why animals--e.g., birds--migrate
6. Why animals (neglect, take care of) their young
7. Why anthropoids--e.g., apes--cannot talk
8. Why certain animals--e.g., ants, bees, termites--act like human beings
9. Why apes have no tails
10. Why birds sing
11. Why birds have no teeth
12. Why (female) worker bees do not lay eggs
13. Why camels have humps
14. Why canine teeth are so called
15. Why cats are said to have nine lives
16. (Major) Effects of confinement (as in a zoo) upon animals
17. Why cows chew their cuds

18. Why Utopia (does, does not) teach evolution
19. Why (fresh, salt) water fish cannot live in (salt, fresh) water
20. Why fish (do, do not) run in "schools"
21. Why the giraffe has no voice
22. Why (guinea pigs, monkeys, etc.) are used in scientific experiments
23. Why homing pigeons go home
24. Why hyenas "laugh"
25. Why the ladybug is so named
26. Why lemmings "commit suicide"
27. Why man has survived
28. Why man stands upright
29. Why man and apes cannot be crossed
30. Why the mule is sterile
31. (Major) Causes of neuroticism in zoo animals
32. Why opossums hang upside down
33. Why ostriches cannot fly
34. Why pigeons are monogamous
35. Why rattlesnakes rattle
36. Why animals--e.g., cats, dogs--have tails
37. Why people do not have tails
38. Why worms appear after a rain

CLASSIFICATION

Kinds/Types of:

1. Amphibians
2. Anthropoids
3. Ants
4. Apes
5. Bees
6. Birds
7. Bugs
8. Canines
9. Cats
10. Cattle
11. Chickens
12. Cows
13. Crabs
14. Dogs
15. Elephants
16. Equines
17. Fish
18. Fowls
19. Goats
20. Hogs
21. Horses
22. Insects
23. Monkeys
24. Parrots
25. Pigeons
26. Primates
27. Rabbits
28. Reptiles
29. Rodents
30. Sheep
31. Snakes
32. Swine
33. Turtles
34. Whales
35. Zoos

COMPARISON and CONTRAST

1. Airplane and bird
2. Alligator and crocodile
3. Animal and plant
4. Ant colony and (socialist, communist) community
5. Ape and man

6. Bat and bird
7. Bee hive and modern city
8. Bird, fish, and reptile
9. Birth control: among animals and among human beings
10. Bridge and spider web
11. Bug and insect
12. Butterfly and moth
13. Buzzard, falcon, eagle, hawk, and/or vulture
14. Carniverous, herbiverous, insectiverous and omnivorous
15. Caterpillar, grasshopper, tadpole, and/or worm
16. Clam, oyster, scallop, and/or snail
17. Class, family, genus, order, phylum, and species
18. Claw, hoof, and nail
19. Courting customs: of animals and of human beings
20. Cow and tree
21. Dolphin and porpoise
22. Ear of cat and of cricket
23. Eel and snake
24. Electric battery and electric eel
25. Electric light and lightning bug
26. Embryos: animal and human
27. Estivation and hibernation
28. Evolution: animal and human
29. Eye of insect and of man
30. Family life: among animals and among human beings
31. Fin and wing
32. Fish and submarine
33. Frog and toad
34. Gill and lung
35. Goldfish, silverfish, and starfish
36. Group behavior: among animals and among human beings
37. Harmful (birds, reptiles, rodents, worms) and useful (birds, reptiles, rodents, worms)
38. House cat and tiger
39. Hummingbird and helicopter
40. Hybrids: animal and plant
41. Instinct and love
42. Man and protozoa
43. Mole and worm
44. Morality: in animals and men
45. Prairie chicken and prairie dog
46. Purebred and thoroughbred
47. Sea cow, sea horse, and sea lion
48. Sexual reproduction: animal and plant
49. Snake and worm
50. Terrapin, tortoise, and turtle
51. Trilobite and whale

DEFINITION

1. Batty
2. Beeline
3. Behavior
4. Catty
5. Chicken-livered
6. Crabby

7. Crocodile tears
8. Evolution
9. Fishy
10. Foxy
11. Genes
12. Genetic code
13. Harelip
14. Host
15. Human
16. Imprinting
17. Instinct
18. Kingdom
19. Leech
20. Mermaid
21. Metamorphosis
22. Mimicry
23. Missing link
24. Pattern
25. Pigeon-toed
26. Play possum
27. Shrimp
28. Snail's pace
29. Sponge
30. Swan song
31. Toady
32. Waspish
33. White elephant
34. Zodiac

DESCRIPTION

Equipment and/or facilities used by an agency, organization, or institution--local, state, federal; public, private--devoted to the subject of zoology, either directly or indirectly--for example,

A. An ant farm
B. An aviary
C. A bee-hive
D. Equipment and/or facilities of Utopia's Department of Zoology

PROCESS

1. How animals--snowshoe rabbits, chameleons--adapt to changes in environment
2. How amphibians--e.g., frogs--develop
3. How animals--e.g., lobsters, dogs--assimilate food
4. How animals attract other animals--in courtship; as prey
5. How man (controls, disturbs, destroys) the balance of nature
6. How bats (navigate, see) in the dark
7. How beavers build dams
8. How bees make honey
9. How to bird-watch
10. How birds build their nests
11. How birds fly
12. How birds get their names
13. How the bumblebee flies
14. How animals camouflage themselves
15. How to skin a cat (or some other animal)
16. How a caterpillar becomes a butterfly
17. How the chameleon changes its color
18. How animal cells (are formed; grow; are destroyed; fight disease, etc.
19. How animals communicate with each other
20. How crabs walk backward

21. How animals digest their food
22. How earthworms (breathe, eat)
23. How fish (breathe, swim)
24. How homing pigeons find their way home
25. How animal hybrids are produced
26. How insects carry diseases
27. How invertebrates--e.g., jellyfish, oysters, etc.--(breathe; digest food; move; reproduce)
28. How the leopard got its spots
29. How lightning bugs light
30. How mammals--e.g., kangaroos, whales, etc.--(breathe, digest food; move; reproduce)
31. How man has survived
32. How to assemble a menagerie
33. How moths are born
34. How animals--e.g., horses--(move, run)
35. How oysters make pearls
36. How animals--e.g., porcupines, skunks--protect themselves
37. How salmon (breathe, digest food, move, reproduce)
38. How silkworms make silk
39. How spiders (breathe, digest food, move, reproduce, spin webs)
40. How squids swim
41. How tadpoles become (frogs, toads)
42. How to feed the animals at a zoo
43. How zoos are kept
44. How to plan a zoological garden
45. How to (collect; preserve; display) zoological specimens

ARGUMENTATION

PROPOSITIONS OF FACT*

1. Are animals (amoral, immoral, moral)?
2. Do animals--e.g., dogs--dream?
3. Are animals capable of love--for man; for other animals?
4. Are all animals parasites?
5. Can animals--e.g., monkeys, rats--reason?
6. Do animals have souls?
7. Do animals talk to each other?
8. Is artificial insemination of animals (moral, immoral)?
9. Do bulls see red?
10. Is caging birds--e.g., canaries--a form of cruelty to animals?
11. Which came first--the chicken or the egg?
12. Do crocodiles cry?
13. Does meat make a dog mean?
14. Is the dog man's best friend?
15. Is the dolphin the most intelligent animal next to man?
16. Is (the eagle, the turkey) a fitting national emblem for the United States?

*Cf. Animal Psychology, 151.3

17. Do elephants (ever, never) forget?
18. Are elephants afraid of mice?
19. Is Darwin's theory of evolution (sound, unsound)?
20. Is the female of the species more deadly than the male?
21. Are fish "brain food"?
22. Can horses be trusted?
23. Do hyenas really laugh?
24. (Can, Will) insects take over the world?
25. Is the jellyfish (useful, useless) to man?
26. Is the lion "king of beasts"?
27. Is man descended from apes?
28. Is man God's noblest work?
29. Will man evolve into a superman?
30. Will man destroy himself?
31. Is meat eating (immoral, unclean, unhealthful)?
32. Are all men created equal?
33. Is the practice of keeping animals in menageries (humane, inhumane)?
34. Do (mice, rats) serve any useful purpose?
35. Is nature (amoral, immoral, moral; kind, indifferent, malevolent)?
36. Are owls wise?
37. Are people parasites?
38. Are people animals?
39. Are pigs unclean?
40. Do sea monsters exist?
41. Is self-preservation the first law (of man; of nature)?
42. Are the sexes equal--among animals; among human beings?
43. Is the language of zoology necessary?
44. Is confinement in zoos (beneficial, harmful) to animals?

PROPOSITIONS OF POLICY

1. Should "animal instincts" be (curbed, encouraged) in human beings?
2. Should Utopis (promote, prohibit) the study of evolution?
3. Should human beings be bred scientifically?
4. Should scientists attempt to alter nature's balance?
5. Should a pet skunk be de-scented?
6. Should state laws pertaining to vivisection be (enforced, repealed)?
7. Should Utopia require zoology for graduation?
8. Should (tame, wild) animals be placed in zoos?

EVALUATION

OBJECTS

An object of use to an individual or to an organization in the study of zoology--for example,

A. A cage
B. A microscope
C. A trap
D. Some other piece of equipment found in a zoology laboratory

POLICIES

A policy, in effect or proposed, of an organization devoted to the general subject of Zoology and related fields--for example,

A. A (local, state, federal) policy relating to
   1. fisheries
   2. game laws
   3. wild-life preservation
B. A policy of the Audubon Society
C. A policy of the SPCA
D. A policy of Utopia's Zoology Department

MEDICAL SCIENCES 610-619.99

Thought Starters for ANALYSIS

What about:

1. Abortion
2. Accident prevention
3. Adolescence: human physiology
4. Age: human physiology
5. Alcoholism
6. Alimentary tract
7. Allergies
8. Anemias
9. Antibiotics
10. Antidotes
11. Antisocial compulsions: psychiatry
12. Appendix, vermiform
13. Arctic hygiene and medicine
14. Arteries
15. Arthritis
16. Artificial respiration
17. Automobile accident prevention
18. Aviation medicine
19. Bacteriology, medical
20. Barbiturates
21. Biliary tract
22. Biological products: pharmacology
23. Biopsies
24. Birth control
25. Bladder
26. Blood
27. Blood transfusions
28. Blood vessels
29. Body care: hygiene
30. Bone diseases
31. Bones
32. Botanical drugs: pharmacology
33. Brain
34. Burns: first-aid treatment
35. Cancers
36. Capillaries
37. Cardiovascular system
38. Cavities: dental treatment
39. Cells: human cytology
40. Child development: physiology
41. Child psychiatry
42. Childbirth
43. Chiropody
44. Chiropractic
45. Cholesterol
46. Circulation
47. Cleanliness: hygiene
48. Climatology, medical
49. Clothing: hygiene
50. Color blindness
51. Common cold
52. Comparative medicine
53. Conception
54. Contagious diseases: medicine
55. Convulsions: symptomatology
56. Deformation: human teratology
57. Dental anatomy
58. Dental medicine and physiology
59. Dermatology
60. Diabetes
61. Diet
62. Digestion, human
63. Dipsomania
64. Disease carriers
65. Disease control and prevention
66. Domestic medicine
67. Dreams: physiology
68. Drug addiction
69. Drugs: medicine
70. Ductless glands
71. Dwarfism
72. Ear
73. Embryology, human
74. Emergency treatment: first aid
75. Endocrinology
76. Environment: hygiene
77. Enzymes
78. Epidemics
79. Epilepsy
80. Eugenics

81. Euthanasia: medical ethics
82. Excretion, human
83. Exercise: hygiene
84. Experimental medicine
85. Eye
86. Faith healing
87. Fall-out, radioactive: physiological effects; public health measures
88. Fevers
89. First aid
90. Fluoridation: public health measures
91. Folk medicine
92. Food and drug control: public health
93. Food assimilation, human
94. Food: hygiene
95. Fractures: first-aid treatment
96. Gallstones
97. Genetics
98. Geriatric medicine
99. Germ theory of disease
100. Gerontology: human physiology
101. Glands
102. Growth
103. Gustatory organs
104. Gynecology
105. Heart
106. Heatstroke: first-aid treatment
107. Hereditary factors: hygiene
108. High blood pressure
109. Highway safety: public health
110. Hippocratic Oath
111. Homeopathy
112. Hormones
113. Human anatomy
114. Human anomalies
115. Human biochemistry
116. Human biophysics
117. Human cytology
118. Human histology
119. Human physiology
120. Human teratology
121. Hygiene
122. Hypnotherapy
123. Hypochondriasis
124. Hysteria
125. Immature personalities: psychiatry
126. Infectious diseases: treatment and control
127. Injuries: first-aid treatment
128. Insanity
129. Insomnia
130. Integumentary system: human physiology
131. Intestines
132. Joints: human anatomy and physiology
133. Kidneys
134. Laboratory animals: experimental medicine
135. Larynx
136. Laws and regulations: public health
137. Laxatives
138. Leprosy
139. Light: hygiene
140. Liver
141. Locomotion, human
142. Longevity
143. Lungs
144. Lymphatic system
145. Malformations: human teratology
146. Malnutrition
147. Manias
148. Maturation: human physiology
149. Meat: hygiene
150. Medical care: economics
151. Medical entomology
152. Medical ethics
153. Medical meteorology
154. Medical parasitology
155. Medical superstitions
156. Menopause
157. Mental illness
158. Metabolism
159. Microbiology, medical
160. Midwifery
161. Military hygiene and medicine
162. Motion sickness
163. Motor system
164. Mouth
165. Multiple personality: psychiatry
166. Multiple sclerosis

167. Muscles
168. Muscular dystrophy
169. Music therapy
170. Nails: human anatomy and physiology
171. Narcotics
172. Naturopathy
173. Naval hygiene
174. Neck
175. Nervous system
176. Neuroses
177. Noise control: public health measures
178. Nose
179. Nudism: hygiene
180. Nurses
181. Nursing
182. Nutrition
183. Obesity
184. Obstetrics
185. Occupational therapy
186. Ophthalmology
187. Optometry
188. Osteopathy
189. Pancreas
190. Pathology
191. Pediatrics
192. Personal hygiene
193. Personality disorders
194. Perversion, sexual
195. Pharmacology
196. Phobias
197. Physical culture
198. Physicians
199. Plasma
200. Plastic surgery
201. Podiatry
202. Poisons
203. Population control
204. Pregnancy
205. Prenatal hygiene
206. Prescriptions
207. Preventive medicine
208. Psychiatry
209. Psychosomatics
210. Puberty: physiology
211. Public health
212. Pure food and drug laws
213. Quackery
214. Race improvement: eugenics
215. Radium therapy
216. Reflexes: physiology
217. Reproduction
218. Respiration
219. Rheumatic fever
220. Safety measures: public health
221. Sanitation: public health
222. Secretion, human
223. Sedatives
224. Senescence
225. Sense organs
226. Sex hormones
227. Sexual deviations
228. Shipboard hygiene
229. Sight preservation: medicine
230. Skeleton
231. Skin
232. Sleep
233. Smog and smoke control: public health
234. Space medicine
235. Stammering and stuttering
236. Sterilization, human: eugenics
237. Stillbirths
238. Stimulants
239. Stomach
240. Streams, pollution: public health measures
241. Submarine medicine
242. Sun bathing: hygiene and therapy
243. Surgeons
244. Surgery: medicine
245. Symptomatology
246. Teeth
247. Temperature
248. Throat
249. Tobacco products: hygiene
250. Toxicology
251. Tranquilizers
252. Tropical hygiene and medicine
253. Ulcers
254. Underweight
255. Urinary system
256. Urology
257. Vacations: hygiene
258. Vaccines
259. Vegetarianism
260. Veins
261. Venereal diseases

262. Veterinary medicine (see under AGRICULTURE, 630-639.99)
263. Viruses
264. Vivisection
265. Vocal organs
266. Water: hygiene
267. Water safety
268. Wounds, first aid for
269. X-ray

CAUSE and EFFECT

1. (Major) Effects of state abortion laws--on the medical profession; on morality, etc.
2. (Major) Causes of acne--e.g, in adolescents
3. Why human beings have (adenoids, appendixes, tonsils)
4. (Major) Effects--mental; physiological; psychological, etc.--of aging
5. (Major) Effects of air conditioning on health
6. (Major) Causes of automobile accidents--generally; regionally; locally
7. Why children wet their beds
8. (Major) Effects of (alcoholic; carbonated; hot, cold) beverages on health
9. (Major) Effects--physiological, psychological, social, economic, etc.--of birth control
10. Why blood is typed
11. Why blood banks are necessary
12. (Major) Causes of boating accidents
13. (Major) Effects of candy on health
14. (Major) Effects of (chewing tobacco, cigars, cigarettes) on health
15. Why childbirth (is, need not be) painful
16. (Major) Effects of (climate, weather) on health
17. (Major) Effects of clothing--e.g., belts, collars, girdles, hats, shoes, support hose, etc.--on health
18. (Major) Causes of convulsions--in infants; in children; in adults
19. (Major) Causes of deafness
20. (Major) Causes of a common disease--e.g., cancer, heart disease
21. Why I (want to be, could never be) a doctor
22. Why reputable doctors do not advertise
23. Why I (would, would not) like to be a doctor's wife
24. Why most Russian doctors are women
25. Why many people distrust doctors
26. Why many doctors (are, seem to be) "unfeeling"
27. Why people dream
28. (Major) Effects of (state, federal) laws on drug addiction
29. Why (men, women, adolescents) drink excessively
30. (Major) Effects--physiological, psychological, etc.--of excessive drinking
31. (Major) Effects of (proper, improper; too much, too little) exercise on health
32. (Major) Effects of television on eyesight
33. (Major) Effects of radioactive fall-out--on people; on animals; on plant life; on milk; on drinking water, etc.

34. Why fevers are necessary to medical (diagnosis, treatment)
35. Why (local, state, federal) food and drug laws are necessary
36. (Major) Causes of simple headaches
37. (Major) Effects of (adequate, inadequate; proper, improper) housing on health
38. Why (men, women) become hypochondriacs
39. (Major) Causes of hysteria--in men, in women, in children
40. (Major) Causes of insomnia
41. (Major) Causes of malnutrition in the United States
42. Why the cost of medical care is high--generally; regionally; locally
43. Why I would like to be a medical missionary
44. Why milk is pasteurized
45. (Major) Effects of (music, noise) on health
46. Why (children, adolescents, adults) bite their nails
47. (Major) Effects of narcotics on health
48. Why I would like to be a nurse
49. (Major) Causes of (overweight, underweight)--in infants; in children; in adolescents; in men and women
50. (Major) Effects of (smog, smoke) on health--e.g., on the lungs
51. (Major) Effects of space travel on health--e.g., on the circulation; on the equilibrium
52. Why (children, adults) (stammer, stutter)
53. (Major) Effects of sunspots on (mental, physical) health
54. Why 98.6 degrees is considered normal temperature
55. Why children suck their thumbs
56. (Major) Causes of tooth decay
57. (Major) Causes of train accidents
58. (Major) Causes of ulcers
59. (Major) Effects of X-rays on health

CLASSIFICATION

Kinds/Types of:

1. Abortion
2. Allergies
3. Anesthetics
4. Birth control
5. Blood
6. Burns
7. Dentists
8. Disease carriers
9. Doctors
10. Drinkers
11. Drugs/druggists
12. Fractures
13. Glands
14. Hormones
15. Hospital visitors
16. Hospitals
17. Medicine
18. Muscles
19. Nerves
20. Nurses/nursing
21. Orderlies
22. Pain-killers
23. Patients
24. Pharmacists
25. Physicians
26. Poisons
27. Prescriptions
28. Quackery/quacks

COMPARISON and CONTRAST

1. Abortion: here and there; yesterday and today--e.g., in the United States and in Sweden
2. Alcoholism and social drinking
3. Allopath, chiropractor, homeopath, osteopath, and/or naturopath
4. Arteries, capillaries, and veins
5. Artificial respiration: conventional and mouth-to-mouth
6. Birth control and death control
7. Blood: animal and human
8. Bottle feeding and breast feeding
9. Brain: of ape and of man
10. Christian Science and medical science
11. Cold pack and hot pack
12. Corpuscles: red and white
13. Contact lenses and conventional eyeglasses
14. Dentifrice and "elbow grease"
15. Dr. Jekyll and Mr. Hyde
16. Diagnosis and hunch
17. Doctor of medicine and witch doctor
18. Doctors: in fact and in fiction--e.g., on television
19. Drives and instincts
20. Embryo: animal and human
21. Experimental medicine: here and there; yesterday and today--e.g., in the U.S.A. and in the U.S.S.R.
22. Faith healer and medicine man
23. Folk medicine and modern medicine
24. Geriatrics and pediatrics
25. Guinea pigs and patients
26. Gynecologist and obstetrician
27. Healing: by faith and by (medicine, surgery)
28. Insanity and sanity
29. Isolation and quarantine
30. Instinct and will
31. Insulin: by injection and by mouth
32. Iron lung and natural lung
33. Limbs: artificial and natural
34. Man and monkey
35. Medicine: here and there; yesterday and today--e.g., in the U.S.A. and in the U.S.S.R.
36. Mineral drugs and organic drugs
37. Neurosis and psychosis
38. Nurses: in fact and in fiction (e.g., on television)
39. Oculist, optician, optometrist, and ophthalmologist
40. Personalities: mature and immature
41. Polio vaccines: Sabin and Salk
42. Psychologist and psychiatrist
43. Quack doctor and witch doctor
44. Saccharin and sugar
45. Sex: in medicine and in religion
46. Standards of medicine: here and there; yesterday and today--e.g., in the U.S.A. and in Britain
47. Toothbrush: electric and manual

DEFINITION

1. Anthropology
2. Autopsy
3. Biopsy
4. Birth
5. Congenital
6. Death
7. Disease
8. Emotion
9. Ethics
10. Evidence
11. Expert
12. Faith healing
13. Genes
14. Health
15. Hippocratic Oath
16. Humours
17. Intelligence
18. Kleptomania
19. Malpractice
20. Materia medica
21. Negligence
22. Nostrum
23. Panacea
24. Patent medicine
25. Phrenology
26. Specialist

DESCRIPTION

I. A piece of equipment used in the private or public promotion of health, either in the home, or in a physician's office, or in a hospital--for example,
   A. A stethoscope
   B. A vaporizer
   C. A vehicle used by a local rescue squad
   D. An X-ray machine

II. Facilities used in administering first aid or in the practice of medicine--for example,
   A. Facilities of a clinic
   B. Facilities of the emergency room of a local hospital
   C. Facilities of a local rescue squad
   D. Facilities of a local pharmacy

III. An organ or some other component of the human body--for example,
   A. A human brain
   B. A human heart
   C. A skeleton

PROCESS

1. How acne is treated (at home; professionally)
2. How we age
3. How the aging process (can be, is) stemmed
4. How airlines promote safety
5. How to solve the problem of air pollution--generally; in our community
6. How to treat (alcoholism, the alcoholic)--at home; professionally
7. How the alimentary tract functions
8. How to provide antidotes for common poisons found in the home
9. How to (detect, give first-aid treatment for) appendicitis

10. How artificial eyes are manufactured
11. How to give artificial respiration--conventionally; mouth-to-mouth
12. How to treat athlete's foot
13. How to deliver a baby (in or out of a taxi)
14. How to combat bad breath
15. How to treat baldness
16. How to take a bath
17. How to practise beach safety
18. How to eliminate bed-wetting in children
19. How to treat the "bends"
20. How the biliary tract functions
21. How to treat a black eye
22. How the bladder functions
23. How to stop minor bleeding
24. How to live with blindness
25. How the blood coagulates
26. How blood is typed
27. How a blood transfusion is given
28. How to prevent boating accidents
29. How the body assimilates food
30. How the body controls temperature
31. How the brain functions
32. How we breathe
33. How to set a broken (arm, leg, etc.)
34. How to remove (bunions, corns) safely
35. How to treat minor burns
36. How to watch calories
37. How to have a painless childbirth
38. How the circulatory system functions
39. How to treat a cold
40. How communicable diseases are communicated
41. How to treat convulsions
42. How to treat croup
43. How to live with deafness
44. How to visit the dentist
45. How the digestive system functions
46. How diseases are classified
47. How to select a doctor
48. How to establish the proper doctor-patient relationship
49. How to save a person from drowing
50. How to treat a minor earache
51. How the electrocardiograph works
52. How the human embryo develops
53. How to select a mate eugenically
54. How to exercise
55. How doctors make up their fee schedules
56. How to reduce fever (gradually, quickly)
57. How to care for the finger nails
58. How to administer first aid--in, for example, an automobile accident
59. How to stay alive in a fall-out shelter
60. How to remove a foreign object from the eye
61. How to (determine, prepare) a baby's formula

62. How to treat frostbite
63. How our glands function
64. How we grow
65. How to (prevent, treat) a hangover
66. How to treat hay fever
67. How to treat a minor headache
68. How we hear
69. How to select a hearing aid
70. How the heart functions
71. How to live with heart disease
72. How to make our highways safe--generally; locally
73. How hormones function
74. How to go to the hospital
75. How to visit in the hospital
76. How to improve our local hospital(s)
77. How hypnotism is used in medicine
78. How to treat the hypochondriac
79. How to treat insomnia
80. How our intestines function
81. How the kidneys function
82. How medical schools, etc., procure laboratory animals
83. How to select a reading lamp
84. How the larynx functions
85. How the liver functions
86. How to promote longevity
87. How the lungs function
88. How the lymphatic system functions
89. How to provide better medical care--generally; regionally; locally
90. How to reduce the cost of medical care
91. How to equip a medicine cabinet
92. How to treat motion sickness
93. How to live with (multiple sclerosis, muscular dystrophy)
94. How to treat nail-biting
95. How the nervous system functions
96. How to (control, eliminate) noise--generally; in our community; in our home
97. How to treat a minor nosebleed
98. How to improve the nursing profession
99. How to treat nymphomania
100. How to be a good orderly
101. How the pancreas functions
102. How to be a good patient
103. How to treat phobias
104. How to treat (poison ivy, poison oak, poison sumac)
105. How to promote good posture
106. How to (avoid, ensure) pregnancy
107. How to take a pulse
108. How to spot a quack doctor
109. How to improve the (black, white, yellow; human) race eugenically
110. How to relax
111. How the reproductive system functions

112. How we see
113. How to (influence, predict) the sex of a baby
114. How to treat shock
115. How shock therapy is administered
116. How to give a shot--to oneself; to someone else
117. How to care for the skin
118. How to sleep (with, without) medication
119. How to make a sling (as for a broken arm)
120. How we smell
121. How to (control, eliminate) smog--generally; in our community
122. How to stop smoking
123. How to make a splint
124. How to remove a splinter
125. How to treat a sprained ankle
126. How to treat (stammering, stuttering)
127. How to treat a simple stomach ache
128. How to take a sun bath
129. How to treat sunburn
130. How we talk
131. How we taste
132. How to clean the teeth
133. How to take the temperature of (an infant, a child, an adult)
134. How to read a thermometer
135. How to cure thumb-sucking
136. How to (make, apply) a tourniquet
137. How to reduce traffic accidents--on our highways; on our streets; generally, locally
138. How to treat ulcers
139. How to treat an upset stomach
140. How to take a vacation (for reasons of health)
141. How our veins function
142. How to (avoid, induce) vomiting
143. How to remove warts
144. How water is purified
145. How to (gain, lose) weight
146. How to (dress, bandage) a wound

ARGUMENTATION

PROPOSITIONS OF FACT

1. Is air conditioning (beneficial, harmful) to health?
2. Does air pollution cause disease--e.g., cancer?
3. Is air travel safe?
4. Does the American Medical Association serve (well, ill) the cause of medicine in the United States?
5. Will an apple a day keep the doctor away?
6. Is artificial (birth control, insemination, respiration) immoral?
7. Are birth-control pills (effective, safe)?
8. What does blood tell?

9. Are blood transfusions (immoral, sinful)?
10. Is calorie counting (necessary, unnecessary) in weight control?
11. Is cancer caused by a virus?
12. Are carbonated beverages detrimental to health?
13. Do men go through a "change of life"?
14. Are children "little adults"?
15. Are children's toys (safe, unsafe)?
16. Does (cigarette, cigar, pipe) smoking cause lung cancer?
17. Do cigarettes stunt growth?
18. Is cleanliness next to Godliness?
19. Is modern clothing--for men, for women--(beneficial, harmful) to health?
20. Are onions good for colds?
21. Are (doctors, nurses) overpaid?
22. Is the drinking water in our community safe?
23. Is the cost of drugs (reasonable, excessive)?
24. Is (the manual, the electric) toothbrush effective?
25. Is the electrocardiograph (reliable, unreliable)?
26. Are our State's examinations for physicians and surgeons (reasonable, unreasonable)?
27. Does faith healing heal?
28. Is fasting (detrimental, beneficial) to health
29. Are fat people happy?
30. Is fee-splitting (a defensible, an indefensible) practice?
31. Are (state, federal) food and drug laws (adequate, inadequate; obsolete, up-to-date)?
32. Do Americans give (too little, too much; proper, improper) attention to health?
33. Is (heredity, stress, tension) the chief cause of heart disease?
34. Is the Hippocratic Oath (obsolete, still vital)?
35. Are (25, 50, 75) percent of human ailments imaginary?
36. Is the jargon of medicine necessary?
37. Are (state, Federal) laws governing (quackery, malpractice) (adequate, effective)?
38. Are laxatives (beneficial, harmful)?
39. Are liver extracts beneficial to health?
40. Can medicine make people live forever?
41. Is longevity (acquired, inherited)?
42. Do male doctors understand women (not at all, all too well)?
43. Are three meals a day (necessary, unnecessary)?
44. What's (right, wrong) with the (medical, nursing) profession?
45. Is all medicine experimental?
46. Are mercy killings (defensible, indefensible; moral, immoral)?
47. Are our (motels, tourist courts) (sanitary, unsanitary)--generally; locally?
48. Is nudism (healthful, immoral)?
49. Do men belong in nursing?
50. Is orthodontic treatment (a necessity, a luxury)?
51. Are patent medicines medicinal?

52. Is perfect health possible?
53. Are industries polluting our (streams, rivers)--generally; locally?
54. Is a "ram-rod" posture (beneficial, detrimental) to health?
55. Is the value of psychiatry over-rated?
56. Are (state, Federal) pure food and drug laws (adequate inadequate; effective, ineffective)?
57. Do seat belts (save, destroy) lives?
58. Are our service station rest rooms (sanitary, unsanitary)--generally, locally?
59. Can the sex of a baby be (predetermined, predicted)?
60. Is shock therapy (beneficial, harmful) to health?
61. Does everyone need eight hours' sleep?
62. Is socialized medicine (beneficial, detrimental) to (medicine, the public)?
63. Is space travel (beneficial, detrimental) to health?
64. Is (God, man, nature) responsible for stillbirths?
65. Is sunbathing (beneficial, detrimental) to health?
66. Are surgeons "scalpel-happy"?
67. Are the (public, private) swimming pools in our community (safe, unsafe)?
68. Is the topless bathing suit (for men, for women) beneficial to health?
69. Are Americans "hooked" on tranquilizers?
70. Are vitamin pills (necessary, unnecessary) to health?
71. Is vivisection inhumane?
72. Is our local water supply (pure, impure)?
73. Do our medical schools discriminate against women?
74. Do women make better (physicians, specialists, surgeons) than men?
75. Are women physiologically superior to men?

PROPOSITIONS OF POLICY

1. Should human abnormalities--e.g., Mongoloids--be destroyed?
2. Should abortions be legalized (in our state, in the United States)?
3. Should automobile drivers be required to take periodic physical examinations?
4. Should a father be present at the birth of his baby?
5. Should birth control (devices, information) be available to the general public?
6. Should blood (plasma) be labeled according to race?
7. Should women wear bras?
8. Should a mother breast-feed her baby?
9. Should doctors advertise?
10. Should doctors charge what the traffic will bear?
11. Should drug addicts be (hospitalized, imprisoned)?
12. Should euthanasia be legalized?
13. Should (men, women) wear girdles in the interest of health?
14. Should (gynecologists, obstetricians) be (male, female)?

15. Should hospitals refuse service to those unable to pay?
16. Should one's mate be selected eugenically?
17. Should medical care (for the aged, for all) be financed (privately, publicly)?
18. Should doctors make night calls?
19. Should our community have a nudist camp?
20. Should parenthood be planned?
21. Should patients with incurable diseases be told?
22. Should seat belts for automobiles be (compulsory, voluntary)?
23. Should (men, women) be sterilized (compulsorily, voluntarily)?
24. Should all children have their tonsils removed?
25. Should public water supplies be fluroidated?

EVALUATION

OBJECTS

I. An article useful (or supposed to be useful) in the promotion of health--for example,
   A. A rowing machine
   B. A steam cabinet
   C. An electric toothbrush
II. A piece of equipment used by an individual in the home or by a physician, either in his office or in a clinic or hospital, for medical purposes--for example,
   A. A medicine cabinet
   B. A wheelchair
   C. A physician's bag
III. Facilities of an organization devoted to health--for example,
   A. Facilities of a local health club
   B. Facilities of a school gymnasium
IV. Facilities of an organization--local, state, federal; public, private--devoted to medicine or surgery--for example,
   A. Facilities of a clinic
   B. Facilities of a hospital
   C. Facilities of a sanitarium

POLICIES

1. A policy of a local hospital, clinic, or sanitarium--e.g., a policy involving the admission, care, or discharge of patients
2. A policy, in effect or proposed, of an individual engaged in the practice of medicine or surgery--e.g., a private physician's policy regarding night calls
3. A policy of an organization devoted to medicine or surgery--e.g., the A.M.A.

ENGINEERING 620-629.99

Thought Starters for ANALYSIS

What about:

1. Acoustics
2. Adhesives: engineering properties and tests
3. Aeronautics
4. Air conditioning: airplanes, railroad cars, and ships
5. Air navigation
6. Aircraft engineering: civil, military, and naval
7. Airports
8. Alloys: engineering properties and tests
9. Ancient and medieval ships
10. Arms and armaments: military engineering
11. Atomic power
12. Automation
13. Automotive engineering
14. Biological and chemical warfare: military engineering
15. Bombs: military engineering
16. Bridges: engineering and construction
17. Broadcasting stations: radio and television engineering
18. Ceramic materials: engineering properties and tests
19. Civil engineering: technology
20. Construction engineering
21. Covered bridges
22. Dams
23. Defense: military engineering
24. Design: structural engineering
25. Diesel engines
26. Drainage engineering
27. Electric lighting engineering
28. Electric power engineering
29. Electrification, rural
30. Electronic engineering
31. Engineering industries: technology
32. Engineering materials
33. Engineering properties and tests
34. Engines
35. Erosion control: engineering
36. Extractive industries: technology
37. Factory engineering
38. Flight engineering
39. Flights around the world
40. Flood-control engineering
41. Flying saucers: aeronautics
42. Fortifications and forts: military engineering
43. Foundations: highway and railroad
44. Germ warfare: military engineering
45. Guided missiles: military engineering
46. Guns: military engineering
47. Harbor engineering
48. Heat, engine
49. Heating: electrical engineering
50. High fidelity sound reproduction
51. House wiring: electrical engineering

NOTE: See also such related fields as ARCHITECTURE (720-729.99), BUILDING CONSTRUCTION (690-699.99), and PHYSICS (530-539.99)

52. Hydraulic engineering
53. ICBM: military engineering
54. Industrial sanitation
55. Inertial navigation: engineering
56. Insulating materials: engineering properties and tests
57. Interplanetary flight: inertial navigation
58. Irrigation engineering
59. Jet engines
60. Journals, engineering
61. Lake engineering
62. Laminates: engineering properties and tests
63. Land reclamation
64. Lighter-than-air craft
65. Lubrication: mechanical engineering
66. Machine tools: mechanical engineering
67. Marine engineering
68. Masonry materials: engineering properties and tests
69. Materials: engineering
70. Materials, strength of
71. Mechanical engineering
72. Metals: engineering properties and tests
73. Military engineering
74. Mining engineering
75. Models: automobiles, aircraft, railroads, and ships
76. Moon, flights to: inertial navigation
77. Motor vehicle design and construction
78. Motor vehicle engineering
79. Motors: engineering
80. Municipal engineering
81. Municipal sanitation
82. Naval engineering
83. Navigation: air and sea
84. Noise control engineering
85. Nuclear engineering
86. Nuisances, industrial
87. Ordnance: military and naval engineering
88. Phonograph recording: electronic engineering
89. Pipes and pipelines: engineering
90. Plastics: engineering properties and tests
91. Pollution control: sanitary engineering
92. Power plants: engineering
93. Precious metals and stones: mining engineering
94. Primitive firearms: military engineering
95. Public health engineering
96. Public works engineering
97. Pumps: engineering
98. Quarrying
99. Radar engineering
100. Radiation: nuclear engineering
101. Radio and television engineering
102. Railroad engineering
103. Refrigeration engineering
104. River engineering
105. Road and highway engineering
106. Rocket engineering
107. Rural electrification engineering
108. Rural sanitary engineering
109. Sanitary engineering: civil and military
110. Sea water distillation
111. Seamanship
112. Sewerage engineering
113. Ships: engineering
114. Smog control: industrial sanitation
115. Soils: engineering
116. Solar engineering
117. Sound engineering
118. Space flight engineering
119. Steam engineering
120. Strain and stress: structural engineering
121. Strength tests: engineering materials
122. Structural engineering

123. Supersonic flying: aeronautics
124. Telecommunication engineering
125. Telephones and telegraphs
126. Thermodynamics: engineering
127. Tools: engineering
128. Transit systems: engineering
129. Tunnels: engineering and construction
130. Turbines: motor vehicle engineering
131. Underwriter requirements
132. Vibrations: motion and sound engineering
133. Warning systems: military engineering
134. Warships: engineering
135. Waterways engineering
136. Weapons: military engineering
137. Wells: water-supply engineering
138. Wire and wireless communication: electrical engineering
139. Wreckage studies: aeronautics and motor vehicle engineering

CAUSE and EFFECT

1. (Major) Causes of aircraft accidents
2. (Major) Effects--cultural; economic; social--of the automobile on America--generally; locally
3. (Major) Causes of automobile accidents
4. (Major) Effects of public taste on automobile design and engineering
5. (Major) Effects of (high, low) automobile horsepower--on accidents; on highway safety
6. Why bridges collapse
7. Why cement adheres to brick, stone, etc.
8. Why a classic car is considered a classic
9. Why the clipper ship was (built, discontinued)
10. Why the coal locomotive is obsolete in modern America
11. Why the DC-3 aircraft was discontinued
12. Why dams burst
13. Why Death Valley is arid
14. Why the dirigible died
15. (Major) Effects of the electric light on modern America
16. Why the ferryboat is obsolescent in the United States
17. (Major) Causes of floods in America
18. Why (radio, television) sets need to be grounded
19. Why I (am, would like to be) a "ham" operator
20. (Major) Effects of (heat, cold) on materials--e.g., metals in space flight
21. (Major) Causes of mining accidents
22. Why collecting and assembling model (airplanes, automobiles, ships, trains) is an (interesting, educational) hobby
23. Why man feels compelled to go to the moon
24. Why women drive motorcycles
25. (Major) Effects--economic, social, etc.--of (adequate, inadequate) municipal lighting
26. Why people race cars

27. (Major) Causes of railroad accidents
28. (Principal) Causes of short circuits--e.g., in home appliances; in house wiring
29. Why (men, women, adolescents) (buy, drive) sports cars
30. Why the steam locomotive is obsolescent
31. Why the streetcar is obsolescent
32. (Major) Effects of the submarine in (World War I, World War II)
33. (Major) Effects--cultural; economic; military, etc.--of Telstar
34. (Major) Effects of time on (metals, plastics, rubber, wood, etc.)
35. (Major) Effects of vibration on materials

CLASSIFICATION

Kinds/Types of:

1. Acoustical materials
2. Adhesives
3. Aircraft engines
4. Alloys
5. Automobile engines
6. Bombs
7. Bridges
8. Canals
9. Dams
10. Electric lighting
11. Engineers
12. Engines
13. Fasteners
14. Foundations
15. Guided missiles
16. Guns
17. Heating
18. Highway materials
19. Insulating materials
20. Laminates
21. Lighter-than-air craft
22. Lubricants
23. Masonry materials
24. Metals
25. Pipes
26. Power plants
27. Pumps
28. Rockets
29. Ships
30. Steam engines
31. Structural materials
32. Submarines
33. Telecommunication
34. UFO's
35. Warships

COMPARISON and CONTRAST

1. Aircraft engine design: jet, prop, and prop jet
2. Air conditioner, fan, and refrigerator
3. Aqueducts: here and there; yesterday and today--e.g., in ancient Rome and in modern America
4. Artillery: here and there; yesterday and today--e.g., in ancient times and today
5. Autogyro and helicopter
6. Automatic pilot and human pilot
7. Automobile assembly: custom-built and mass-produced
8. Automobile body design: convertible top and rigid top; two-door and four-door
9. Automobile brakes: hydraulic and mechanical
10. Automobile chokes: automatic and manual
11. Automobile engine designs: air-cooled and water-cooled; front-wheel and rear-wheel drive; external and internal

combustion; gas turbine and internal-combustion gasoline; "in-line" and "V"-type.
12. Automobile engine location: in front and in rear
13. Automobile engine lubrication: periodic and "lifetime"
14. Automobile engine materials: aluminum and cast-iron block
15. Automobile suspension systems: coil and leaf springs and torsion bar
16. Automobile tires: tube and tubeless
17. Automobile transmissions: automatic, semi-automatic, and manual
18. Blunderbuss and M-1
19. Boat materials: aluminum, plastic, and wood
20. Boat motors: inboard and outboard
21. Bolt and rivet
22. Bridge and spider web
23. Carburetor and fuel injection
24. Christopher Columbus and John Glenn
25. Coal locomotive and diesel locomotive
26. Telegraphic codes: continental, Morse, and Phillips
27. Dial telephone and manual telephone
28. Drilling for oil and drilling for water
29. Driving: an automobile, a plane, and a truck
30. Engineer and physicist
31. Fort and fortress
32. Garbage collector and sanitary engineer
33. Girder, beam, and truss
34. Guided aircraft and guided missile
35. Gunnery: here and there; yesterday and today--e.g., under Napoleon and under Eisenhower
36. Heating fuels and systems: coal, electric, gas, oil, and solar
37. Heavier-than-air craft and lighter-than-air craft
38. High fidelity and low fidelity
39. Horse and tractor
40. Hydrogen and helium
41. Jeep: civilian and military
42. Lighting: electric, gas, and oil
43. Locomotives: electric, diesel, and steam
44. Maps: aeronautic, maritime, and road
45. Mayflower and Queen Elizabeth
46. Model T and VW
47. Merrimac, Monitor, and Nautilus
48. Radio: long-wave and short-wave
49. Shipbuilding: here and there; yesterday and today--e.g., among the Phoenicians and among the British
50. Telegraphy: wire and wireless
51. Transistor and tube

DEFINITION

1. Bearing
2. Cell
3. Circuit
4. Clutch

5. Condenser
6. Conduit
7. Dead reckoning
8. Drag
9. Dynamo
10. Filament
11. Gear
12. Generator
13. Jig
14. Joint
15. Kinescope
16. Meter
17. Power
18. Rheostat
19. Strength
20. Switch
21. Tensility
22. Transformer
23. Transmission
24. Tube
25. Turbine
26. Valve
27. Vibration
28. Weightlessness

DESCRIPTION

I. Equipment found in a firm, organization, or plant devoted to some aspect of engineering, either for peace or for war--for example,
   A. Equipment found in an (aircraft, automobile) plant
   B. Equipment found in a (railroad, ship) yard
   C. Equipment found in a (radio, television) studio
   D. Equipment found in a local sewage disposal plant

II. Facilities used by an organization or plant--local, state, or federal; public or private--devoted to some phase of engineering (experimentation, testing, production, or manufacturing)--for example,
   A. Facilities of a brick-making plant
   B. Facilities of a commercial airline
   C. Facilities of a mining company
   D. Facilities of a space center--e.g., Cape Kennedy
   E. Facilities of Utopia's Department of Engineering

PROCESS

1. How to improve the (equipment, facilities, service) of our local airport
2. How to construct (an air-raid, fall-out) shelter
3. How the ancient Romans constructed (aqueducts, bridges, roads)
4. How artificial earth satellites are (assembled, launched, kept in orbit, returned to earth)
5. How to reduce the number of fatal automobile accidents
6. How to select an automobile mechanic
7. How to change an automobile tire
8. How to replace an automobile windshield (or other glass)
9. How antique automobiles are restored
10. How to build a small boat
11. How to make a bow and arrow
12. How (bricks, tiles, etc.) are made
13. How to construct a small (rigid, non-rigid) bridge
14. How a modern bridge is built
15. How the (Erie, Panama, Suez) Canal was built

16. How to make a concrete (walk, wall)
17. How to build a small dam
18. How a modern dam is built
19. How to make a flagstone (patio, walk)
20. How to build a glider
21. How the Great Wall of China was built
22. How guided missiles are (launched, guided)
23. How to select a heating system for a house
24. How a modern highway is built
25. How to improve our (highways, roads)--generally, locally
26. How the Holland (or other) Tunnel was built
27. How to build the hottest hot rod in the neighborhood
28. How industries control (odors, smoke, waste)
29. How the jeep originated
30. How the jet plane flies
31. How to (make, fly) a kite
32. How to install a light switch
33. How materials are protected against (corrosion, deterioration, weather)
34. How materials--metals, wood, etc.--are tested for strength
35. How missiles are (aimed, fired, controlled)
36. How to build model (airplanes, automobiles, ships, trains)
37. How to make a Molotov cocktail
38. How to make a better mouse trap
39. How to (control, eliminate) noise in a (plant, home)--generally; locally
40. How phonograph records are made
41. How the Pyramids were built
42. How railroad ties are made
43. How to construct a retaining wall
44. How to improve (local, municipal) sanitation
45. How to install seat belts
46. How to install a septic tank
47. How the sewers of Paris were built
48. How to make a slingshot
49. How to (control, eliminate) smog--generally; locally
50. How a solar furnace works
51. How Robert Fulton built his steamboat
52. How subways are built
53. How the tape recorder records
54. How (the telegraph, the telephone) works
55. How Telstar works
56. How to dig a well
57. How to wire a house

ARGUMENTATION

PROPOSITIONS OF FACT

1. Is the (aircraft carrier, battleship, bomber) obsolescent?

2. Are our (airports, landing fields) adequate--generally; locally?
3. Do Americans worship the automobile?
4. Is (a new, a used) automobile a good investment?
5. What's (right, wrong) with (American, foreign) automobiles?
6. Is the (cavalry, infantry) obsolete?
7. Can the world's (arid lands, deserts) be reclaimed?
8. Is driver training a proper function of our schools?
9. Do flying saucers exist?
10. Is the (fort, fortress) obsolete?
11. Are our (highways, roads) (adequate, safe)--generally; locally?
12. Is interplanetary flight worth (the cost, the risk)?
13. Are (local, state) laws governing (inspection, operation) of motor vehicles (adequate, effective)?
14. Is the Morse Code obsolescent?
15. Is radar effective (in peace, in war)--e.g., in defense; in navigation; on our highways?
16. Is there a satisfactory substitute for the railroad tie?
17. Can our rivers--e.g., the Mississippi--be (saved, tamed)?
18. Do seat belts in (automobiles, planes) (save, destroy) lives?
19. Is the automobile speed trap (fair, just, legal)?
20. Is the Suez Canal obsolete?
21. Is all fair in love and war?
22. Is our local water supply (adequate, safe)?
23. Are the weapons used by our armed forces (satisfactory, unsatisfactory; superior, inferior)?
24. Is what they say about women drivers true?

PROPOSITIONS OF POLICY

1. Should all (civilian, private) aircraft be equipped with (radar, radio)?
2. Should we train female astronauts?
3. Should automobiles be equipped with governors?
4. Should all automobile drivers be required by law to take periodic tests and examinations?
5. Should America's communications industries--e.g., newspapers; radio and television; telephone and telegraph, etc.--be nationalized?
6. Should Utopia (establish, abolish) a Department of Engineering?
7. Should our community set up a drag strip for hot-rodders?
8. Should the age for obtaining a driver's license be (raised, lowered)?
9. Should flood control be the responsibility of (private enterprise; state or federal government)?
10. Should our local airport(s) establish helicopter service?
11. Should liability insurance be (voluntary, compulsory) for all motorists?

12. Should (mental, physical) tests be required of all <u>motorists</u>?
13. Should (a bridge, a tunnel) be constructed at every <u>railroad crossing</u>?
14. Should America's (<u>railroads</u>, airlines) be nationalized?
15. Should <u>seat belts</u> be required for all passenger cars?

EVALUATION

OBJECTS

I. <u>Equipment</u> created as a result of an engineering process--for example,
   A. Equipment related to consumer goods: e.g., an automobile, a telephone
   B. Equipment related to the national defense: e.g., a military or naval aircraft; a small arm
   C. Equipment connected with a public service: e.g., a fire truck and/or related equipment; a garbage truck
   D. Tools related to an engineering process: e.g., a lathe; a power saw

II. <u>Facilities</u> of a firm or plant devoted to an engineering process--for example,
   A. Facilities of a local engineering concern
   B. Facilities of a local construction company

III. <u>Materials</u> used, or considered for use, in carrying out an engineering process--for example,
   A. An alloy
   B. A metal
   C. A plastic
   D. A wood

POLICIES

Evaluation of a policy, in effect or proposed, by a company, firm, or organization--local, state, or federal; public or private--engaged in the manufacture or use of a product or products which are the result of an engineering process--for example,

A. A policy of a government aeronautical agency
B. A policy of an aircraft company
C. A policy of a regional or national airline
D. A policy of an automobile association (such as the AAA)
E. A policy of a local automobile agency or dealer
F. A policy of a railroad
G. A policy of a local sanitation department
H. A policy of a local shipyard
I. A policy of the local telegraph or telephone company
J. A policy of a local transit company
K. A policy of a local utility company

AGRICULTURE 630-639.99

Thought Starters for ANALYSIS

What about:

1. Agricultural bacteriology
2. Agricultural chemistry
3. Agricultural climatology
4. Agricultural equipment and machinery
5. Agricultural pathology
6. Agricultural pests
7. Agricultural physics
8. Agronomy
9. Animal hunting and trapping industries
10. Animal husbandry
11. Bees: apiculture
12. Birds: aviculture
13. Blacksmithing
14. Blights: crop production
15. Breeding: animal husbandry; crop production
16. Bulbs: field crops and horticulture
17. Business management, farm
18. Cats: domestic animals
19. Cattle: animal husbandry
20. Cereals: field crops
21. Citrus fruits
22. Clams: fishing industries
23. Conservation, soil
24. Corn: field and garden crops
25. Cotton: fiber crops
26. Country life
27. Crabs: fishing industries
28. Crop diseases
29. Crop production
30. Dairy farming
31. Dairy industry
32. Disease control: agriculture
33. Diseases, animal: veterinary medicine
34. Dogs: domestic animals
35. Dogs, hunting
36. Domestic animals
37. Drugs: veterinary medicine
38. Dry farming
39. Engineering, agricultural
40. Erosion control
41. Farm industries: technology
42. Farm life
43. Farm management
44. Farming
45. Fertilizers
46. Fiber crops
47. Field crops
48. First-aid: veterinary hygiene
49. Fish culture
50. Fisheries
51. Floriculture
52. Flower gardening
53. Food supply: agriculture
54. Forage crops
55. Forest fires
56. Forestry and forestry engineering
57. Fowls: animal husbandry
58. Fresh-water fishing industries
59. Fruit culture
60. Fungicides: agricultural use
61. Fur-bearing animals: hunting and trapping industries
62. Game birds: hunting industries; poultry husbandry
63. Garden crops and flowers
64. Gardens and gardening
65. Grafting, plant
66. Grange

NOTE: See also such related fields as CHEMISTRY (540-549.99), CHEMICAL TECHNOLOGY (660-669.99), BOTANICAL SCIENCES (580-589.99) and ZOOLOGY (590-599.99)

67. Harvesting
68. Hatcheries: fish; poultry
69. Herbicides: agricultural use
70. Horses: animal husbandry
71. Horticulture
72. Hunting industries
73. Hybrids: animal and plant
74. Hygiene, veterinary
75. Insecticides: agricultural use
76. Insects, injurious: crop production and forestry
77. Insects, useful
78. Irrigation: agriculture and floriculture
79. Land drainage and reclamation
80. Livestock
81. Lobster fishing industries
82. Medicinal plants
83. Mildews and molds: agricultural pathology
84. Nurseries: floriculture and silviculture
85. Nuts: culture
86. Oats: field crops
87. Orchards
88. Oyster fishing industries
89. Parasitic diseases and plants
90. Patrons of Husbandry
91. Pest control
92. Pesticides: agricultural use
93. Plant care
94. Plant diseases
95. Poultry: animal husbandry
96. Produce markets
97. Reforestation
98. Reptiles: farming and hunting
99. Resources, natural: forestry
100. Rodents: animal husbandry
101. Rotation, crop
102. Rubber plantations
103. Rural electrification
104. Salt water fishing industries
105. Sheep: animal husbandry
106. Shrimp fishing industries
107. Soils
108. Submarginal lands
109. Surgery: veterinary medicine
110. Swine: animal husbandry
111. Tobacco: field crops
112. Tree surgery
113. Trees: forestry
114. Truck gardening
115. Vegetable gardening
116. Veterinary medicine
117. Vineyards
118. Wasteland reclamation
119. Weed killers; agricultural use
120. Whaling industries
121. Wheat: field crops

CAUSE and EFFECT

1. Why the (promotion, study) of agriculture is important (to the United States; to the rest of the world)
2. Why American agriculture (needs, does not need) government aid
3. (Major) Effects of government aid--e.g., crop supports--on American agriculture
4. (Major) Causes of the near-extinction of the American buffalo
5. Why country life has (great, little) appeal for me
6. Why crop rotation is necessary (for crops; for soils)
7. (Major) Causes of (damage to, destruction of) crops--generally; regionally; locally

8. (Major) Causes of disease in (animals, crops, plants, trees)--generally; locally
9. (Major) Effects--agricultural; economic, etc.--of (a) drought
10. (Major) Causes of farm (failure; success)--generally; locally
11. Why farmers (farm; move to the city)
12. (Major) Causes of floods--generally; locally
13. (Major) Causes of forest fires--generally; regionally; locally
14. (Major) Effects of forest fires--e.g., on plant and wild life
15. Why hunters hunt
16. (Major) Effects of music on domesticated animals--e.g., in milk production; in egg production
17. (Major) Causes of soil erosion
18. Why I (would, would not) like to be a veterinarian
19. Why preservation of America's wildlife is essential
20. (Major) Effects of (scientific, wanton) destruction of wildlife

CLASSIFICATION

Kinds/Types of:

1. Bees
2. Cattle
3. Cereals
4. Crops
5. Dairy products
6. Dogs
7. Erosion
8. Farm pests
9. Farmers
10. Farming
11. Farms
12. Feed
13. Fertilizers
14. Fishermen
15. Fodder
16. Forests
17. Fruits
18. Gardens
19. Grasses
20. Horses
21. Hunters
22. Hunting dogs
23. Irrigation
24. Medicinal plants
25. Nurseries
26. Orchards
27. Poultry
28. Sheep
29. Soil
30. Swine
31. Trees
32. Useful birds
33. Useful insects
34. Useful reptiles
35. Useful rodents

COMPARISON and CONTRAST

1. Agricultural (equipment, machinery, tools): here and there; yesterday and today--e.g., in 1800 and today
2. Agriculture: here and there; yesterday and today--e.g., in the U.S.A. and in the U.S.S.R.; in ancient Egypt or Rome and in modern America
3. Ante-bellum Southern plantation and modern farm-estate
4. Apiary and aviary
5. Cat, poison, and rat-trap

6. Cattle: beef, dairy, and dual-purpose
7. Cattle-raising: here and there; yesterday and today--e.g., in 1890 and today; in Argentina and in the United States
8. City life and country life
9. Commercial produce and "home-grown" produce
10. Cotton-raising: here and there; yesterday and today--e.g., in the Old and the New South
11. Country life: here and there; yesterday and today--e.g., in the U.S.A. and in the U.S.S.R.
12. Crop production: here and there; yesterday and today--e.g., in Red China and in the United States
13. Dairy industry: here and there; yesterday and today--e.g., in the United States and in Switzerland
14. Dirt farmer and gentleman farmer
15. Farmer's daughter--here and there; yesterday and today, in fact and in fiction
16. Farming: here and there; yesterday and today--e.g., in ancient Egypt and in modern America
17. Fertilizers: natural and synthetic
18. Fishing industry: here and there; yesterday and today--e.g., in Japan and in the United States
19. General practitioner and veterinarian
20. Gentleman farmer: in fact and in fiction
21. Harvesting: here and there; yesterday and today--e.g., c. 1800 and today
22. Hatcheries: fish and poultry
23. Horse and tractor
24. Hunting: here and there; yesterday and today; for business and for pleasure
25. Insects: harmful and useful
26. Irrigation: here and there; yesterday and today--e.g., in ancient Egypt and in modern America
27. Milking: by hand and by machine
28. Mushroom and toadstool
29. Ocean fishing and lake or stream fishing
30. Poison oak, poison ivy, and poison sumac
31. Poultry raising: here and there; yesterday and today
32. Reptiles: harmful and useful
33. Rodents: harmful and useful
34. Soil conservation: here and there; yesterday and today
35. Soybean: yesterday and today--e.g., c. 1860 and today
36. Spice trade--here and there; yesterday and today--e.g., c. 1700 and today
37. Stockbreeding: here and there; yesterday and today
38. Tobacco farming: here and there; yesterday and today--e.g., c. 1840 and today
39. Veterinary (medicine, surgery): here and there; yesterday and today--e.g., c. 1900 and today
40. Whaling: here and there; yesterday and today--e.g., c. 1850 and today

DEFINITION

1. Agriculture
2. Bang's disease
3. Condiment
4. Contour planting
5. Fallow
6. Glanders
7. Herb
8. Husbandry
9. Kapok
10. Legume
11. Parity
12. Plow
13. Praying mantis
14. Ruminant
15. Sharecropping
16. Silage
17. Silviculture
18. Timber stand
19. Tuber
20. Watershed

DESCRIPTION

I. Equipment, machinery, or tools used in agriculture--as on a farm--or in the practice of veterinary medicine--for example,
   A. A butter churn
   B. A fishing boat
   C. A threshing machine
   D. A piece of equipment used in the practice of veterinary medicine
II. Facilities used by an individual engaged in farming, by an agricultural agency or industry--local, state, or federal; public or private--or by a veterinarian--for example,
   A. Facilities found on a private farm
   B. Facilities made available to agriculture by the Department of Agriculture
   C. Facilities of a seafood industry
   D. Facilities of a veterinary hospital

PROCESS

1. How to determine the age of a domesticated animal--e.g., a horse
2. How to raise alligators
3. How to care for a sick domesticated animal until the doctor comes
4. How to treat a bee sting
5. How to keep bees
6. How to grow (black, rasp, huckle) berries--for home consumption; for sale
7. How bloodhounds are trained
8. How to grow cactus at home
9. How to (select, raise) cattle--for home consumption; for profit
10. How the holes get into Swiss cheese
11. How to make a compost
12. How to raise (hybrid) corn--for home use; for profit
13. How to milk a cow (by hand; by machine)

14. How a cream separator works
15. How to (hunt, trap) crocodiles
16. How (field, garden) crops are (planted, rotated, harvested)
17. How to select a dog--as a pet; for work
18. How to build a dog-house
19. How to train a falcon
20. How to make (a dairy, a truck, etc.) farm pay
21. How to select a farm
22. How to erect a fence
23. How to clean fish
24. How fish are raised commercially
25. How to build a fish-pond
26. How to raise flowers--for pleasure; for profit
27. How to (prevent, fight) forest fires
28. How to be a forest ranger
29. How our forests are preserved
30. How to get free farm land from the government
31. How to (raise, catch) frogs
32. How to raise fruit--for home consumption; for profit
33. How to raise fur-bearing animals--e.g., mink
34. How to (plan; plant) a (formal, rock) garden
35. How to select garden tools
36. How to (select, care for) goldfish
37. How to graft (branches, trees)
38. How to grow grapes--for home consumption; for profit
39. How to build a greenhouse
40. How to (plant, trim) a hedge
41. How to (select, harness, saddle, shoe, ride, train) a horse
42. How to raise house plants
43. How to hunt (big, small) game
44. How to train a hunting dog
45. How to (select seed for, plant, care for, cut) a lawn
46. How to raise prize livestock
47. How maple sugar is produced
48. How to give an animal (liquid, solid) medication
49. How milk goes from cow to consumer
50. How to be a good (milkman, milkmaid)
51. How to build a better mouse trap
52. How to grow mushrooms
53. How to tell mushrooms from toadstools
54. How to protect orchards from frost
55. How to open an oyster shell
56. How to rid (a home, a farm) of pests
57. How to (select, train, care for) a household pet
58. How to select (plants, shrubs, trees) for one's home
59. How to transplant (plants, shrubs, trees)
60. How to raise poultry--for home use; for profit
61. How to raise a few rabbits
62. How rain is produced artificially
63. How to make a scarecrow
64. How seafood--e.g., clams, crabs, lobsters, oysters, shrimp, etc.--is harvested commercially

65. How to shear sheep
66. How to handle snakes
67. How to distinguish between harmless and poisonous snakes
68. How soil erosion is controlled
69. How to set a trap
70. How to remove a tree stump
71. How to (select, cut) trees for timber
72. How to raise turkeys
73. How to (plan, plant) a vegetable garden
74. How to train a watchdog
75. How to control weeds
76. How to dig a well
77. How whales are (hunted, caught)
78. How to make a windmill
79. How to make a window box for flowers
80. How to raise worms

ARGUMENTATION

PROPOSITIONS OF FACT

1. Is agriculture "the only honest way" to wealth?
2. Is animal (hunting, trapping) (beneficial, harmful; humane, inhumane)?
3. Is artificial insemination of animals (moral, immoral)?
4. Is artificial rain-making sinful?
5. Is scientific breeding of animals immoral?
6. Are chemical weed-killers harmful (to other plants; to wildlife)?
7. Is conservation of our natural resources--e.g., forests; rivers; wildlife--the proper responsibility of (localities, states, the federal government)?
8. Is everything about the cow useful except the moo?
9. Does the dairy industry set prices (fairly, unfairly)--in our community; in our state?
10. Is the Department of Agriculture (the friend, the foe) of the American farmer?
11. Are American farms overmechanized?
12. Is the farm boy healthier than the city boy?
13. Are parity farm prices (fair, unfair; effective, ineffective)?
14. Can America's "farm problem" be solved?
15. Does farming pay?
16. Do good fences make good neighbors?
17. Are America's forests being exploited?
18. Are (fungicides, insecticides, pesticides, etc.) a threat to (agriculture, wildlife)?
19. Does a home garden pay?
20. Is the horse obsolete on the modern farm?
21. Who owns the land?
22. Is science cruel to animals?
23. Is water pollution destroying America's wildlife--generally; regionally; locally?

PROPOSITIONS OF POLICY

1. Should agriculture in America be nationalized?
2. Should the bow-and-arrow be the only legal weapon against small game?
3. Should the CCC (Civilian Conservation Corps of New Deal days) be reactivated?
4. Should crop production be regulated by (government; normal supply-and-demand)?
5. Should America share its food supply with needy (friendly, unfriendly) countries?
6. Should our national forests be (returned to the states; sold to private industry)?
7. Should Utopia (abolish, expand) its (School, Department) of Agriculture?
8. Should American farmers be unionized?

EVALUATION

OBJECTS

I. Equipment, machinery, or tools used in agriculture or in veterinary medicine--for example,
   A. An electrified fence
   B. A windmill
   C. A water pump
   D. A tractor

II. Facilities used by an individual or organization devoted to agricultural pursuits--for example,
   A. Facilities of an agricultural cooperative
   B. Facilities of a 4-H Club
   C. Facilities of a veterinary hospital

POLICIES

Evaluation of a policy, in effect or proposed, by an individual, agency, or organization--local, state, or federal; public or private--devoted to agriculture or to veterinary medicine--for example,

A. A policy of an agricultural college
B. A policy of a local or state dairy association
C. A policy of the Department of Agriculture
D. A policy of a local florist
E. A policy of a 4-H Club
F. A state or federal game law
G. A policy of a local garden club
H. A policy of a local hunt club
I. A policy of a (State, National) Park Service
J. A policy of a local nursery
K. A policy of the local SPCA
L. A policy of a seafood industry
M. A policy of a local veterinarian or veterinary hospital

HOME ECONOMICS 640-649.99

Thought Starters for ANALYSIS

What about:

1. Amusements: child care
2. Appetizers
3. Arctic and cold weather cooking
4. Army and navy cooking
5. Baby-sitting
6. Baking
7. Barbecuing
8. Bathrooms: home furnishing
9. Beauty culture
10. Beds and bedding
11. Beverages
12. Body care
13. Bread: cooking and nutrition
14. Broiling
15. Budgets: household management
16. Buying food
17. Calories: nutrition
18. Camp cooking
19. Candies: cooking and nutrition
20. Canning food
21. Catering
22. Cereals: cooking and nutrition
23. Charm
24. Child care
25. Cleaning
26. Clothing construction
27. Clothing and dress
28. Consumer education: household management
29. Cookbooks
30. Cooking techniques
31. Cooling systems: home economics
32. Cosmetology
33. Cost of living: home economics
34. Dairy products
35. Decoration: home; table
36. Design, clothing
37. Desserts: cooking
38. Dietetics
39. Diets
40. Domestic finance
41. Domestic service
42. Dressmaking
43. Dyeing textiles
44. Entertaining
45. Fabrics and textiles
46. Fashions, clothing
47. Feeding infants and children
48. Floor covering: home furnishing
49. Food
50. Food costs
51. Food preservation
52. Food values
53. Frozen foods
54. Fungicides and pesticides
55. Furnishings: home economics
56. Game: cooking
57. Garden furnishings
58. Groceries
59. Hairdressing
60. Heating systems: home economics
61. Home arrangement
62. Home decoration
63. Home furnishing
64. Home nursing
65. Home planning
66. Hospital cookery
67. Housecleaning
68. Household appliances and equipment
69. Household management
70. Household pests
71. Household repairs
72. Household sanitation
73. Household storage
74. Institutional cooking
75. Jam and jelly making
76. Laundering
77. Lighting, home
78. Make-up: home and professional use

79. Meals: planning, preparation, and service
80. Meats: cooking and nutrition
81. Mending
82. Nails, care of
83. National cooking
84. Nutrition
85. Parties: entertaining
86. Personal appearance
87. Pest control, household
88. Poultry: cooking
89. Recipes
90. Reducing diets
91. Refrigeration: food
92. Regional cooking
93. Salads: cooking and nutrition
94. Sandwiches
95. Sauces
96. Sea food: cooking
97. Seasoning
98. Sewing
99. Shoppers' guides
100. Skin care: home and professional
101. Slip covers: sewing and home furnishing
102. Spices
103. Supermarkets
104. Training infants and children
105. Travel cooking
106. Tropical cooking
107. Upholstery: home furnishing
108. Vegetables: cooking and nutrition
109. Vegetarianism: nutrition
110. Ventilation, home
111. Wall paper: home furnishing
112. Water supply, home
113. Weight control
114. Wine: cooking
115. Yard and garden improvement: home economics

CAUSE and EFFECT

1. (Major) Causes of accidents in the home
2. (Major) Causes of jaded appetites (inside, outside) the home
3. Why good baby-sitters are hard to find
4. Why baby-sitters are (hired, fired)
5. Why beauty is important in the home
6. Why (men, women, adolescents) buy
7. Why (men, women, adolescents) wear clothes
8. (Major) Causes of the high cost of living--generally; locally
9. Why (men, women, adolescents) diet
10. Why a good domestic servant is hard to find
11. (Major) Effects of racial tension on domestic service
12. Why women "follow fashion"
13. (Major) Effects of home freezers on American food habits
14. Why women (like, dislike) house cleaning
15. (Major) Effects of household appliances on the American housewife
16. (Major) Effects of commercial laundering on the home
17. Why personal appearance is important (inside, outside) the home
18. Why it pays to shop around
19. Why "weight-watching" is important

CLASSIFICATION

Kinds/Type of:

1. Amusements for children
2. Appetites
3. Baby-sitters
4. Beauty
5. Beauty aids
6. Campers
7. Charm
8. Cooks
9. Diets
10. Domestic servants
11. Fashion
12. Hairdressers
13. Housecleaners
14. Housewives
15. Shoppers
16. Vegetarians

COMPARISON and CONTRAST

1. A la carte and table d'hote
2. American Plan and European Plan
3. Barber shop and beauty salon
4. Beauty, charm, and sex appeal
5. Beauty culture: here and there; yesterday and today--e.g., in ancient Egypt and in modern America
6. Building, buying a ready-built, and renting a home
7. Buying: cash and credit
8. Cafeteria system and waiter system
9. Chain store (supermarket) and independent store
10. Chef and cook
11. Closets: hers and his
12. "Clothes horse" and dandy
13. Clothing and dress: here and there; yesterday and today--e.g., in eighteenth-century France and in modern America
14. Clothing: ready-made and tailor-made
15. Cooking with charcoal, electricity, gas, and wood
16. Cosmetics: here and there; yesterday and today--e.g., in America c. 1900 and today
17. Cost of living: here and there; yesterday and today--e.g., in the U.S.S.R. and in the U.S.A.
18. Depilatory and electrolysis
19. Dietary laws: Hindu and Jewish
20. Dining out: at the Waldorf and at the "Greasy Spoon"
21. Domestic servants: here and there; yesterday and today--e.g., in America and in Europe; in the ante-bellum and modern South
22. Doors: Dutch, French, and standard
23. Dressmaking: home and factory
24. Eating: in the Arctic and in the tropics
25. Eating to live and living to eat
26. Entertainment: here and there; yesterday and today
27. Fad and fashion
28. Fashion and taste
29. Fashion: here and there; yesterday and today--e.g., in (Elizabethan, eighteenth-century) England and in modern America
30. Foods: canned, dehydrated, fresh and frozen

31. Gourmand and gourmet
32. Heating: by coal, electricity, fire place, gas, oil, sun
33. Home and house
34. Home care and hospital care
35. Home laundry and laundromat
36. Housecleaning : here and there; yesterday and today--e.g., in Colonial and in modern America
37. Houses: Ranch style and traditional
38. Impulse buying and planned buying
39. Institutional cooking and mother's cooking
40. Merchandise: "name-brand" and "off-brand"
41. Operation of a business, a government, and a home
42. Paint, paneling, and wallpaper
43. Nurses: practical and registered
44. Razors: electric, safety, and straight
45. Shower and tub

DEFINITION

1. Accessory
2. Attractiveness
3. Bargain
4. Bundling
5. Cleanliness
6. Compromise
7. Conscientiousness
8. Cost
9. Discipline
10. Domesticity
11. Duty
12. Economy
13. Efficiency
14. Epicureanism
15. Esthetics
16. Etiquette
17. Happiness
18. Health
19. Leisure
20. Luxury
21. Malnutrition
22. Manners
23. Necessity
24. Privacy
25. Property
26. Recreation
27. Taste
28. Thrift
29. Togetherness
30. Value

DESCRIPTION

1. An appliance or other piece of equipment found in a home--e.g., a dishwasher, a furnace, a refrigerator, a stove
2. A beauty salon or barber shop
3. A campsite
4. A cafeteria, or part thereof
5. A piece or suite of furniture found in a home
6. A garden
7. A home
8. A shopping center, or part thereof

PROCESS

1. How to treat acne
2. How to be a good baby-sitter

3. How to bake (bread, a cake, etc.)
4. How to barbecue (indoors, outdoors)
5. How to bathe (a baby, an invalid)
6. How to be beautiful (with, without) a budget
7. How to make a bed
8. How to balance the family budget
9. How to dress well on a budget
10. How to eat well on a budget
11. How to entertain on a budget
12. How to furnish a home on a budget
13. How to treat minor burns
14. How to can (fruits, vegetables, etc.) at home
15. How to lay (a carpet, a tile floor)
16. How to carve (a roast, a turkey, etc.)
17. How to (kill, pluck, dress) a chicken
18. How to (buy, select) clothes (for men; for women; for teenagers; for children)
19. How to make an article of clothing--e.g., a hat, a dress--at home
20. How to make (cocoa, coffee, tea, etc.)
21. How to make a pair of curtains
22. How to darn a sock
23. How to (go on, stick to) a diet
24. How to make a doll
25. How to unclog a (sink, toilet) drain
26. How to make an inexpensive dress look otherwise
27. How to dye (clothing, curtains, etc.)
28. How to reduce the consumption of (electricity, gas, heat, water) around the home
29. How to build a fire (in a brazier; in a fireplace)
30. How to buy food
31. How to prepare food--for the finicky; for an invalid; for a person on a special diet--e.g., a diabetic
32. How to make an article of (indoor, outdoor) furniture--e.g., a bookcase; a bench
33. How to (slipcover, upholster) a piece of furniture
34. How to cut grass
35. How to cultivate a green thumb
36. How to (cut, shampoo) hair at home
37. How to (select, buy, pay for) a home
38. How to break into one's own home
39. How to make simple repairs on a home appliance--e.g., repair an electric cord; replace a fuse, etc.
40. How to make simple home repairs--e.g., replace a doorknob; replace a broken step; unstick a sticking door, etc.
41. How to clean house
42. How to cut household expenses
43. How to make ice cream at home
44. How to care for an invalid at home
45. How to iron an article of clothing--e.g., a shirt, a skirt
46. How to keep (up with, ahead of, behind) the Joneses
47. How to be a good (landlord, tenant)

48. How to (grow, water) a lawn
49. How to (make, break) a lease
50. How to use leftovers
51. How to apply make-up
52. How to give oneself a (manicure, pedicure)
53. How to (plan, prepare, serve) a meal
54. How to protect clothing from moths
55. How to select (neighbors, a neighborhood)
56. How to (plan, equip) an infant's nursery
57. How to (give, break up) a party
58. How to give oneself a home permanent
59. How to rid a home of (human, insect, animal) pests
60. How to make pickles
61. How to prepare a picnic lunch
62. How to make a (patchwork) quilt
63. How to improve home safety
64. How to make a tempting and unusual (salad, sandwich, etc.)
65. How to be a good domestic servant
66. How to keep a servant
67. How to shop--for clothing; for food; for furniture
68. How to care for the skin
69. How to keep slender and healthy
70. How to construct a solarium
71. How to prepare a special--e.g., English, French, Hungarian, Russian, Spanish, other--dish
72. How to (set, decorate) a table
73. How to make a simple toy for a child
74. How to leave a home during vacation
75. How to hang wallpaper with two arms
76. How to (gain, lose) weight

ARGUMENTATION

PROPOSITIONS OF FACT

1. Do American homes have (too many, too few) appliances?
2. Is a private bath necessary?
3. Is the practice of "block-busting" (defensible, indefensible)?
4. Are American women excessively "beauty conscious"?
5. Are brand-name products--consumer goods, foods, etc.--best?
6. Is the cost of beauty care (reasonable, unreasonable)?
7. Is cleanliness next to Godliness?
8. Do clothes make (the man, the woman)?
9. Do too many cooks always spoil the broth?
10. Is the cosmetics industry a racket?
11. Are all (detergents, soaps) alike?
12. Is a separate dining room a luxury?
13. Is the domestic servant becoming extinct in America?
14. Are American women slaves to fashion?
15. Do good fences make good neighbors?
16. Is the fireplace a luxury?

17. Is the cost of food excessive?
18. Is the price of haircuts excessive--generally; locally?
19. Is the modern American home a bargain?
20. Is the modern American man's home his castle?
21. Are American homes over-heated?
22. Does a home freezer pay?
23. Is a house a home?
24. Is the cost of household appliances (reasonable, unreasonable)?
25. Is housewife a dirty word?
26. Does housework degrade the modern American wife?
27. Is the electric light bulb a bargain?
28. Is man's place outside the home?
29. Are two meals a day enough?
30. Is the millinery business a racket?
31. Are servants worth it?
32. Are slenderizing salons a racket?
33. Are soap and water enough for personal cleanliness?
34. Is (family, neighborhood, world) togetherness (a blessing, a curse)?
35. Are our utility rates--e.g., electricity, gas, water, telephone--(reasonable, unreasonable)?
36. Is woman's place in the home?
37. Do women belong in business?
38. Do women dress (for men, for other women, for themselves)?

PROPOSITIONS OF POLICY

1. Should baby-sitters be unionized?
2. Should bedridden invalids be (institutionalized, cared for at home)?
3. Should each member of a family have his own private bedroom?
4. Should a home be child-centered?
5. Should children be seen and not heard?
6. Should (men, women) use cosmetics?
7. Should a father change diapers?
8. Should one "crash-diet"?
9. Should domestic servants be unionized?
10. Should one fence in one's property?
11. Should (men, women) wear girdles?
12. Should one (build a new, buy a ready-made, rent a) home?
13. Should Utopia require a course in home economics for its (male students, coeds)?
14. Should a husband stay out of the kitchen?
15. Should parents be pals to their children?
16. Should husbands shop with their wives?
17. Should a wife be paid for her services to home and family?
18. Should a wife go to bed with her hair in curlers?
19. Should wives buy their husbands' clothes?
20. Should wives work outside the home?

OBJECTS

I. Facilities of a home, or part thereof--for example,
   A. Bathroom facilities
   B. Eating facilities
   C. Kitchen facilities
   D. Laundry facilities
   E. Recreational facilities

II. A useful object connected with some phase of home management or personal grooming--for example,
   A. A home air conditioner
   B. An article of clothing
   C. An article of furniture
   D. An article used in personal grooming--e.g., a hair dryer
   E. A kitchen appliance or utensil--e.g., a can opener, A dishwasher
   F. A sewing machine

POLICIES

A policy, in effect or proposed, of an agency, firm, or organization--local, state, or federal; public or private--concerned, directly or indirectly, with home management or personal grooming--for example,

A. A policy of a baby-sitter or baby-sitting agency
B. A policy of a barber shop or beauty salon
C. A policy of a charm school
D. A policy of an employment agency relating to domestic service
E. A policy of a Madison (or other) Avenue fashion house
F. A policy of the Federal Housing Authority relating to the construction and financing of a home
G. A policy of a local Household Finance Company
H. A policy of an independent grocer or grocery store
I. A policy of a day nursery
J. A policy of a supermarket

BUSINESS AND BUSINESS METHODS 650-659.99

Thought Starters for ANALYSIS

What about:

1. Accounting
2. Advertising
3. Auditing: accounting
4. Automation: business and industry
5. Bill collecting
6. Book industries
7. Book trade
8. Bookbinding: technology
9. Bookkeeping
10. Business communications
11. Business ethics (Cf. ETHICS, 174)
12. Business and industrial management
13. Business methods
14. Business machines
15. Business records
16. Business technology
17. Chain stores
18. Charge accounts
19. Consumer research
20. Copywriting: advertising
21. Copying processes: business technology
22. Copyright
23. Credit: business and industrial management
24. Department stores
25. Discharge of personnel: business and industry
26. Employees and employers: business and industrial management
27. Employment practices: business and industry
28. Fashion modeling
29. Graphic arts: technology
30. Hiring: business and industry
31. Industrial management
32. Installment plans
33. Labeling: advertising
34. Magazine advertising
35. Mail order houses
36. Management
37. Market research and analysis
38. Marketing
39. Mass production
40. Merit ratings: business, industrial management
41. Morale: personnel management
42. Motivational research
43. Newspaper advertising
44. Office equipment
45. Office management
46. On-the-job training
47. Outdoor advertising
48. Ownership: business and industry
49. Packaging
50. Paper money: engraving
51. Partnerships: business and industry
52. Pay: business and industry
53. Personnel: business and industry
54. Postage stamps: printing and engraving
55. Premiums and trading
56. Printing: technology
57. Production management
58. Production research and development
59. Promotion, personnel
60. Promotion, sales
61. Public relations
62. Publishing and book-selling techniques
63. Quality control
64. Radio advertising
65. Retirement
66. Safety measures: industry
67. Sales management

NOTE: See also such related fields as JOURNALISM (070-079.99), ETHICS (170-179.99), and ECONOMICS (330-339.99)

68. Salesmanship
69. Secretarial practice
70. Shopping centers
71. Shorthand systems
72. Success in business
73. Supermarkets
74. Taxation: business expenses
75. Telephone sales
76. Television advertising
77. Traveling salesmen
78. Typography: printing
79. Wholesale marketing
80. Working conditions: business and industry

CAUSE and EFFECT

1. Why businessmen (do, do not) advertise
2. (Major) Effects of advertising--on production; on consumption; on the economy
3. Why (billboard, magazine, newspaper, radio, television) advertising benefits (the customer, the distributor, the manufacturer)
4. (Major) Effects of automation--on business and industry; on labor; on the economy
5. Why books (sell, do not sell)
6. Why people (buy, do not buy) by brand
7. Why businessmen go to church
8. Why people (buy, do not buy)
9. (Major) Effects of chain stores--on consumption generally; on independent stores
10. (Major) Effects of the coffee break on business and industry--e.g., on morale; on efficiency
11. (Major) Effects of mass production--on consumption; on quality of product, etc.
12. Why (employee, management) morale at _________ Company is (high, low)
13. Why I believe in (private, public) ownership of business and industry--e.g., the steel industry; railroads; communications, etc.
14. Why business partnerships are (entered into, dissolved)
15. Why I (like, do not like) to shop in a particular (store, community, shopping center)
16. (Major) Causes of (success, failure) in business
17. (Major) Effects of (local, state, federal) taxation on business
18. (Major) Effects of trading stamps (on costs, on trade)
19. Why women are (satisfactory, unsatisfactory; successful, unsuccessful) in business

CLASSIFICATION

Kinds/Types of:

1. Accounting systems
2. Advertising media
3. Advertisements
4. Bookkeeping systems
5. Business machines
6. Charge accounts
7. Collection methods
8. Copyrights
9. Credit
10. Credit risks
11. Customers

12. Duplicating methods
13. Fashion models
14. Marketing/markets
15. Office bores
16. Office parties
17. Ownership
18. Printing processes
19. Salesmen/saleswomen
20. Secretaries
21. Selling
22. Shoppers
23. Shorthand systems
24. Success in business
25. Taxes/taxation
26. Type

COMPARISON and CONTRAST

1. Advertisements: black and white and color
2. Advertising: here and there; yesterday and today--e.g., c. the 1880's in America and today
3. Advertising media: magazine, newspaper, radio, television, and/or other
4. American coffee break and British tea time
5. Book binding: by hand and by machine
6. Books: clothbound, leatherbound and/or paperbound
7. Brand-name and "off-brand" merchandise
8. Business ethics: here and there; yesterday and today--e.g., c. 1900 and today in the United States
9. Business ethics and political ethics
10. Cash-and-carry and charge account
11. Chain store and independent store
12. Copyright, patent, and trade mark
13. Copy writing: for magazines, newspapers, radio, television
14. Country store and supermarket
15. Fair business practices and unfair business practices
16. Fraudulent advertising and misleading advertising
17. Hard-sell and soft-sell
18. Labeling: dishonest, honest, and misleading
19. Lockout and strike
20. Marketing: here and there; yesterday and today--e.g., United States and in the Common Market countries
21. Monopolies: private and public
22. Office equipment: here and there; yesterday and today--e.g., in 1800, in 1900, and today in the United States
23. Packaging: attractive and unattractive; practical and impractical; dishonest, honest, and misleading
24. Printing: here and there; yesterday and today--e.g., in 1500, in 1800, and today
25. Push and pull
26. Salesmanship: here and there; yesterday and today--e.g., c. 1900 and today in the United States
27. Shorthand and dictaphone
28. Success in business: in a controlled economy and in a free economy
29. Trade mark and trade name
30. Traveling salesmen: in fact and in fiction; here and there; yesterday and today--e.g., c. 1900 and today in the United States
31. Working: for the boss and for oneself

DEFINITION

1. Blurb
2. C.P.A.
3. Caveat emptor
4. Control
5. Display
6. Efficiency
7. Ethics
8. Fair employment
9. Fair trade
10. Fraud
11. Good will
12. Guarantee
13. Honesty
14. Layout
15. Linotype
16. Living wage
17. Lottery
18. Morality
19. Quality
20. Risk
21. Ruthlessness
22. Skywriting
23. Standardization
24. Success
25. Work

DESCRIPTION

I. Equipment found in the office(s) or plant of a (local, state, federal; public, private) business establishment --for example,
   A. Equipment found in an advertising agency--e.g., a drawing board
   B. Equipment found in a department store
   C. Equipment found in a printing plant or bindery
II. Facilities of a business firm--for example,
   A. Facilities of an accounting firm
   B. Facilities of an employment agency
   C. Facilities of a mail-order house

PROCESS

1. How to write a classified advertisement
2. How advertising aids (the manufacturer; the middleman; the consumer; the economy in general)
3. How to (plan, conduct) a successful advertising campaign
4. How to collect a bill--and keep the customer
5. How books are bound
6. How to keep books at home
7. How to be a good boss
8. How to give the boss his money's worth
9. How to marry the boss's (daughter, son)
10. How to improve business (in our community; in our town; in our city)
11. "How to succeed in business without really trying."
12. How to write a business letter
13. How to (open, use, keep) a charge account
14. How to educate the consumer
15. How to secure a copyright
16. How to (get, keep) a good credit rating
17. How to (dictate a letter, take dictation)
18. How to dress at the office

19. How to (fire, hire, retire) an employee
20. How to improve employee-employer relations--generally; at ________ Company
21. How to be a fashion model
22. How to (improve, simplify) filing in business--generally; at ________ Company
23. How to conduct an interview
24. How to get a job
25. How to handle the office bore
26. How to increase office efficiency--generally; at ________ Company
27. How improve office morale
28. How to manage an office (full of women, full of men, with men and women)
29. How to have fun at an office party--with no regrets
30. How to select a business partner
31. How to (organize, dissolve) a partnership
32. How to promote public relations in business-generally; at ________ Company
33. How to (ask for, get, deserve) a raise
34. How to retire
35. How to get one's foot in the door--as a prospective employee; as a salesman
36. How to be a good salesman
37. How to be a good secretary--and a good girl
38. How to sell oneself
39. How to learn shorthand at home
40. How to answer the telephone
41. How to learn typing at home
42. How to improve working conditions (for employees, for management)--generally; at ________ Company

ARGUMENTATION

PROPOSITIONS OF FACT

1. Does (billboard, magazine, newspaper, radio, television) advertising (bear in mind, insult) the intelligence of the American people?
2. Does advertising (raise, lower) the cost of merchandise?
3. What's (right, wrong) with advertising in the United States?
4. Is American enterprise free?
5. Does automation (create, eliminate) jobs?
6. Does the local Better Business Bureau promote better business?
7. Are our (state, federal) highways "billboard jungles"?
8. Do local Blue Laws make sense?
9. Are brand-name products best?
10. Is American business (over, under) mechanized?
11. Are business codes (worth while, worthless; reasonable, unreasonable)--generally; locally?
12. Are modern business methods (effective, ineffective)?

13. Is American business taxed (fairly, unfairly)--generally; locally?
14. Are businessmen literate?
15. Are chain stores monopolistic?
16. Is the charge account (a blessing, a curse) to (business, the consumer)?
17. Is the coffee break (beneficial, detrimental)--to management; to employees?
18. Are (local, national) contests and lotteries rigged?
19. Are (national, international) copyright laws (fair, unfair; effective, ineffective)?
20. Is the customer always right?
21. Is America's credit system (sound, unsound; beneficial, harmful)?
22. Is the so-called "fair (price, profit, wage") fair?
23. Is "fair trade" fair?
24. Is all fair in business?
25. Is the Good Housekeeping Seal of Approval (meaningful, meaningless)?
26. Is so-called "government interference in business" justified?
27. Is the guaranteed annual wage (sound, unsound; proper, improper)?
28. Is honesty the best policy in business?
29. Is the jargon of business (i.e., "businessese") necessary?
30. Do package labels misrepresent?
31. Is material success enough?
32. Is monopoly a dirty word?
33. Can one get something for nothing?
34. Is packaging (intentionally, unintentionally) deceptive--generally; specifically with reference to a particular product?
35. Does one always get what one pays for?
36. Is profit a dirty word?
37. What's (right, wrong) with public relations in American business--generally; in a particular business or company?
38. Are American businessmen retired too soon?
39. Is the art of salesmanship dead?
40. Are the (salesmen, saleswomen) of the __________ (Company, Store) (effective, polite)?
41. Are secretaries (competent, literate)--generally; at ____ Company?
42. Is selling by telephone an invasion of privacy?
43. Is a "soak-the-rich" tax policy (necessary, fair)?
44. Do trading stamps benefit (the consumer, the distributor)?
45. Do women belong in business?
46. Are women (discriminated against: given preferential treatment) in business?

PROPOSITIONS OF POLICY

1. Should alcoholic beverages be advertised in the mass media--e.g., television?
2. Should billboards be outlawed on interstate highways?

3. Should one be neither a borrower nor a lender?
4. Should we do business with Communist countries--e.g., Red China?
5. Should (alcoholic beverages, cigarettes) be labeled as being dangerous to health?
6. Should employers be unionized?
7. Should the loyalty oath be a requirement for (employment, tenure)?
8. Should mail order houses be allowed to mail certain products--e.g., contraceptive devices, guns?
9. Should the United States set up a national lottery?
10. Should (newscasts, telecasts) be sponsored?
11. Should management share the profits with employees?
12. When should an executive retire?
13. Should "top executives" receive pensions when they retire?
14. Should the sponsors of (radio, television) programs control the content of those programs?
15. Should merchants (encourage, discourage) the use of trading stamps?
16. Should women in business receive equal pay for equal work?

EVALUATION

OBJECTS

I. Evaluation of facilities found in a business establishment--for example,
   A. Facilities of an advertising agency
   B. Facilities of a book-publishing concern
   C. Facilities of an employment agency
   D. Facilities of a fashion-modeling agency
II. Evaluation of a useful object found in a business firm --for example,
   A. A beverage dispenser found in an office
   B. A charge plate
   C. A duplicating machine
   D. A package or other container for merchandise
   E. A postage machine
   F. A printing press
   G. A telephone

POLICIES

Evaluation of a policy, in effect or proposed, of a business firm--local, state, or federal; public or private--for example,

A. A policy of the local Better Business Bureau
B. A policy of a book store
C. A copyright law or laws
D. A policy of a department store--e.g., a store's credit policies
E. A firm's policy regarding (firing, hiring, retiring) of personnel
F. A policy of a local market

BUILDING CONSTRUCTION 690-699.99

Thought Starters for ANALYSIS

What about:

1. Air conditioning: buildings and engineering
2. Asbestos: construction material
3. Asphalt roofing
4. Bathrooms
5. Blast-resistant construction
6. Bombproof construction
7. Bricklaying
8. Bricks
9. Building construction industry
10. Building construction materials
11. Building construction systems
12. Building laws and codes
13. Built-in furniture
14. Carpentry
15. Ceilings
16. Central heating systems
17. Ceramic materials: building construction
18. Concrete building construction
19. Concrete: construction material
20. Construction business practices
21. Construction materials
22. Contracts: building construction
23. Costs: building construction
24. Dampproof, moistureproof, and waterproof construction: buildings
25. Doors: carpentry
26. Drawings: building construction
27. Earthquake-resistant construction
28. Fiberglass: building construction and material
29. Fireplaces, indoor
30. Fireproof construction
31. Fixtures, plumbing
32. Flashings: roof construction
33. Floor coverings: building construction
34. Floors
35. Furnaces
36. Gas heating
37. Glass: construction material
38. Gutters, roof
39. Heat pump
40. Heating engineering
41. Heating systems
42. Hot water heating
43. House painting: building construction and maintenance
44. Insulating materials: building construction
45. Interior details: carpentry
46. Joinery
47. Lathwork
48. Masonry adhesives: construction materials
49. Masonry construction
50. Metals: construction material
51. Nuclear heating
52. Oil heating systems
53. Ornamental woodwork
54. Painting trades
55. Paper hanging
56. Pest-resistant construction
57. Pipe-fitting: building construction
58. Plans: building construction

NOTE: See also such fields as ENGINEERING (620-629.99), HOME ECONOMICS (640-649.99), and ARCHITECTURE(720-729.99)

59. Plastering
60. Plastics: construction material
61. Plumbing
62. Prefabricated houses
63. Prefabricated housing materials
64. Radiant panel heating
65. Reflection and refraction: heating engineering
66. Reinforced concrete: construction material
67. Remodeling
68. Roofing
69. Roofing materials
70. Scaffolding: building construction
71. Solar heating
72. Stairs: carpentry
73. Steel, structural: construction material
74. Stone: construction material
75. Structural elements
76. Structural woodworking
77. Temperature control engineering
78. Ventilation engineering
79. Walls
80. Water supply: plumbing
81. Windows
82. Wood: construction material
83. Wood finishing

CAUSE and EFFECT

1. (Major) Causes of accidents in the home
2. (Major) Effects of air conditioning on health
3. Why asbestos does not burn
4. Why basements (are damp; leak)
5. Why brick (or some other building material--e.g., wood) is popular--generally; in our community
6. Why building laws and codes are necessary
7. (Major) Effects of (lax, strict; reasonable, unreasonable) building laws and codes--generally; locally
8. Why ceilings (crack, sag)
9. Why chimneys catch fire
10. Why concrete (crumbles, cracks, flakes)--in foundations; in walks
11. Why a contract is necessary in building
12. Why the cost of building (commercially, privately) is (high, low)--generally; locally
13. Why doors (sag, stick, warp)
14. Why fireplaces smoke
15. (Major) Causes of fires in the home
16. Why floors (sag, squeak)
17. Why (coal, electric gas, oil) heat is (superior, inferior)
18. Why (interior, exterior) paint (flakes, peels)
19. Why pipes (burst, sweat)
20. Why plaster (cracks, falls)
21. Why plastic is (a satisfactory, an unsatisfactory) building material
22. Why plumbers usually work in pairs
23. Why plumbing fixtures--faucets, etc.--(break down, leak)
24. Why plumbing laws and codes are necessary
25. (Major) Effects of prefabrication on building construction--e.g., on costs; on design

26. Why roofs leak
27. Why windows stick
28. Why wood (decays, rots, warps)
29. Why wood is (a satisfactory, an unsatisfactory) building material

CLASSIFICATION

Kinds/Types of:

1. Air conditioning systems
2. Architects
3. Bricks
4. Builders
5. Building materials
6. Building stones
7. Carpenters
8. Ceilings
9. Ceramic materials
10. Contractors
11. Contracts
12. Doors
13. Electricians
14. Fireplaces
15. Fireproof materials
16. Flashing
17. Flooring
18. Furnaces
19. Glass
20. Heat
21. Heating systems
22. House paint
23. Insulating materials
24. Lumber
25. Masonry
26. Paint
27. Plastics
28. Plumbers
29. Pipe
30. Roofing materials
31. Roofs
32. Sidewalk superintendents
33. Ventilation
34. Walls
35. Windows
36. Waterproofing materials
37. Wood

COMPARISON and CONTRAST

1. Architect, builder, and contractor
2. Artisan, craftsman, and jackleg
3. Asbestos and asphalt
4. Building construction: here and there; yesterday and today--e.g., in the United States and in Japan
5. Building laws and codes: here and there; yesterday and today--e.g., in the U.S.A and in the U.S.S.R.
6. Building materials: here and there; yesterday and today --e.g., in the United States and in Asia
7. Building materials: aluminum, brick, glass, steel, etc.
8. Building upon rock and building upon sand
9. Contract price and "cost-plus"
10. Doors: flush and panel; French and Dutch
11. Fireproof and fire-resistant
12. Flashing: aluminum, copper, and tin
13. Flooring: concrete, stone, tile, wood, etc.
14. Guttering and downspouts: aluminum, copper, and tin
15. Heating fuels: coal, electricity, gas, oil
16. Heating systems: here and there; yesterday and today--e.g., in ancient Rome and in modern America
17. Houses: one-story, two-story, and split-level
18. Housing: prefabricated and conventional

19. Insulating materials: asbestos, rock wool, wall-board
20. Lathe and plasterboard
21. Louis Sullivan and Thomas Jefferson
22. Piping: copper, cast iron, and plastic
23. Prefabrication: in automobile manufacturing and in building construction
24. Public sewer and septic tank
25. Roof design: flat and gable
26. Roofing material: aluminum, asphalt or asbestos shingles, slate, tin, etc.
27. Wall construction, exterior: brick, aluminum siding, wood, etc.
28. Wall construction, interior: dry-wall, plaster, panel, etc.
29. Window design: casement and sash
30. Window materials: aluminum, steel, and wood

DEFINITION

1. Adobe
2. Bargain
3. Bay
4. Beam
5. Caveat emptor
6. Column
7. Convector
8. Cupola
9. Damper
10. Frame
11. Fraud
12. Header
13. Integrity
14. Jamb
15. Jerry-built
16. Joint
17. Joist
18. Level
19. Mortise
20. Partition
21. Plumber
22. Polyethylene
23. Rafter
24. Stretcher
25. Sill
26. Tenon
27. Terra cotta
28. Value

DESCRIPTION

I. Equipment found in a private dwelling, commercial establishment, or office building--for example,
   A. Air-conditioning equipment or system
   B. Bathroom fixtures
   C. Built-in furniture
   D. A fireplace
   E. A furnace
   F. A staircase
II. A piece of equipment used in private or public construction--for example,
   A. A bulldozer
   B. A cement-mixer
   C. A crane
   D. A ditch- or well-digger
III. Facilities of an individual or a concern engaged in some phase of building construction--for example,

A. An architect's or contractor's office, or part thereof
B. A lumber dealer's establishment, or part thereof
C. A plumbing or heating concern, or part thereof

IV. A tool used by an individual engaged in building construction--for example,
A. A carpenter's brace-and-bit
B. A civil engineer's transit
C. A plumber's wrench

PROCESS

1. How to make an adobe hut
2. How to (select, install) a home air-conditioner
3. How to select (an architect, a builder, a contractor)
4. How to plan (a bathroom, a bedroom)
5. How to waterproof (a new, an old) basement
6. How a building is made (bombproof, blast-resistant, earthquake-resistant)
7. How to read a blueprint
8. How to lay bricks
9. How to (determine, reduce) the building costs of a home
10. How to improve our building laws and codes--generally; locally
11. How to build a piece of built-in furniture--e.g., a bookcase
12. How to build a cabin retreat
13. How to build a carport
14. How to (select, install) an acoustical ceiling--as in a recreation room
15. How to mix cement at home
16. How to clean a chimney
17. How to (read, write) a contract for a house
18. How to (select, install) (a door, a door frame)
19. How to repair (a sagging, a stuck) door
20. How to unclog a (sink, toilet) drain
21. How to construct a fallout shelter in one's home
22. How to repair a leaking faucet
23. How to construct an (indoor, outdoor) fireplace
24. How timber is made fire-resistant
25. How to (select, install) flooring
26. How to (plan, dig, erect) the foundation for a house
27. How to build a garage
28. How to install a pane of glass
29. How to select window glass
30. How to (install, repair) gutters and downspouts
31. How to (select, install) a heating system for a house
32. How to cut corners, not quality, in home construction
33. How a modern house is built
34. How to inspect a house under construction
35. How to (select, install) insulation--for a wall; for a ceiling
36. How to get a home loan

37. How to select nails in building construction
38. How to select paint for a house
39. How to paint a house (inside, outside)
40. How to hang paper
41. How to plan a house
42. How to mix plaster
43. How to plaster a room
44. How a prefabricated home is (designed assembled)
45. How to install (an asphalt an asbestos, a tin, a tile, a slate) roof
46. How to select roofing material for a home
47. How to build a scaffold for a house
48. How to select a site for a home
49. How to make a home termite-resistant
50. How to (select, install) (bathroom, ceiling, drain, floor) tile
51. How to build a tool house
52. How to (clean, paint, varnish) woodwork

ARGUMENTATION

PROPOSITIONS OF FACT

1. Is central home air-conditioning (a luxury; a necessity)?
2. Is an architect (necessary, unnecessary; a luxury)?
3. Is that extra bathroom worth it?
4. Are building costs (reasonable, unreasonable)--generally; locally?
5. Are building laws and codes (adequate, inadequate; obsolete)--generally; in our community?
6. Is (brick, wood, etc.) the best building material for home building?
7. Are building methods in home construction obsolete?
8. Is a contractor "an architect without an imagination"?
9. Is (dry-wall construction, paneling, plaster, etc.) best for (private, commercial) building?
10. Does it pay to (enlarge, remodel, move)?
11. Is a fireplace worth the cost?
12. Is (block-masonry; poured concrete) best for foundations in home construction?
13. Does (electricity, hot air, hot water) provide the best heat?
14. Is (electricity, gas, oil, etc.) the best heating source?
15. Is (a new, an old) home a good buy?
16. Are American homes overheated?
17. Is a plumber's helper necessary?
18. Are our plumbing laws and codes (adequate, inadequate; obsolete)?
19. Is prefabrication the answer to high building costs?
20. Is (asphalt, slate, etc.) the best roofing material?
21. Is the "shell home" a good investment?

PROPOSITIONS OF POLICY

1. Should one hire an architect?
2. Should the federal government provide bomb shelters for the public?
3. Should one (build, buy, enlarge, remodel, rent)?
4. Should our building laws and codes be (relaxed, strengthened)--generally; locally?
5. Should one be his own contractor?
6. Should our plumbing laws and codes be revised?
7. Should one buy (a conventional, a prefabricated) home?
8. Should (our community; our state. the federal government) undertake a slum-clearance project?
9. Should our city undertake an urban redevelopment program (on its own; with state or federal aid)?

EVALUATION

OBJECTS

1. An air conditioner or air conditioning system
2. A building material--e.g., aluminum, concrete, glass, masonry blocks, steel, stone
3. A heating fuel or source--e.g., coal, electricity, gas, oil, sunlight
4. A heating system--e.g., hot air, hot water, radiant
5. An insulating material--e.g., asbestos, rock wool, wallboard
6. Piping materials--e.g., cast iron, copper, plastic
7. Roofing materials--e.g., aluminum, gravel, slate, tin
8. Tools and equipment used by an architect, by a builder or contractor, or by a plumber
9. Wall materials--e.g., dry wall, masonry block, paneling, plaster, wood
10. Window materials--e.g., aluminum, steel, wood

POLICIES

Evaluation of a policy, in effect or proposed, of an individual, an agency, a firm, or an organization--local, state, or federal; public or private--having to do, directly or indirectly, with building construction--for example,

A. A policy of a local architectural association or firm
B. A policy of a local bank with reference to home loans
C. A policy of a local builder or contractor
D. A local building code
E. A policy of the F.H.A.
F. A policy of a local hardware dealer
G. A policy of a local lumber dealer
H. A policy of a local plumbing establishment
I. A local plumbing law or code

ARCHITECTURE 720-729.99

Thought Starters for ANALYSIS

What about:

1. Aegean architecture, ancient
2. American Indian architecture
3. Ancient architecture
4. Apartment houses
5. Architectural construction
6. Architectural design and decoration
7. Baroque architecture
8. Botanical gardens
9. Byzantine architecture
10. Carvings: architectural decoration
11. Castles
12. Cathedrals
13. Ceilings: architectural design
14. Christian architecture, medieval
15. Church buildings
16. Church furniture: design and decoration
17. Civic architecture
18. Classical architecture
19. Classical revival
20. Clubhouses
21. College and university buildings
22. Commercial buildings
23. Composition: architectural design
24. Construction, architectural
25. Courthouses
26. Decoration: architecture
27. Design, architectural
28. Doors
29. Dormers
30. Ecclesiastical furniture: design and decoration
31. Ecclesiology
32. Educational buildings
33. Etruscan architecture
34. Farm buildings
35. Fireplaces, indoor
36. Floors
37. Foundations: buildings
38. Functional architecture, modern
39. Georgian architecture
40. Gothic architecture: medieval and revival
41. Government buildings
42. Greek architecture, ancient
43. Gymnasiums
44. Hospital buildings
45. Hotels
46. Houses
47. Industrial buildings
48. Inns
49. Islamic architecture, medieval
50. Jails
51. Laboratory buildings
52. Log cabins
53. Mayan architecture, ancient
54. Medieval architecture
55. Military buildings
56. Mills
57. Modern architecture
58. Moorish architecture, medieval
59. Mortuary buildings
60. Mosques
61. Motels
62. Municipal buildings
63. Office buildings
64. Oriental architecture, ancient
65. Ornamentation: architecture
66. Palaces

NOTE: See also such related fields as PHYSICS (530-539.99), ENGINEERING (620-629.99), and BUILDING CONSTRUCTION (690-699.99)

67. Pre-Columbian American architecture
68. Prefabricated houses
69. Prison buildings
70. Queen Anne architecture
71. Recreation buildings
72. Reformatories
73. Religious architecture
74. Residential buildings
75. Resorts
76. Restaurants
77. Revivals, architectural
78. Roman architecture: ancient and revival
79. Roofs
80. Sacramental furniture
81. Sanitariums
82. Saracenic architecture
83. School buildings
84. Service stations
85. Shopping centers
86. Skyscrapers
87. Stadiums
88. Stained glass: architectural decoration
89. Stairs
90. Structural elements: design and construction
91. Supermarkets
92. Swimming pools
93. Temples
94. Terminal buildings
95. Theaters
96. Tombs
97. Tourist courts
98. Towers
99. Town halls
100. Transportation buildings
101. Walls: architectural design
102. Walls: buildings
103. Welfare buildings
104. Windows

CAUSE and EFFECT

1. (Major) Effects of air conditioning on architectural design--e.g., in commercial buildings; in private homes
2. (Major) Effects of ancient architecture--e.g., Greek, Roman--on American architecture
3. (Major) Effects of (the arch, the dome) on architectural (design, progress)
4. Why an architect is necessary
5. Why America (adapted, adopted) (classical, Gothic) architecture
6. (Major) Effects of (classical, Gothic) architecture on (private homes, commercial buildings) in America
7. (Major) Effects of climate on architectural design
8. (Major) Effects of the column on architectural (design, progress)
9. (Major) Effects of concrete on architectural (design, progress)
10. (Major) Effects of (crime, fear) on architectural design
11. (Major) Effects of form on function--and vice versa--in architectural design
12. (Major) Effects of mass leisure on architectural (design, progress)
13. (Major) Effects of materials--e.g., brick, cast iron, cinder (or other) block, marble, steel, wood, etc.--on architectural design
14. Why cathedrals were built in the Middle Ages
15. (Major) Effects of the Middle Ages upon the architecture of (private homes, commercial buildings, etc.) in America

16. (Major) Effects of the Orient--e.g., Japan--on American architecture
17. (Major) Effects of prefabrication on American architecture
18. (Major) Effects of public pressure on American architecture--e.g., in the design of private homes
19. Why one of the Seven Wonders of the World was built
20. Why the skyscraper evolved in America
21. (Major) Effects of space--i.e., the availability and cost of land--on architectural design
22. (Major) Effects of topography on architectural design
23. (Major) Effects of transportation on architectural design --e.g., in commercial buildings; in private homes

CLASSIFICATION

Kinds/Types of:

1. Architects
2. Architectural styles
3. Architecture
4. Buildings
5. Cathedrals
6. Ceilings
7. Columns
8. Curved construction
9. Doors
10. Dormers
11. Ecclesiastical buildings
12. Floors
13. Foundations
14. Monastic buildings
15. Non-Christian temples and shrines
16. Ornamentation
17. Revivals
18. Roofs
19. Stairs
20. Structural elements
21. Towers
22. Walls

COMPARISON and CONTRAST

1. African primitive architecture and American Indian architecture
2. Amphitheaters: here and there; yesterday and today--e.g., in ancient Greece or Rome and in modern America
3. Ante-bellum Southern mansion and medieval feudal manor
4. Arch, dome, niche, and vault
5. Architect, builder, contractor, and engineer
6. Architect: as artist and as scientist
7. Architecture: Classical, Colonial, Georgian, Gothic, and Modern
8. Baroque and Rococo
9. Building "out" and building "up"
10. Bungalow and cottage
11. Capital and capitol
12. Castle, mansion, palace, and villa
13. Church, shrine, and temple
14. Classical Revival and Romanesque Revival
15. Compressive strength and tensile strength
16. Convents: medieval and modern
17. Dome, spire, steeple, and tower
18. Dormer and gable
19. Duke or Princeton University and University of Virginia

20. Egyptian pyramid and Medieval cathedral
21. Eighteenth-century English inn and modern American tourist court
22. Eighteenth-century English tavern and modern American restaurant
23. Factories: nineteenth-century and twentieth-century
24. Half-timber and timber
25. Home and house
26. Houses: colonial "salt-box" and modern ranch
27. Igloo and tepee
28. Inn, hotel, and motel
29. Libraries: here and there; yesterday and today--e.g., in Colonial America and today
30. Little red schoolhouse and modern school building
31. Medieval castle and modern fort or fortress
32. Medieval cathedral and modern skyscraper
33. Minaret and mosque
34. Monasteries: medieval and modern
35. Pantheon and Parthenon
36. Prefabrication and conventional home construction
37. Roman and Romanesque
38. Roofs: flat and gabled
39. Shops: here and there; yesterday and today--e.g., in ancient Pompeii and in modern America
40. Temples: Greek, Indian, Oriental, and Roman
41. Villas: modern and Roman

DEFINITION

1. Aesthetics
2. Baptistry
3. Beauty
4. Blueprint
5. Cantilever
6. Casino
7. Chancel
8. Clerestory
9. Colonnade
10. Column
11. Cornice
12. Curve
13. Design
14. Elevation
15. Entablature
16. Facade
17. Flying buttress
18. Form
19. Frieze
20. Function
21. Gable
22. Imagination
23. Integrity
24. Light
25. Minaret
26. Mosaic
27. Nave
28. Niche
29. Obelisk
30. Ornament
31. Pagoda
32. Patio
33. Pediment
34. Pilaster
35. Portico
36. Post and lintel
37. Purlin
38. Pylon
39. Relief
40. Sacristy
41. Shinto
42. Space
43. Structure
44. Style
45. Taste
46. Transept
47. Vault
48. Ziggurat

DESCRIPTION

I. Major characteristics of the--(public, private) buildings of an architectural period--for example,
   A. Classical architecture
   B. Colonial architecture
   C. Georgian architecture
   D. Gothic architecture
   E. Modern architecture

II. Interior or exterior detail of an architectural structure --historical or contemporary; local, state, or federal; public or private--for example,
   A. A City or Town Hall
   B. A famous historical structure--e.g., the Palace of Versailles, St. Paul's Cathedral
   C. A private home, or part thereof
   D. A skyscraper

III. The office, or part thereof, belonging to an architect or to an architectural firm

IV. A tool, or other article, used by an architect--e.g., a brick scale, a parallel rule

PROCESS

1. How one becomes an architect
2. How an architect designs a building
3. How the architect uses (light, materials, space)
4. How to read a blueprint
5. How to design a cabin
6. How medieval (castles, cathedrals) were (designed, built)
7. How to (design, make) a piece of church furniture
8. How to (design, build) a clubhouse
9. How computers are used in architectural drafting
10. How to design an attractive courthouse
11. How to (design, build) one's dream house
12. How foundations are rendered earthquake-proof
13. How to design a (school, college, university) gymnasium
14. How to return the Leaning Tower of Pisa to its original position
15. How a moon house will be built
16. How to design a mortuary
17. How (the Pantheon, the Parthenon) was (designed, built)
18. How to (draw up, read) house plans
19. How prefabricated houses are designed
20. How a private residence is built
21. How the Pyramids were (designed, built)
22. How to design (a mountain, a seashore) resort on a (limited, unlimited) budget
23. How the Romans (designed, built) their (aqueducts, bridges, roads)
24. How the Romans built the Colosseum
25. How one of the Seven Wonders of the World was (designed, built)

26. How to design a shopping center--generally; locally
27. How the site for a building is selected
28. How a skyscraper is built
29. How a stadium is (designed, built)
30. How to design a better supermarket
31. How to design a swimming pool
32. How the Taj Mahal was (designed, built)
33. How the U.N. Building was (designed, built)

ARGUMENTATION

PROPOSITIONS OF FACT

1. Are our airport terminals well designed?
2. Is an architect necessary?
3. What is "American" architecture?
4. Is America architecturally (arid, ugly)?
5. What's (right, wrong) with American architecture?
6. Does American architecture sacrifice beauty for (efficiency, function)?
7. Are architects impractical dreamers?
8. Is architecture (an art, a science)?
9. Is our (auditorium, coliseum) adequately designed?
10. Does our community need (an auditorium, a coliseum)?
11. Is an efficient building "automatically beautiful"?
12. Are our local building codes obsolete?
13. Do we have (too many, too few) churches--generally; locally?
14. Is our (City, Town) Hall an eyesore?
15. Is our home adequately designed?
16. Are our hospitals designed for the convenience of (the hospital staff, the patients)?
17. Are our hotels adequately designed--generally; locally?
18. Are our (jails, prisons, reformatories) adequately designed?
19. Does our community need (a new, an enlarged) library?
20. Is our Main Street an eyesore?
21. Must mortuary buildings be dead?
22. Is our local post office building adequately designed?
23. Is our local (radio, television) station adequately designed?
24. Does our community need (a new, an enlarged) restaurant?
25. Is our local sanitarium adequately designed?
26. Are our local school buildings adequately designed?
27. Does our community need (new, enlarged) school facilities?
28. Must all service stations look alike?
29. Is the skyscraper obsolete?
30. Is our local stadium adequate?
31. Are our municipal swimming pools adequate?
32. Does our community need (a new, an enlarged) theater?
33. Are our local transportation buildings--e.g., bus depots; railroad stations, etc.--satisfactory?
34. Are our local welfare buildings adequate?

PROPOSITIONS OF POLICY

1. Should one hire an architect?
2. Should one follow (modern, traditional) architectural design when building a home?
3. Should educational buildings follow (modern, traditional) architectural design?
4. Should a home have a fireplace?
5. Should one (build his own; buy a ready-built) home?
6. Should one buy (a new, an old) home?
7. Should one invest in a prefabricated home?
8. Should our Town Hall be (razed, rebuilt)?

EVALUATION

OBJECTS

The architectural design of a specific building--for example,
A. An apartment building or house
B. A castle
C. A church or Sunday School building
D. A college or university building--e.g., a dormitory
E. A courthouse
F. A farm building--e.g., a barn
G. A hospital
H. A hotel
I. A jail
J. A motel
K. An office building
L. A prison
M. A recreation hall
N. A restaurant
O. A sanitarium
P. A school building
Q. A service station (including its rest rooms)
R. A shopping center
S. A skyscraper
T. A stadium
U. A supermarket
V. A theater
W. A town or city hall

POLICIES

A policy, in effect or proposed, of an agency, a firm, or an organization--local, state, or federal; public or private--devoted to architecture or to building design--for example,
A. A policy of a local architect or architectural firm
B. A policy of the American Institute of Architects
C. A policy of a state regarding the licensing of architects

SCULPTURE 730-739.99

Thought Starters for ANALYSIS

What about:

1. African sculpture
2. Ancient sculpture
3. Armor: art metalwork
4. Arms: art metalwork
5. Art metalwork
6. Baroque sculpture
7. Bas-relief
8. Bone carvings
9. Byzantine sculpture
10. Cameos
11. Carving techniques
12. Casting
13. Ceramic arts
14. Chinaware
15. Classical Revival
16. Classical sculpture
17. Clay: ceramic arts
18. Coins
19. Composition
20. Diamonds: cutting and polishing
21. Diamonds: jewelry
22. Earthenware
23. Engravings
24. Equestrian sculpture
25. Firearms: art metalwork
26. Gothic sculpture
27. Grotesque sculpture
28. Ironwork
29. Ivory carvings
30. Jewelry: art metalwork
31. Medieval sculpture
32. Metalwork
33. Modeling
34. Modern sculpture
35. Naturalism
36. Numismatics
37. Potters' marks
38. Pottery
39. Precious metals and stones
40. Primitive sculpture
41. Pyrography
42. Relief sculpture
43. Restoration of sculpture
44. Rings: jewelry
45. Scrollwork
46. Sculptors
47. Shell carvings
48. Shields
49. Side arms: art metalwork
50. Snow carving
51. Soap carving
52. Stone carving
53. Tableware: ceramic arts
54. Tableware: metalwork
55. Talismans
56. Terra cotta: ceramic arts
57. Tools: sculpture
58. Vases: ceramic and metal
59. Whittling
60. Wood-carving arts
61. Wood sculpture
62. Wrought iron: art metalwork

CAUSE and EFFECT

1. (Major) Effects of the invention of gunpowder on the manufacture of armor
2. (Major) Effects of technology on the making of chinaware
3. (Major) Causes of (the rise, the decline) of the Classical Revival in (Europe, America)
4. Why people collect coins
5. Why coins are generally round
6. (Major) Causes of the (rise, decline) of Gothic sculpture
7. (Major) Effects of insanity on sculpture
8. (Major) Effects of technology on the making of jewelry
9. (Major) Effects of technology on metalwork

10. (Major) Effects of (nationalism, patriotism) on sculpture
11. (Major) Effects of technology on numismatics
12. (Major) Effects of poverty on (the sculptor, sculpture)
13. Why precious metals are precious
14. (Major) Effects of prejudice on sculpture
15. (Major) Effects of prosperity on (sculpture, the sculptor)
16. (Major) Effects of (paganism, Puritanism) on sculpture
17. (Major) Effects of race on sculpture
18. Why certain religions object to sculpture
19. (Major) Effects of (Christian, non-Christian) religion on sculpture
20. Why sculptors sculpt
21. (Major) Effects of sex on sculpture--e.g., in primitive cultures, in civilized societies, among Christians, among non-Christians
22. (Major) Effects of superstition on sculpture
23. (Major) Effects of technology on the making of (ceramic, metal) tableware

CLASSIFICATION

Kinds/Types of:

1. Armor
2. Busts
3. Ceramics
4. Coins
5. Earthenware
6. Enamelware
7. Jewelry
8. Masks
9. Materials used in sculpture
10. Medallions
11. Modeling
12. Monuments
13. Numismatists
14. Porcelainware
15. Pottery
16. Sculptors
17. Sculpture
18. Statues
19. Tokens
20. Urns
21. Vases

COMPARISON and CONTRAST

1. African sculpture and Afro-American sculpture
2. Ancient sculpture and primitive sculpture
3. Atlantes and caryatides
4. Carving and whittling
5. Carving, casting, and modeling
6. Carving: in marble, limestone, stone, and/or wood
7. Ceramics: by hand and by machine
8. Classic, Gothic, and Renaissance
9. Coin and token
10. Coins: counterfeit and genuine
11. Diamond and zircon
12. Earthenware, enamelware, and porcelain
13. Emboss and engrave
14. Fashion model and sculptor's model
15. Figurine and monumental sculpture
16. Helmets: medieval and modern

17. <u>High relief</u> and low relief
18. <u>Jewelry</u>: costume and precious
19. <u>Medal</u> and medallion
20. <u>Medieval</u> breastplate and modern bullet-proof vest
21. <u>Medieval suit of armor</u> and modern space-suit
22. <u>Numismatist</u> and philatelist
23. <u>Painter</u> and sculptor
24. <u>Piece mold</u> and waste mold
25. <u>Sculpture</u>: as art and as technology
26. <u>Sculpture</u>: classical and neo-classical
27. <u>Sculpture</u>: colossal and heroic
28. <u>Sculpture</u>: modern and primitive
29. <u>Sculpture</u>: in relief and in the round

DEFINITION

1. Art
2. Beauty
3. Bust
4. Grotesque
5. Idealism
6. Intaglio
7. Mask
8. Naturalism
9. Patina
10. Plasticine
11. Primitivism
12. Realism
13. Romanticism
14. Sculpture
15. Token

DESCRIPTION

1. A suit of <u>armor</u>
2. A piece of <u>sculpture</u>
3. A sculptor's <u>studio</u>, or part thereof
4. A <u>tool</u> used in sculpture--e.g., a chisel
5. An <u>urn</u> or vase

PROCESS

1. How a <u>bronze statue</u> is cast
2. How to <u>carve</u> (a bust, a statue)
3. How to <u>carve</u>--e.g., a ship model--in a bottle
4. How <u>chinaware</u> is made
5. How to make an article of <u>clay</u>--e.g., a bowl
6. How to collect <u>coins</u> (for pleasure, for profit)
7. How <u>coins</u> are made
8. How a piece of sculpture is <u>copied</u>
9. How to tell a <u>counterfeit</u> from a genuine coin
10. How to <u>educate</u> Americans to appreciate sculpture
11. How paper money is <u>engraved</u>
12. How the <u>Great Sphinx</u> was created
13. How "<u>junk jewelry</u>" is made
14. How to construct a <u>kiln</u>
15. How to make a <u>mask</u>--e.g., a Halloween mask
16. How <u>medieval armor</u> was made

17. How medieval arms--e.g., swords--were made
18. How to be a sculptor's model
19. How a mold is made in sculpture
20. How monumental sculpture is created
21. How to make a piece of pottery
22. How sculptors harden clay figures
23. How to make a snowman
24. How to carve an object from soap
25. How the Statue of Liberty was made
26. How to whittle

ARGUMENTATION

PROPOSITIONS OF FACT

1. Is modern sculpture nonsense?
2. Are statues of the nude human body evil?
3. Can anyone be a sculptor?
4. Are sculptors' models immoral?

PROPOSITIONS OF POLICY

1. Should our coins be debased?
2. Should the fine arts be subsidized by the federal government?
3. Should the human body be sculptured in the nude?
4. Should our (city, town) have an avenue of monuments?
5. Should nude statues be clothed in fig-leaves?
6. Should the sculptor (idealize, treat realistically) his subject?

EVALUATION

OBJECTS

1. A suit of armor
2. A coin
3. A piece of earthenware
4. A piece of pottery
5. A ring
6. A piece of (ceramic, metal, plastic) tableware
7. A tool used in sculpture

POLICIES

Evaluation of a policy, in effect or proposed, of an agency, association, or organization--local, state, federal; public or private--devoted to the fine arts (especially sculpture) --for example:

1. A policy of a patriotic organization regarding the commissioning of a work of sculpture
2. A policy of Utopia's Fine Arts Department

DRAWING; DECORATIVE ARTS; HANDICRAFTS 740-749.99 and PAINTING 750-759.99

Thought Starters for ANALYSIS

What about:

1. Advertising illustration: commercial art
2. Anatomy for artists
3. Ancient painting
4. Animated cartoons
5. Arts and crafts
6. Baroque painting
7. Biblical characters: art representation
8. Byzantine painting
9. Caricature drawing
10. Cartoons
11. Christian churches: interior decoration
12. Classicism: painting
13. Color
14. Comic strips
15. Commercial art
16. Cubism
17. Dadaism
18. Drawing arts
19. Engineering drawing
20. Fashion drawing
21. Finger painting
22. Flowers, plants, and trees: art representation
23. Folk art
24. Fur handicrafts
25. Furniture arts
26. Glassware arts
27. God: art representation
28. Gothic painting
29. Greeting cards: commercial art
30. Handicrafts: decorative and useful arts
31. Heraldic design
32. Holy Family: art representation
33. Home: interior decoration
34. Human figure: art representation
35. Illustrations: books and magazines
36. Impressionism
37. Industrial art and design
38. Interior decoration
39. Jesus Christ: art representation
40. Lamps: useful and decorative arts
41. Landscapes: art representation
42. Leather handicrafts
43. Legendary characters: art representation
44. Life drawing techniques
45. Magazine illustration
46. Mary, Virgin: art representation
47. Medieval painting
48. Mediums: drawing and painting
49. Metal handicrafts
50. Methods: drawing and painting
51. Modern painting
52. Monograms: decorative arts
53. Motion picture cartoons
54. Murals
55. Naturalism: drawing and painting
56. Navaho rugs: handicrafts
57. Newspaper illustrations: commercial art
58. Nude figure: art representation
59. Oil painting techniques
60. Painting: art and interior decoration
61. Paper handicrafts

NOTE: See also ENGINEERING (620-629.99), HOME ECONOMICS (640-649.99), BUSINESS AND BUSINESS METHODS (650-659.99), and BUILDING CONSTRUCTION (690-699.99)

62. Peasant art
63. Pen and ink drawing
64. Pencil drawing
65. Plastics: handicrafts
66. Portraits
67. Primitive painting
68. Public buildings: interior decoration
69. Queen Anne furniture
70. Restoration of paintings
71. Rubber handicrafts
72. Rugs
73. Seascapes: art representation
74. Shell handicrafts
75. Shinto art
76. Sketching
77. Still life art
78. Styles: furniture
79. Taoism: art representation
80. Textiles: handicrafts
81. Theatrical scenery
82. Wallpaper: interior decoration
83. Water color painting
84. Wax handicrafts
85. Wire handicrafts
86. Woodcraft
87. Woodwork: interior decoration

CAUSE and EFFECT

1. (Major) Effects of aesthetics on (drawing, painting) the human figure
2. Why a knowledge of anatomy is necessary for artists
3. (Major) Effects of Christianity--e.g., Puritanism--on (drawing, painting)
4. (Major) Effects of Christianity on the representation of figures of (mythology, non-Christian religions)
5. Why some Christians disapprove of depicting the nude human figure
6. (Major) Effects of commerce upon art
7. (Major) Effects of education on interior decoration
8. (Major) Effects of eye disorders on (drawing, painting)
9. (Major) Effects of (fear, hope) on medieval painting
10. Why God is rarely represented in art
11. (Major) Effects of mass production on art
12. Why painters paint
13. (Major) Effects of photography on portrait painting
14. (Major) Effects of politics on the interior decoration of public buildings
15. (Major) Effects of (religion, secularism) on greeting cards
16. (Major) Effects of sex on advertising illustration
17. (Major) Effects of sex on fashion drawing
18. (Major) Effects of technology on furniture arts
19. (Major) Effects of technology on handicrafts--e.g., metal, textile
20. (Major) Effects of technology on (drawing, painting)

CLASSIFICATION

Kinds/Types of:

1. Calendar art
2. Cartoons
3. Drawing
4. Furniture
5. Glassware

6. Greeting cards
7. Handicrafts
8. Interior decorators
9. Mediums in drawing and painting
10. Monograms
11. Paintings
12. Portraits
13. Rugs
14. Sketches
15. Stained glass
16. Styles, furniture
17. Wallpaper
18. Watercolors

COMPARISON and CONTRAST

1. African painting: ancient and modern
2. Ancient furniture and modern furniture
3. An art and a craft
4. Artificial flowers: paper and wax
5. Artisan and manufacturer
6. Calendar art and fine art (e.g., painting)
7. Caricature and cartoon
8. Cartoons: here and there; yesterday and today--e.g., c. 1890 and today in the United States
9. Catholic church and Quaker meeting house
10. Christ: in medieval art and in modern art
11. Classicism and impressionism in painting
12. Commercial art and fine art
13. "Contemporary" (i.e., sophisticated) greeting cards and traditional greeting cards
14. Copy and forgery
15. Copy and original
16. Crocheting and embroidery
17. Eve and Mary in art
18. Fashion art and fine art
19. Fashion drawing: here and there; yesterday and today--e.g., c. 1890 and today in the United States; in the U.S.A. and in the U.S.S.R.
20. God(s) in art: Christian and (Greek, Roman)
21. Handicrafts: here and there; yesterday and today--e.g., in Europe and in the United States
22. Hogarth and Nast
23. Motion-picture cartoons: here and there; yesterday and today--e.g., c. 1920 and today in the United States
24. Painted glass and stained glass
25. Painting: here and there; yesterday and today
26. Paper and papier-mâché
27. Portrait painting and still-life painting
28. Portrait and photograph
29. Rug making: here and there; yesterday--e.g., in Persia (Iran) and in the United States
30. Tapestries: here and there; yesterday and today
31. Theatrical scenery: here and there; yesterday and today --e.g., c. 1500 and today
32. Virgin Mary: in medieval art and in modern art

DEFINITION

1. Anthropomorphism
2. Art
3. Caricature
4. Comedy
5. Craft
6. Encaustic
7. Epic
8. Fashion
9. Forgery
10. Fresco
11. Genre
12. Heraldry
13. Heroic
14. Humor
15. Legend
16. Modern
17. Mosaic
18. Myth
19. Panorama
20. Primitivism
21. Raffiawork
22. Tempera
23. Wit

DESCRIPTION

I. An art gallery, or part thereof
II. Equipment or tools used in drawing, handicrafts, or painting--for example,
   A. An easel
   B. A loom
   C. A palette
III. The interior of a building distinctive for its decoration--for example,
   A. The interior of a church
   B. The interior of a home
   C. The interior of a theater
IV. The studio, or other place of operation, used by
   A. A cartoonist
   B. A commercial artist
   C. A greeting-card manufacturer
   C. An interior decorator

PROCESS

1. How animated cartoons are made
2. How to prepare for a career in art
3. How artificial (flowers, fruits) are made
4. How to make artificial flowers
5. How to make a basket
6. How to make a bath mat
7. How to make a string of beads
8. How to make a bedspread
9. How to make a blanket
10. How to make a candle
11. How to make a (cane, pair of crutches, walking stick)
12. How to make a (carpet, rug)
13. How to make a simple chair
14. How to repair a rush-bottom chair
15. How to make a coaster
16. How to tell a copy from the real thing

17. How to make a decal
18. How to make draperies
19. How forgeries are detected in painting
20. How to make a simple piece of furniture--e.g., an end table; a bookcase
21. How to decorate a piece of furniture
22. How to (slipcover, reupholster) an article of furniture
23. How to wrap a gift
24. How glass is blown
25. How glass is (colored, stained)
26. How to collect glassware
27. How to make greeting cards--e.g., for Christmas or other occasions
28. How to decorate the interior of a home
29. How to make a lamp
30. How to make an article of leather--e.g., a belt
31. How to monogram an article--e.g., a towel, a shirt
32. How paintings are cared for and preserved
33. How to collect paintings on a budget
34. How paintings are copied
35. How paintings are restored
36. How to make an article of paper--e.g., a paper doll
37. How to make a poster
38. How to make a pot-holder
39. How to collect sea shells
40. How to make an article of sea shells--e.g., a necklace
41. How to make slip covers (for an automobile; for a piece of furniture)
42. How to paint a tray
43. How to hang wallpaper
44. How to make a wax figure--e.g., a bust

ARGUMENTATION

PROPOSITIONS OF FACT

1. "But is it art?"
2. Is the artist appreciated in America?
3. Are artists immoral?
4. Is calendar art art?
5. Is Christ (properly, improperly) depicted in art?
6. Is Christianity (beneficial, detrimental) to art?
7. Are comic strips art?
8. Can anyone learn to (draw, paint)?
9. Is antique furniture worth it?
10. Do (book, magazine) illustrations destroy the imagination?
11. Is a professional interior decorator necessary?
12. Is modeling in the nude evil?
13. Is modern art art?
14. Is painting the nude figure sinful?
15. In painting, is determination enough?
16. Is one picture worth a thousand words?

PROPOSITION OF POLICY

1. Should every home have original art?
2. Should the federal government subsidize the arts in America?
3. Should Christian churches place (less, more) attention on interior decoration than they do?
4. Should commercial establishments--e.g., barber shops, garages, etc.--displaying lewd calendar art be denied licenses to carry on their businesses?
5. Should one send greeting (e.g., Christmas) cards?
6. Should the human figure be (drawn, painted) in the nude?
7. Should one hire an interior decorator?
8. Should modeling in the nude be forbidden in our art schools?
9. Should the portrait painter flatter his subject?

EVALUATION

OBJECTS

I. A piece of equipment or a tool used in drawing, handicrafts, interior decoration, or painting--for example:
   A. A brush
   B. A canvas
   C. An easel
   D. A ladder
   E. A loom
   F. A stool
II. Facilities of an agency or organization devoted to drawing, handicrafts, interior decoration, or painting--for example:
   A. Facilities of a Department or School of Art
   B. Facilities of an artist's studio
   C. Facilities of a commercial artist
   D. Facilities of an interior decorator
   E. Facilities of an establishment devoted to handicrafts

POLICIES

Evaluation of a policy, in effect or proposed, of an agency, a firm, or an organization--local, state, or federal; public or private--devoted to drawing, handicrafts, interior decorating, or painting--for example:

A. A policy of a Christian church relating to the display of art
B. A policy of a Department or School of Art
C. A policy of a firm devoted to commercial art
D. A policy of an interior decorator

PHOTOGRAPHY 770-779.99

Thought Starters for ANALYSIS

What about:

1. Aerial photography
2. Amateur motion picture photography
3. Amateur photography
4. Animated cartoons
5. Apparatus, photographic
6. Astrophotography
7. Binocular photography
8. Cameras
9. Cinematography
10. Close-up photography
11. Cold weather photography
12. Color photography
13. Darkrooms
14. Facsimile production
15. Films
16. Fluoroscopy
17. High speed photography
18. Indoor photography
19. Infrared photography
20. Lenses, photographic
21. Microphotography
22. Motion picture photography
23. Night photography
24. Optics
25. Outdoor photography
26. Panoramic photography
27. Photographers
28. Photographic chemistry
29. Photographic projection
30. Photographs: collection
31. Photostats
32. Portraits
33. Retouching photographs
34. Radiography
35. Silhouette photography
36. Sound, motion pictures: recording
37. Stereopticons: photographic projection
38. Stereoscopic photography
39. Still life art
40. Studios, photographic
41. Submarine photography
42. Sunlight photography
43. Table top photography
44. Telephotography
45. Trick photography
46. Tropical photography
47. Underwater photography
48. X-ray photography

CAUSE and EFFECT

1. (Major) Effects of (atmosphere, motion, temperature, etc.) on aerial photography
2. (Major) Effects of (atmosphere, light, etc.) on astrophotography
3. Why a camera has (a lens, a diaphragm, a shutter)
4. (Major) Effects of (moisture, temperature, time) on a camera
5. (Major) Effects of (adequate, inadequate; inferior, superior) equipment on photography
6. (Major) Effects of temperature on film developing
7. (Major) Effects of (proper, improper) light on picture taking
8. Why photography is a rewarding (hobby, business)
9. (Major) Causes of (good, bad) photographs

NOTE: See also such related fields as PHYSICS (530-539.99) and CHEMISTRY (540-549.99)

10. Why photographs fade
11. Why people (like, do not like) to have their pictures taken
12. (Major) Effects of (pressure, temperature, motion) on underwater photography

CLASSIFICATION

Kinds/Types of:

1. Aerial photographs
2. Camera attachments
3. Cameras
4. Film
5. Filters
6. Lenses
7. Photographers
8. Photographs
9. Photography
10. Trick photography
11. Underwater photography

COMPARISON and CONTRAST

1. Aerial photography and underwater photography
2. Aerial photography: in peace and in war
3. Amateur photographer and professional photographer
4. Animated cartoons: here and there; yesterday and today --e.g., c. 1925 and today in the United States
5. Art and pornography (in photography)
6. Artificial light photography and natural light photography
7. Box camera and motion picture camera
8. Camera and eye
9. Cameraman and photographer
10. Cameras: here and there; yesterday and today--e.g., c. 1870 and today in the United States
11. Conventional camera and Polaroid camera
12. Dry plate and wet plate
13. Enlarger and slide projector
14. Flashbulb and floodlamp
15. Flashbulb photography and available light photography
16. Kinetoscope and Kodak
17. Laboratory and studio
18. Macrophotography and microphotography
19. Matthew Brady and Margaret Bourke-White
20. Motion picture photographers: amateur and professional
21. Motion picture photography: here and there; yesterday and today--e.g., c. 1920 and today in the United States; in Germany and in America
22. Negative and positive
23. Overexposure and underexposure
24. Painter and photographer
25. Painting and photograph
26. Photograph and story
27. Photography as an art and as a science
28. Photography: black-and-white and color
29. Photography: as a hobby and as a profession
30. Photography: here and there; yesterday and today--e.g., c. 1865 and c. 1945 in the United States

31. Portraiture: in painting and photography
32. Still-life art: in painting and in photography
33. X-ray photography: here and there; yesterday and today

DEFINITION

1. Art
2. Camera obscura
3. Daguerreotype
4. Focus
5. Light
6. Microfilm
7. Optics
8. Photogrammetry
9. Photomural
10. Pigment
11. Pornography
12. Safelight
13. Science

DESCRIPTION

I. Apparatus, equipment, or tools useful in some phase of photography--for example,
   A. A camera
   B. A dryer
   C. An enlarger
   D. A tripod
II. An enclosure useful in photography--for example,
   A. A darkroom
   B. A laboratory used in the field of photography
   C. A commercial photographer's studio

PROCESS

1. How aerial photographs are taken
2. How the camera takes a picture
3. How to select a camera
4. How to care for a camera
5. How motion picture cartoons are made
6. How to photograph (children, animals)
7. How contact prints are made
8. How to (build, equip) a darkroom
9. How to work in a darkroom
10. How to develop film
11. How heavenly bodies are photographed
12. How to make a lantern slide
13. How the photographer (controls, uses) light
14. How a light meter measures light
15. How motion picture film is edited
16. How to make home motion pictures
17. How to select a home movie projector
18. How to read a negative
19. How to judge a photograph
20. How a photograph is made
21. How photographic film is made
22. How photographic prints are (enlarged, reduced)

23. How photographs are preserved
24. How photographs are retouched
25. How photography is used in advertising
26. How photography is used by the armed forces (in defense, in offense)
27. How photography is used in astronomy
28. How photography is used in (crime prevention, crime detection)
29. How photography is used in (primary, secondary, higher) education
30. How photography is used in industry
31. How photography is used in journalism
32. How photography is used in medicine
33. How a photostatic copy is made
34. How to take a picture
35. How positives are made from negatives
36. How to make a print
37. How to make a silhouette
38. How to (make, mount) slides
39. How stereo photography works
40. How to take trick photographs
41. How underwater pictures are taken

ARGUMENTATION

PROPOSITIONS OF FACT

1. Is aerial photography--e.g., over enemy territory--effective?
2. Do cameras ever lie?
3. Is fashion photography ever erotic?
4. Can anyone be a photographer?
5. Is the photographer an invader of privacy?
6. Is photography (an art, a science)?
7. Is one picture always worth a thousand words?

PROPOSITIONS OF POLICY

1. Should the United States (continue, discontinue) flights over enemy territory for the purpose of taking aerial photographs?
2. Should earth satellites take the place of manned planes taking aerial photographs?
3. Should cameras be banned from such places as courtrooms and military installations?
4. Should motion pictures be censored?
5. Should photographers associated with the mass media be be bound by a code of ethics?
6. Should (magazines, newspapers) containing lewd photographs be banned (from the newsstands, from the mails)?

OBJECTS

I. Equipment, materials, or supplies used in photography--for example,
   A. A camera: still or movie
   B. A chemical or other substance used in photography
   C. A particular brand or type of film
   D. A lens
   E. A photographic attachment

II. Facilities of an individual, firm, agency, or organization engaged in some phase of photography, either for pleasure or for profit--for example,
   A. A darkroom
   B. A photographic laboratory
   C. A photographer's studio

POLICIES

Evaluation of a policy, in effect or proposed, of an individual, a firm, or an organization devoted to making and selling photographs or photographic supplies--for example,

   A. A policy of a private photographer
   B. A policy of a firm devoted to photographic supplies
   C. A policy of a national organization or society devoted to photography--e.g., the National Geographic Society

MUSIC 780-789.99

Thought Starters for ANALYSIS

What about:

1. Arrangement: music composition and performance
2. Ballet music
3. Band music
4. Battle songs
5. Blind, music notation for
6. Bowed string instruments
7. Brass wind instruments
8. Carols: sacred music
9. Chamber music: instrumental and vocal
10. Children's songs
11. Choral singing
12. Christmas music
13. Church choirs
14. Comic opera
15. Composers
16. Composition, music
17. Concerts
18. Conducting
19. Congregational singing: sacred music
20. Criticism, musical
21. Dance music
22. Dramatic music
23. Drinking songs
24. Drum and bugle corps
25. Drum majors
26. Electric musical instruments
27. Ensembles
28. Esthetics: music
29. Folk songs
30. Grand opera
31. Harmony
32. High fidelity sound reproducers
33. Hymns: sacred music
34. Instrumental music
35. Jazz
36. Keyboard musical instruments
37. Lullabies: folk music
38. Mechanical musical instruments
39. Melody
40. Military band music
41. Music and society
42. Music appreciation
43. Musical comedies
44. Musical instruments
45. Musicians
46. Musicology
47. National songs
48. Negro spirituals
49. Opera
50. Operettas
51. Orchestra: musical ensemble
52. Organ music
53. Patronage of music
54. Percussion instruments
55. Phonograph recordings
56. Piano music
57. Plagiarism, musical
58. Popular songs
59. Psalms: sacred music
60. Psychology of music
61. Publishing, music
62. Radio music
63. Records, phonograph
64. Reed instruments
65. Religious music
66. Rhythm
67. Scales
68. School band: musical ensemble
69. School songs
70. Scores, musical
71. Secular music
72. Singing
73. Songs, sacred and secular
74. String instruments
75. Student songs
76. Talking books and machines
77. Television programs: background music
78. Theory, music

NOTE: See also PHYSICS (530-539.99)

79. Time
80. Tuning: musical instruments
81. Vocal music
82. Voice training
83. Wind instruments
84. Woodwind instruments

CAUSE and EFFECT

1. Why I (like, dislike) band music
2. (Major) Effects of commercialism on Christmas music
3. Why church congregations (do, do not) sing
4. Why I (like, dislike) a certain composer
5. Why (men, women) attend (concerts, operas)
6. (Major) Effects of ear disorders on musical composition
7. Why a particular musical instrument (appeals, does not appeal) to me
8. Why the Jew's harp was so named
9. (Major) Effects of military band music on (enlistment, patriotism)
10. Why music hath charms
11. Why Utopia needs a course in music appreciation
12. (Major) Psychological effects of music--e.g., in commerce (as in a bank, a supermarket, a department store, etc.)
13. (Major) Effects of music on animals--as on the farm in milking cows
14. Why music is often called an "international language"
15. (Major) Effects of music on health
16. Why I (like, dislike) music teachers
17. Why Negroes (sang, sing, no longer sing) Negro spirituals
18. Why I (like, dislike) opera
19. Why a piano keyboard normally has eighty-eight keys
20. (Major) Effects of (poverty, prosperity) on musical composition
21. (Major) Effects of racial (discrimination, prejudice) on musical composition
22. Why record collecting is (an interesting, a profitable) hobby
23. (Major) Effects of religion--e.g., Puritanism--on musical composition
24. (Major) Effects of sex on popular music
25. Why singing in the bathtub is a popular pastime

CLASSIFICATION

Kinds/Types of:

1. Arrangements
2. Ballet
3. Bands
4. Bowed string instruments
5. Brass wind instruments
6. Choirs
7. Choir singers
8. Composers
9. Compositions
10. Dance music
11. Drum major(ette)s
12. Electric musical instruments
13. Jazz

14. Keyboard musical instruments
15. Mechanical musical instruments
16. Music
17. Music critics
18. Musical instruments
19. Musicians
20. Opera
21. Orchestras
22. Percussion instruments
23. Recording instruments
24. Reed instruments
25. Singers
26. String instruments
27. Wind instruments
28. Woodwind instruments

COMPARISON and CONTRAST

1. African music and rock-'n'-roll music
2. African Negro music and American Negro music
3. Art songs and popular songs
4. Band and orchestra
5. Battle songs: here and there; yesterday and today--e.g., in ancient, medieval, and modern times
6. Blues, ragtime, and swing
7. Caruso and Crosby
8. Children's songs: here and there; yesterday and today--e.g., in Soviet Russia and in the United States
9. Christmas music: here and there; yesterday and today--e.g., in a European country and in the United States
10. Comic opera, grand opera, and operetta
11. Concerto and symphony
12. Dance band and symphony orchestra
13. Disc, tape, and wire recorders
14. Folk song and spiritual
15. Grand piano and spinet
16. Improvised music and written music
17. Jazz: here and there; yesterday and today--e.g., in the United States and in modern Japan
18. Liberace and Liszt
19. Mathematician, musician, and physicist
20. Mouth organ and pipe organ
21. Music and noise
22. Music: as an art and as a science
23. Music: "live" and recorded or transmitted
24. Music: sacred and profane
25. Musical instruments: here and there; yesterday and today
26. Musical plagiarism: legitimate and illegitimate
27. Musician and musicologist
28. Opera and play
29. Organs: electronic and pipe
30. Patronage of music: here and there; yesterday and today--e.g., in Europe and in America
31. Phonographs: monaural and stereo
32. Pipes and strings
33. Playing: by ear and by note
34. Point and counterpoint
35. Popular songs: here and there; yesterday and today--e.g., c. 1900 and today in the United States

36. Student songs: here and there; yesterday and today--e.g., in Europe and in America; in medieval and in modern times

DEFINITION

1. A cappella
2. Acoustics
3. Amateur
4. Blues
5. Chant
6. Classical
7. Conservatory
8. Criticism
9. Dance
10. Jive
11. Modern
12. Music
13. Music of the spheres
14. Primitivism
15. Professional
16. Ragtime
17. Swing
18. Taste
19. Tintinnabulation
20. Value

DESCRIPTION

I. A building, room, or other structure in which music is played--for example,
   A. A choir loft, or part thereof
   B. A church
   C. A concert hall
   D. A dance hall
   E. A music hall
   F. A night-club
   G. An opera house
   H. A radio or television studio
   I. A recording studio
   J. A school's band room
II. A musical instrument or a piece of equipment used in music--for example,
   A. A baton
   B. A set of bongo drums
   C. An instrument found in a concert orchestra
   D. An instrument found in a marching band
   E. A tuning fork

PROCESS

1. How to get on the Amateur Hour
2. How the blind read music
3. How to compose a popular hit
4. How to be a drum majorette
5. How jazz originated
6. How to appreciate good music
7. How music began
8. How music is recorded
9. How to select a music (pupil, teacher)
10. How to play a particular musical instrument

11. How to (select, care for) a musical instrument
12. How (bowed string, brass wind, electrical, keyboard, mechanical, percussion, reed, string, wind, woodwind) musical instruments produce sound
13. How to appreciate opera
14. How a piano is tuned
15. How a popular song is recorded
16. How to get a song published
17. How to start a record collection
18. How records are made
19. How to sing
20. How talking (books, machines) talk
21. How the voice is trained

ARGUMENTATION

PROPOSITIONS OF FACT

1. Is Utopia's Alma Mater song (inspiring, uninspiring)?
2. Has the American Negro (raised, lowered) the quality of American (folk, popular) music?
3. Is band instruction a proper function of the (elementary, junior high, high) school?
4. Are children's songs childish?
5. Are church hymns (meaningful, meaningless) to church-goers?
6. Is church music (inspiring, uninspiring)?
7. Can American crooners sing?
8. Is crooning music?
9. Is dance music immoral?
10. Is dancing sinful?
11. Are drum (majors, majorettes) merely exhibitionists?
12. Is government aid the proper cure for the arts in America?
13. Is grand opera always grand?
14. Do our hymns (bore, inspire)?
15. Is jazz music?
16. Are heard melodies always sweet?
17. "Is it music?"
18. Is music (an art, a science)?
19. Can anyone (learn, teach) music?
20. Are courses in music appreciation (effective, ineffective)--generally; at Utopia?
21. Are objective standards in music criticism (possible, impossible)?
22. Are music critics frustrated musicians?
23. Is (music, song) composition and publishing (a monopoly, a racket) in the United States today?
24. Can anyone learn to play a musical instrument--e.g., the piano?
25. Are all musicians odd?
26. Is a musicians' union (necessary, unnecessary)?
27. Is musicology a science?

28. Do Negro spirituals degrade the race?
29. Is (private, federal) patronage of music (desirable, undesirable; necessary, unnecessary)?
30. Can the "picture language" of music be (improved, simplified)?
31. Is the player piano a travesty on music?
32. Is the playing of popular music--e.g., on radio and television, in jukeboxes--a controlled monopoly in the United States?
33. Is popular music music?
34. Are our popular songs an insult to the intelligence of the American people?
35. Does our religious music (encourage, discourage) religion?
36. Is rock-'n'-roll music?
37. Is the Steinway overrated?
38. Can tone-deafness be cured?
39. Can anyone be trained to sing?

PROPOSITIONS OF POLICY

1. Should children be forced to take music lessons?
2. Should choir (directors, singers) be paid for their services?
3. Should choir singers be required to audition?
4. Should Christmas music be played in commercial establishments--e.g., department stores?
5. Should Christmas music be played on radio and television before Thanksgiving?
6. Should church congregations take music lessons?
7. Should church music be abolished?
8. Should Congress establish a National Academy of Music?
9. Should Utopia ban dancing?
10. Should the Federal Government subsidize music in the United States?
11. Should martial music be banned--generally; in our schools--in the interest of peace?
12. Should music critics be psychoanalyzed?
13. Should we have a new national anthem?
14. Should Negro spirituals be sung on radio and television?
15. Should all foreign operas be performed for Americans in translation?
16. Should (music critics, music publishers, popular demand) dictate the popular songs to be heard over the mass media--i.e., radio and television?
17. Should Utopia (abolish, expand) its school band?
18. Should Utopia's school song be (revised, scrapped)?
19. Should singers sing (for their art, for the public)?

OBJECTS

1. A pair of ballet shoes
2. A (conductor's, majorette's) baton
3. A drum
4. a hi-fi set
5. A music box
6. The organ in Utopia's chapel
7. A phonograph
8. A piano

POLICIES

Evaluation of a policy, in effect or proposed, by an agency, a firm, or an organization--local, state, or federal; public or private--devoted to the composition, dissemination, playing, or publication of music--for example,

A. A policy of a ballet company
B. A policy of a school or college band
C. A policy of a church choir
D. A policy of a local dance hall
E. A policy of a (local, national) radio or television station or network relating to music
F. A policy of a (local, national) radio or television station or network relating to the playing of Negro spirituals
G. A policy of the Metropolitan Opera Company
H. A policy of a local music store
I. A policy of a national music-publishing firm

RECREATION 790-799.99

Thought Starters for ANALYSIS

What about:

1. Acrobatics
2. Acting: motion picture, radio, television, and theater
3. Air sports
4. Amateur theatricals
5. Amusement parks
6. Aquatic sports
7. Athletics
8. Automobile racing
9. Ball games
10. Ballet
11. Baseball
12. Basketball
13. Bat games
14. Bicycling
15. Big game hunting
16. Billiards
17. Bingo
18. Bird hunting
19. Boat racing
20. Bow and arrow sports
21. Bowling
22. Boxing
23. Bullfighting
24. Calisthenics
25. Camping
26. Card games
27. Card tricks
28. Carnivals
29. Charades
30. Circuses
31. Clowns
32. Coaching
33. Collecting
34. Combat sports
35. Cycling
36. Dancing
37. Dramatic art
38. Dude ranches
39. Equestrian sports
40. Fishing
41. Folk dances
42. Fresh-water fishing
43. Gambling games
44. Game hunting
45. Games
46. Golf
47. Gymnastics
48. Handball
49. Hiking
50. Hobbies
51. Hockey, field and ice
52. Horse racing
53. Horse shows
54. Horsemanship
55. Horseshoe pitching
56. Hunting
57. Ice sports
58. Judo
59. Kite flying
60. Lacrosse
61. Literary games
62. Lotteries
63. Magic: parlor games
64. Mardi Gras
65. Masquerade balls
66. Medicine shows
67. Minstrel shows
68. Motion pictures
69. Motoring
70. Mountain climbing
71. Musical programs: radio and television
72. National dances
73. Ocean fishing
74. Olympic games
75. Pageants
76. Parades
77. Parlor games
78. Parties
79. Playgrounds
80. Plays: motion picture, radio, stage, and television
81. Polo
82. Pool
83. Punch and Judy
84. Puzzles
85. Quizzes
86. Racing: aircraft, animals, automobiles, boats
87. Radio and television entertainment

88. Rodeos
89. Sailing
90. Salt-water fishing
91. Showers: parties
92. Skating, ice and roller
93. Skeet shooting
94. Skiing, snow and water
95. Skin diving
96. Small game hunting
97. Snow sports
98. Soapbox racing
99. Soccer
100. Softball
101. Sports, athletic
102. Square dancing
103. Summer camps
104. Summer theater
105. Swimming
106. Table tennis
107. Tap dancing
108. Tennis
109. Theater
110. Track: athletics
111. Vaudeville
112. Ventriloquism
113. Volleyball
114. Walking
115. Water sports
116. Winter sports
117. Woodcraft
118. Word games
119. Wrestling
120. Yachting

CAUSE and EFFECT

1. (Major) Causes of accidents among acrobats
2. Why (actors, actresses) act
3. Why women race airplanes
4. Why (amateur, professional) athletes compete
5. (Major) Effects of competition upon athletes
6. (Major) Effects of (academic, financial, social) pressure on athletes
7. (Major) Effects of commercialism on athletes
8. Why baseball is (correctly, incorrectly) called "The Great American Sport"
9. Why (adolescents, men, women) bowl
10. Why (men, women) play bridge
11. (Major) Effects of Broadway on American (customs, morality, etc.)
12. Why clowns don't talk
13. (Major) Effects of (commercialism, competition) on coaching
14. Why cocks fight
15. Why collecting (bottle caps, coins, match-boxes, stamps, etc.) is (an interesting, a profitable) hobby
16. (Major) Effects of (radio, stage, television) drama on American (attitudes, customs, habits, morals, etc.)
17. Why (some, most) Americans are flabby
18. Why (men, women) gamble--e.g., at casinos, at race tracks
19. (Major) Effects of gambling (on the gambler, on his family, etc.)
20. (Major) Effects of Hollywood on American (customs, morals, values, etc.)
21. Why (men, women) hunt (big, small) game
22. (Major) Causes of (good, bad) motion pictures
23. Why today's motion pictures (appeal to me, leave me cold, disgust me)

24. (Major) Effects of (motion pictures, radio, television) on (business, the family, morality, etc.)
25. Why women ride motorcycles
26. (Major) Effects of (radio, television) newscasts on public opinion
27. Why women do not, as a rule, play poker
28. Why I enjoy playing post office
29. Why prize-fighters fight
30. (Major) Effects of commercialism on (prize-fighters, prize-fighting)
31. (Major) Effects of commercialism on sports in America
32. Why sports-car enthusiasts race
33. Why I (support, do not support) our summer theater
34. (Major) Effects of (pressure groups, sponsors) on radio and television (entertainment, newscasts)
35. (Major) Effects of television on (amateur or professional plays; motion pictures)
36. (Major) Causes of (the rise, the decline) of vaudeville in the United States
37. Why Americans don't like to walk

CLASSIFICATION

Kinds/Types of:

1. Aquatic sports
2. Athletes
3. Ballet
4. Bat games
5. Bird watchers
6. Bow-and-arrow sports
7. Card games
8. Combat sports
9. Equestrian sports
10. Gambling games
11. Games of action
12. Games of chance
13. Ice sports
14. Lotteries
15. Motion pictures
16. Parlor games
17. Showers
18. Skis
19. Snow sports
20. Theater
21. Water sports
22. Winter sports
23. Word games
24. Yachting

COMPARISON and CONTRAST

1. Acrobat and trapeze artist
2. Acting: here and there; yesterday and today--e.g., c 1870 and today in the United States
3. Acting: in the movies; on radio; on television; on the stage
4. Amateur and professional--in acting; in sports
5. Arrow and (bullet, shotgun shell)
6. Athletics and athleticism
7. Athletics: here and there; yesterday and today--e.g., in the U.S.A. and in the U.S.S.R.; in ancient Greece, Rome, or in Sparta and in modern America
8. Backgammon, checkers, and chess
9. Badminton and lawn tennis

10. Ballet: in America, in Britain, and/or in Russia
11. (Baseball, basketball, boxing, etc.): as a business and as a sport
12. Basketball and volleyball
13. Battledore and shuttlecock
14. Big-game hunting and small-game hunting
15. Billiards and pool
16. Boat and ship
17. Bread and circuses: here and there; yesterday and today --e.g., in ancient Rome and in modern America
18. Broadway and off-Broadway
19. Bullfighting, cockfighting, and prize-fighting
20. Business and sport
21. Carnival and circus
22. Coin collecting and stamp collecting
23. Coliseums: here and there; yesterday and today--e.g., in ancient Rome and in modern America
24. Collecting: as a business and as a hobby
25. Commercials: radio and television
26. Creation and recreation
27. Cricket, football, and rugby
28. Croquet and golf
29. Deep-sea diving and skin diving
30. Dude ranch and "working" ranch
31. Fishing for bass and hunting for whales
32. Games: of action, of chance, of skill
33. Hot rod and sports car
34. Hunting: for business and for pleasure
35. Hunting: with a camera and with a gun
36. Ice skating and roller skating
37. Land polo and water polo
38. Laurel wreath and loving cup
39. Lawn tennis and table tennis
40. "Live" entertainment and (radio, television) entertainment
41. Make-up: for stage and for television
42. Minstrel shows: yesterday and today
43. Olympic games: ancient and modern
44. Participation sport and spectator sport
45. Pointer and retriever
46. Powder-puff derby and soapbox derby
47. Prize-fighting: here and there; yesterday and today--e.g., in ancient, medieval, and modern times
48. Pro and semi-pro
49. Professional boxing and professional wrestling
50. Rifle and shotgun
51. Roulette and "Russian roulette"
52. Value of recreation and of work
53. Vaudeville: here and there; yesterday and today
54. Wrestling: here and there; yesterday and today--e.g., in ancient, medieval, and modern times; in America and in Japan

DEFINITION

1. Athleticism
2. Blackmail
3. Business
4. Conjuration
5. Craps
6. Derby
7. Empathy
8. Exhibitionism
9. Fan
10. "Fix"
11. Gymnasium
12. Ham
13. Honor
14. Hot rod
15. Magic
16. Numismatics
17. Olympia
18. Philately
19. Puppet
20. Racket
21. Recreation
22. Soapbox
23. Spelunking
24. Sport
25. Sportsmanship
26. Steeplechase
27. Toboggan

DESCRIPTION

I. An article of clothing worn for sports or entertainment --for example,
   A. A clown's costume
   B. A fencing mask
   C. The protective clothing worn by a hockey goalie
II. An enclosure devoted to sports or entertainment--for example,
   A. A boxing arena--e.g., Madison Square Garden
   B. The interior of a circus tent
   C. A football stadium
   D. A race track
   E. A theater
III. A piece of equipment used by an individual or team engaged in a sport--for example,
   A. A sailboat
   B. A pair of skis
   C. A hurdle used in track

PROCESS

1. How to perform an acrobatic stunt--e.g., walk a tightrope
2. How to hunt (alligators, bears, lions, etc.)
3. How to take a trip by automobile
4. How to break the bank (at Monte Carlo, in Reno)
5. How to explain (baseball, football, etc.) to someone unacquainted with the game
6. How to perform a particular move associated with (baseball, golf, tennis, etc.)--e.g., catching a ground ball in baseball; serving in tennis, etc.
7. How to win a beauty contest
8. How to ride a (bicycle, motorcycle)
9. How to play (billiards, pool)

10. How to bird watch
11. How to row a boat
12. How to survive after a boat has (capsized, sprung a leak)
13. How to hunt with a camera
14. How to select a campsite
15. How to make a campfire
16. How to make a (canoe, rowboat)
17. How to play a card game
18. How to play charades
19. How to (plan, give) a children's party
20. How to organize a neighborhood (circus, pageant)
21. How to collect (bottle caps, coins, match-covers, stamps, etc.)
22. How to play croquet
23. How dice are loaded
24. How to dive (from the edge of a pool, from a diving-board)
25. How to prepare a hot rod for a drag race
26. How to exercise when one is not in condition
27. How to land that fish (in a lake or stream, in the ocean)
28. How to defend oneself with one's fists
29. How to tell fortunes (with, without) props--e.g., cards
30. How to go on a hayride
31. How to hike
32. How to cultivate a hobby on a budget
33. How to (feed, groom, harness, mount, ride, saddle, shoe, train) a horse
34. How to play the horses
35. How to pitch horseshoes
36. How to (assemble, fly) a kite
37. How to use one's leisure
38. How to apply (stage, television) make-up
39. How to put on a minstrel show
40. How to improve our (motion pictures; radio and television programs)
41. How to climb a mountain (and return)
42. How to prepare for the Olympics
43. How to perform a simple parlor trick
44. How to give a party for one's age group
45. How to set up a neighborhood playground inexpensively
46. How to play post office
47. How to clean up professional boxing--generally; in our State
48. How to make a puppet
49. How to (plan, build, equip) a recreation room
50. How to give a shower
51. How to (prepare for, win) a soapbox derby
52. How sound effects are produced (on radio; on television)
53. How to spelunk safely
54. How to select a piece of sporting equipment--e.g., a fishing rod; a shotgun
55. How to start a summer theater

56. How to improve summer theater--generally; in our community
57. How to construct a home target range--indoors; outdoors
58. How to pitch a tent
59. How to tour (our state; a foreign country)--by automobile; by bicycle or motorbike
60. How to conquer one's fear of water
61. How to perform a water sport--e.g., skin diving; water polo, etc.
62. How professional wrestlers make it look legitimate

ARGUMENTATION

PROPOSITIONS OF FACT

1. Can anyone learn to act?
2. Do women belong in airplane racing?
3. Are our amusement parks (adequate, inadequate; safe, unsafe)--generally; in our community?
4. Is animal racing (humane, inhumane)?
5. Is automobile racing unnecessarily hazardous?
6. Is the playing of bingo in our churches (proper, improper)?
7. Is card playing sinful?
8. Is the circus obsolete?
9. Are our coaches in (secondary schools, colleges) overpaid?
10. Is dancing immoral?
11. Are drag strips (necessary, unnecessary; beneficial, harmful)?
12. Does exercise (prolong, shorten) life?
13. Is (bull-, cock-, prize-) fighting (humane, inhumane)?
14. Is (amateur, professional) football a dangerous sport?
15. Do Americans know how to have fun?
16. Is gambling a sin?
17. Are games of chance immoral?
18. Is horse-racing a sport?
19. Is hunting "for sport" (rather than for food) defensible?
20. Is hunting with a gun unsportsmanlike?
21. Do Americans have (too little, too much) leisure?
22. Do our (motion pictures, television dramas) accurately depict American life?
23. Are the Olympic Games rigged?
24. Are we "making a playground" out of our (schools, colleges)?
25. Do our young people have (too many, too few) playgrounds?
26. Is professional (baseball, basketball, etc.) a (business, sport)?
27. Are professional baseball players really children at heart?
28. Is professional (baseball, basketball, boxing, football, wrestling) rigged in America?

29. Is professional boxing "legalized murder"?
30. Do Americans spend too much (money, time) on recreation?
31. Is the rodeo a brutal sport?
32. Is the (baby, bridal) shower "extortion legalized by custom"?
33. Are sports overemphasized in America today?
34. Is the stage--i.e., the theater--"the devil's drawing room"?
35. Is the star system (beneficial, detrimental) to American (motion pictures, theater)?
36. Do (minority groups, sponsors) have undue influence on television fare?
37. Do (local, national) radio and television programs (bore, inform, indoctrinate, entertain)?
38. Is the television set an electronic Cyclops?
39. Is walking (an art, a reflex action) in modern America?

PROPOSITIONS OF POLICY

1. Should would-be actors and actresses be psychoanalyzed?
2. Should Utopia's athletic program be (expanded, curtailed)?
3. Should automobile racing be prohibited?
4. Should America legalize bullfighting?
5. Should a coach's job be determined by games won?
6. Should cockfighting be legalized?
7. Should dances at Utopia be racially mixed?
8. Should Utopia ban dancing?
9. Should our church outlaw dancing?
10. Should our community construct a drag strip?
11. Should fireworks be (legalized, outlawed) in our (county, state)?
12. Should Utopia (abolish, institute) football?
13. Should our state legalize gambling?
14. Should our state (abolish, legalize) horse racing?
15. Should hunting (big, small) game with a gun be outlawed?
16. Should the bow-and-arrow replace firearms in (big, small) game hunting?
17. Should we have a national lottery?
18. Should our motion pictures be censored?
19. Should censorship boards for motion pictures be composed of (men only, women only, both sexes)?
20. Should (radio, television) newscasts be sponsored?
21. Should the United States Olympic Team be subsidized by the federal government?
22. Should our (community, state) permit pari-mutuel betting?
23. Should the "powder-puff derby" be abolished?
24. Should professional boxing be abolished?
25. Should rodeos be outlawed?
26. Must the show go on--always?
27. Should (baseball, football) be played in an indoor stadium?
28. Should our town have a summer theater?

29. Should <u>television</u> <u>networks</u> (encourage, spurn) controversial programs?
30. Should <u>television</u> <u>programs</u> be censored?

EVALUATION

OBJECTS

I. <u>Equipment</u>, supplies, or tools used in some phase of recreation or sports--for example,
   A. A pair of ice or roller skates
   B. A boat
   C. A gun
   D. A racing car
   E. A golf bag
   F. A saddle
   G. A fishing rod
   H. A trap for small game

II. <u>Facilities</u> designed for use in recreation or sports--for example,
   A. Facilities of an amusement park
   B. Facilities of a bowling alley
   C. Facilities of a dude ranch
   D. Facilities of a playground
   E. Facilities of a skating rink
   F. Facilities of a stadium--e.g., Houston's Astro-Dome
   G. Facilities of a (motion picture, legitimate) theater

POLICIES

Evaluation of a policy, in effect or proposed, of an agency, institution, or organization--local, state, federal; public or sports--for example,

A. A policy of a local amusement park
B. A policy of an athletic association
C. A policy of a local bowling establishment
D. A policy of a state boxing commission
E. A policy of a traveling circus
F. A policy of a school or college coach
G. A policy of a local dance hall
H. A policy of a dude ranch
I. A policy of a gambling establishment
J. A policy of a private hunt club
K. A policy of a local motion picture theater
L. A policy of the promoters of the Olympic Games
M. A policy of the promoters of the Soapbox Derby
N. A policy of a sporting goods establishment
O. A policy of a summer theater
P. A policy of a private yacht club

HISTORY 900-999.99

Thought Starters for ANALYSIS

What about:

1. Adventure and travel
2. Africa
3. Alaska
4. Algerian history
5. American Revolution
6. Americas: discovery and exploration
7. Ancient European tribes
8. Ancient history
9. Arabian peninsula
10. Archeology
11. Argentina
12. Articles of Confederation
13. Asia
14. Assyrian empire
15. Australasia
16. Australia
17. Austria
18. Autobiographies
19. Azores
20. Aztec Indians
21. Babylonian Empire
22. Balkan peninsula
23. Barbary States
24. Belgian Congo
25. Belgium
26. Bermuda
27. Biographies
28. Bolivia
29. Bolshevik Revolution
30. Boston Massacre
31. Boston Tea Party
32. Brazil
33. Britain
34. British Empire
35. Burma
36. Byzantine Empire
37. Cambodia
38. Canada
39. Caribbean Sea
40. Carthage
41. Central (Equatorial) Africa
42. Central America
43. Ceylon
44. Chili
45. China
46. Chivalry, age of
47. Civil War, Spanish
48. Civil War: U.S. history
49. Civilization
50. Coats of arms
51. Collisions at sea
52. Colonial Period: U.S. history
53. Commonwealth of Nations
54. Commonwealth Period: English history
55. Confederate States of America
56. Constitutional Period: U.S. history
57. Continental Congress
58. Crete
59. Criminals: biography
60. Crusades: European history
61. Cuba
62. Cultural history
63. Cyprus
64. Czechoslovakia
65. Dark Ages: European history
66. Denmark
67. Diaries: biography
68. Disasters
69. Dominican Republic
70. East Africa
71. East Germany
72. Eccentrics: biography
73. Ecuador
74. Egypt
75. Eire
76. El Salvador
77. Emancipation Proclamation: U.S. history

NOTE: See also POLITICAL SCIENCE (320-329.99) and ANTHROPOLOGY (570-579.99)

78. Emperors: biography
79. England
80. Epitaphs: genealogy
81. Ethiopia
82. Euphrates Valley
83. Europe: geography and history
84. Excavation, archeological method
85. Expeditions, archeological
86. Exploration
87. Far East
88. Fascist Italy
89. Fiji Islands
90. Finland
91. Flags: heraldry
92. Flights around the world
93. Flowers: national and state
94. Formosa
95. France
96. Free French Movement
97. French Revolution
98. Gabon
99. Genealogy
100. Geography
101. Germany
102. Ghana
103. Gibraltar
104. Great Wall of China
105. Greece
106. Greenland
107. Guatemala
108. Guiana
109. Guinea
110. Haiti
111. Hawaii
112. Heraldry
113. Hermits: biography
114. Holland
115. Holy Roman Empire
116. Honduras
117. Hong Kong
118. Hungary
119. Iberian Peninsula
120. Iceland
121. Inca Empire
122. India
123. Indian Territory: U.S. history
124. Indians: North, Central, and South America
125. Indochina
126. Indonesia
127. Inventors: biography
128. Iran (Persia)
129. Iraq
130. Ireland
131. Islands: history
132. Israel
133. Italy
134. Jamaica
135. Japan
136. Jews: history
137. Journeys around the world
138. Kenya
139. Kings: biography
140. Knighthood
141. Korea
142. Laos
143. Latin America
144. Lebanon
145. Liberia
146. Libya
147. Little America
148. Local (city, county, state, town) history
149. Louisiana Purchase
150. Low Countries
151. Luxembourg
152. Madagascar
153. Magna Carta
154. Malaya
155. Malta
156. Manchu dynasty
157. Manchuria
158. Maps: geography
159. Martyrs: biography
160. Maya Indians
161. Mecca
162. Median empire
163. Medieval history
164. Mediterranean Sea
165. Mexico
166. Middle Ages
167. Middle East
168. Ming dynasty
169. Monaco
170. Morocco
171. Moslem empire
172. Mutinies, ocean
173. Napoleonic wars
174. Near East
175. Negro Africa
176. Negroes

177. Netherlands
178. New Deal
179. New England Confederation
180. New World
181. New Zealand
182. Nicaragua
183. Nicknames: genealogy
184. Nigeria
185. Norsemen
186. North Africa
187. North America
188. Norway
189. Nullification: U.S. history
190. Nyasaland
191. Obituaries: biography
192. Ocean travel
193. Orient
194. Ottoman Empire
195. Outlaws: biography
196. Pakistan
197. Palestine
198. Panama
199. Paraguay
200. Persia
201. Peru
202. Phillippine Islands
203. Philistines
204. Phoenicia
205. Pirates
206. Pitcairn Island
207. Poland
208. Polar Regions
209. Polynesia
210. Pompeii
211. Portugal
212. Presidents: biography
213. Prussia
214. Puerto Rico
215. Queens: biography
216. Reconstruction: U.S. history
217. Red China
218. Reformation: European history
219. Renaissance: European history
220. Revolution: U.S.S.R.
221. Rhodesia
222. Riviera
223. Roman Empire
224. Roman period: English history
225. Russia
226. Sahara desert
227. Saint Lawrence River and Seaway
228. Samoa
229. Saudi Arabia
230. Scandinavia
231. Scotland
232. Sea voyages
233. Shields: heraldry
234. Shipwrecks: travel accounts
235. Siam
236. Siberia
237. Sicily
238. Slave Coast
239. South Africa
240. South America: geography and history
241. Southeast Asia
242. Southern States
243. Soviet Union
244. Spain
245. Sudan
246. Suez Isthmus
247. Sweden
248. Switzerland
249. Syria
250. TVA
251. Tahiti
252. Tartans: heraldry
253. Texas annexation: U.S. history
254. Thailand
255. Third Reich
256. Tibet
257. Trieste
258. Tunisia
259. Turkey
260. U.S.S.R.
261. Uganda
262. Underground Railroad
263. Union of South Africa
264. United Arab Republic
265. United Kingdom
266. United States
267. Uruguay
268. Vatican City
269. Venezuela
270. Vichy government
271. Vietnam
272. Vikings
273. Virgin Islands
274. Wales

275. Wars
276. West Africa
277. West Indies
278. West: U.S. history
279. Wills: genealogy
280. World Wars I and II
281. Yugoslavia
282. Zionism
283. Zululand

CAUSE and EFFECT

1. Why there has never been a (native literature, written language) in many parts of Africa
2. (Major) Causes and/or effects of the segregation of many American Indians on reservations
3. Why modern Arabs and Jews are enemies
4. Why the study of archeology is important in the study of history
5. Major (causes, effects) of a particular (battle, war) in world history--e.g., the Battle of Hastings; the Battle of the Bulge; the Crimean War, etc., etc.
6. (Major) Cause of the comparative backwardness of certain cultures and peoples in the world today--e.g., peoples of Africa, China, India, etc.
7. (Major) Causes of (the rise and fall; the growth and stagnation) of a particular civilization--e.g., Aztec, Mayan, Incan, Graeco-Roman, African, Indian, Persian, etc.
8. Why civilization seems to move in a westerly direction
9. (Major) Effects of (climate, natural resources, race, topography, weather, religion, etc.) on a particular civilization or culture, ancient or modern--e.g., African, Asian, Central or South American, etc.
10. (Major) Effects of (climate, geography, race, technology, etc.) on cultural change--e.g., in Europe; in the Near or Far East
11. (Major) Causes of cultural lag--generally; with reference to a particular culture or civilization
12. Why cultures (do, do not) change--e.g., those of primitive and modern Africa
13. (Causes/Effects) of a (manmade and/or natural) disaster--e.g., the San Francisco earthquake; the Chicago Fire; the London Plague; the eruption of Vesuvius; a shipwreck; a tidal wave
14. Why a particular historical document is important--e.g., the Code of Hammurabi; the Ten Commandments; the Magna Carta; the Declaration of Independence
15. Why (children, adolescents, adults) dislike geography
16. Why geography is important in the study of history
17. Why historians (agree, disagree)
18. Why the study of history is important
19. Why (children, adolescents, adults) dislike history
20. Why modern Japan emulates the West
21. Why Liberia is a relatively backward country today
22. Major (causes, effects) of a particular (movement, revolution) on world history--e.g., the Free French movement; the Negro Revolution, etc.

23. Why there are different races
24. (Major) (Causes, effects) of the (rise, decline) of States' Rights in American history
25. (Major) Causes of (the rise, the fall) of the Third Reich
26. (Major) Effects of travel--on the one who travels; on the country visited
27. (Major) Causes of war--generally; with reference to a specific conflict

CLASSIFICATION

Kinds/Types of:

1. Artifacts
2. Atlases
3. Biography
4. Civilization
5. Colonialism
6. Colonies
7. Crusades
8. Culture(s)
9. Eccentrics
10. Empires
11. Exploration
12. Expeditions
13. Forces
14. Geography
15. Government(s)
16. Heraldry
17. Historical sources
18. History
19. Ignorance
20. Knowledge
21. Law(s)
22. Maps
23. Missionaries
24. Revolution
25. Slavery
26. States
27. Travelers
28. Tyranny

COMPARISON and CONTRAST

1. Two (or more) actors or actresses--e.g., Barrymore and Burton
2. Two admirals--e.g., Nelson and Halsey
3. Two adventurers--e.g., Marco Polo and John Smith
4. African pygmy and Australian bushman
5. Air warfare: in World War I and in World War II
6. Air warfare: in World War II and in World War III
7. American Indian: c. 1700 and today
8. American Revolution and French (or other) Revolution
9. Ancestor worship: here and there; yesterday and today --e.g., in America, England, Japan, etc.
10. Ancient Africa and modern Africa
11. Ancient Egypt and modern Egypt
12. Ancient Ethiopia and modern Ethiopia
13. Ancient Greece and modern Greece
14. Ancient Japan and modern Japan
15. Ancient mind, medieval mind, and modern mind
16. Ancient Rome and modern Rome
17. Arabia: in the Middle Ages and today
18. Arabian Nights: in fact and in fiction
19. Two architects--e.g., Thomas Jefferson and Louis Sullivan
20. Two artists (musicians, sculptors, painters, etc.)--e.g., Jo Davidson and Phidias

21. Asia: c. 1000 A.D. and today
22. Two assassins--e.g., John Wilkes Booth and Lee Harvey Oswald
23. Two astronomers--e.g., Galileo and Newton
24. Athens and Sparta
25. Two athletes--e.g., "Babe" Didrikson and Jesse Owens
26. Atlas, map, and globe
27. Two bankers--e.g., Rothschild and Morgan
28. Baron Munchausen and Paul Bunyan
29. Berlin Wall and Great Wall of China
30. Two biographers--e.g., Douglas S. Freeman and Carl Sandburg
31. Two biographies--e.g., Ludwig's Napoleon and Froude's Caesar
32. Two biologists--e.g., Aristotle and Agassiz
33. The British Empire: yesterday and today--e.g., c. 1764, c. 1864, and today
34. Capitalism, communism, fascism, and socialism
35. Two capitalists--e.g., George Washington and John D. Rockefeller, Sr.
36. Catholicism: here and there; yesterday and today--e.g., c. 1500 and today
37. Central Africa: c. 1500 and today
38. Chicago Fire, Johnstown Flood, and San Francisco Earthquake
39. China: c. 1000, c. 1900, and today
40. Chinese warlords: c. 1000 and today
41. Chivalry: here and there; yesterday and today--e.g., in the Court of King Arthur and in the Virginia Governor's Mansion during the American Civil War
42. Christopher Columbus and John Glenn
43. Circumnavigation of the globe: during the age of Magellan and today
44. Civilization and culture
45. Two civilizations--e.g., that of ancient Rome and that of modern New York City
46. Coat of arms and pedigree
47. Two criminals--e.g., Jack the Ripper and Caryl Chessman
48. Crossing the Alps: by Hannibal and by Hitler
49. Democracy and republic
50. Two dictators--e.g., Caesar and Castro
51. Two manmade disasters--e.g., the sinking of the Titanic and the sinking of the Thresher
52. Two economists--e.g., Adam Smith and Karl Marx
53. Two emperors--e.g., Napoleon Bonaparte and Haile Selassie
54. English colonizers and (Greek, Phoenician, French, Spanish, etc.) colonizers
55. Two diplomats--e.g., Benjamin Franklin and Adlai Stevenson
56. East Indies and West Indies
57. Two emigrations--e.g., of the ancient Hebrews to the Promised Land; of African slaves to the New World; of the Puritans to America, etc.
58. Eve and Mary

59. Two explorers--e.g., Sir Henry Stanley and Admiral Richard E. Byrd
60. Exploring the New World and exploring the moon
61. Two "fanatics"--e.g., Joan of Arc and John Brown
62. Two farmers--e.g., Virgil and George Washington
63. Flights around the world: yesterday, today, and tomorrow
64. Gentlemen: here and there; yesterday and today--e.g., Sir Philip Sidney and Thomas Jefferson
65. Georgia: U.S.A. and U.S.S.R.
66. Ghandi, King, and Thoreau
67. Greek city-state and the Southern Confederacy
68. Haarlem, the Netherlands; and Harlem, New York
69. Two historians--e.g., George Bancroft and Charles A. Beard
70. History, legend, and myth
71. Two humanitarians--e.g., Florence Nightingale and Albert Schweitzer
72. Two labor leaders--e.g., Samuel Gompers and John L. Lewis
73. Laws: of Hammurabi; of the Medes and the Persians; of Napoleon; of Justinian; of the American Constitution, etc.
74. Two leaders--e.g., Abraham Lincoln and Franklin D. Roosevelt
75. Liberia: c. 1830 and today
76. Mecca and Palestine
77. (Military, naval) campaigns--here and there; yesterday and today--Caesar's Gallic Wars; Jackson's Valley campaigns; Rommel's African campaigns, etc.
78. (Military, Naval) Commanders--here and there; yesterday and today--e.g., JEB Stuart and George Patton
79. Negro slave and wage slave
80. Negroes: in Africa and in the United States
81. Ocean travel: here and there; yesterday and today--e.g., c. 1850 and today
82. Patriot and traitor
83. Two (patriots, statesmen)--e.g., Thomas Jefferson and Moise Tshombe
84. Primary sources and secondary sources
85. Rebellion, revolution, and secession
86. Reconstruction: of Germany after World Wars I and II; of Japan after World War II; of the South following the Civil War
87. Two religious leaders--e.g., Martin Luther and Martin Luther King
88. Two revolutionaries--e.g., Tom Paine and Trotsky
89. Roman Empire: heathen and holy
90. Two settlements--e.g., Monrovia (c. 1830) and Jamestown (c. 1630)
91. Two systems of slavery--e.g., American and Greek
92. Two statesmen--e.g., Benjamin Franklin and Winston Churchill
93. Study of history: here and there; yesterday and today--e.g., in high school and in college; in the U.S.A.; in the U.S.S.R.
94. Two theologians--e.g., Jonathan Edwards and Paul Tillich

DEFINITION

1. Academic freedom
2. Accuracy
3. Aggression
4. Bias
5. Challenge
6. Civilization
7. Colonialism
8. Conquest
9. Culture
10. Decay
11. Fact
12. Fairness
13. Historiography
14. History
15. Law
16. Legend
17. Maturity
18. Modern
19. Myth
20. Objectivity
21. Opinion
22. Patriotism
23. Prejudice
24. Primitivism
25. Progress
26. Race
27. Science
28. State
29. Superstition
30. Theory
31. Truth

DESCRIPTION

1. A site or structure associated with an archeological expedition--e.g., the ruins of an ancient city
2. An artifact found at an archeological site
3. An historic battle site--e.g., the battlefield of Gettysburg
4. An important building or other structure associated with the history of the United States or of a foreign country --e.g., the Alamo, the Palace at Versailles, the Parthenon
5. A local historic site or structure
6. One of the Seven Wonders of the World

PROCESS

1. How we bought Alaska
2. How Alaska became a State
3. How to (display, fold) the American flag
4. How (North, Central, South) America was (discovered, explored)
5. How an ancient civilization--e.g., Babylonia, Mesopotamia, Persia, etc.--(rose, fell)
6. How archaeological expeditions are (planned, carried out)
7. How archaeologists excavate
8. How archaeology helps the study of history
9. How to (uncover, preserve) artifacts
10. How Australia was (colonized, civilized)
11. How Belgium (won, lost) the Belgian Congo
12. How Britain colonized Bermuda
13. How ancient Carthage was destroyed
14. How the age of Chivalry (began, ended)
15. How to secure a coat of arms
16. How collisions at sea are avoided

17. How colonies (are born, survive, die)
18. How the Crusades (began, ended)
19. How Spain (won, lost) Cuba
20. How the Dark Ages (became dark; grew light)
21. How to emigrate to a foreign country
22. How to explore an unknown territory
23. How Fascist Italy (arose, fell)
24. How to (prepare for, take) a flight around the world
25. How (national, state) flowers are chosen
26. How to make the study of geography interesting
27. How the Great Wall of China was built
28. How Hawaii joined the Union
29. How historians re-create the past
30. How to (interpret, understand) history
31. How to improve the teaching of history in our (secondary schools, colleges, and universities)
32. How to (equip, live on) a desert island
33. How to (prepare for, take) a journey around the world
34. How knighthood was de-flowered
35. How Liberia was colonized
36. How Little America was established
37. How the Louisiana Purchase was purchased
38. How the Magna Carta originated
39. How maps are made
40. How medieval history became modern
41. How my (city, county, state, town) was founded
42. How to (prepare for, enjoy) ocean travel
43. How the Panama Canal came into existence
44. How Presidents are (made, unmade)
45. How the Pyramids were built
46. How China became Red
47. How the (American, French, Glorious, Industrial, Negro, Russian, Spanish, other) Revolution began
48. How science helps the student of history
49. How one of the Seven Wonders of the World (was built, was destroyed)
50. How to survive a shipwreck
51. How Stonehenge originated
52. How the Suez Canal was built
53. How Switzerland has maintained its (comparative) independence
54. How Texas was annexed
55. How the Third Reich (rose, fell)
56. How to be a welcome tourist (in another state, in a foreign country)
57. How to travel (intelligently, profitably)
58. How wars (start, end)
59. How the wheel evolved

PROPOSITIONS OF FACT

1. Did civilization begin in Africa?
2. Can the continent of Africa be civilized?
3. Is Alaska (an asset, a liability) to the United States?
4. Was the American Civil War an irrepressible conflict?
5. Is American civilization on the wane?
6. Was the American Revolution avoidable?
7. Is the doctrine of apartheid (defensible, indefensible)?
8. Are the Armenians still starving?
9. Is Asia the next great continent?
10. Was the Battle of Gettysburg the turning point of the American Civil War?
11. Was the Bolshevik Revolution Russia's irrepressible conflict?
12. Was the Boston Tea Party a mistake?
13. Is the British Empire doomed?
14. Is annexation of Canada by the United States inevitable?
15. Did Carthage deserve to be destroyed by Rome?
16. Can central Africa be saved?
17. Is central Africa worth saving?
18. Can central America be united?
19. Will China provide our next great civilization?
20. Does Red China deserve admission into the United Nations?
21. Is chivalry dead?
22. Is a coat of arms (meaningful, meaningless)?
23. Is colonialism (beneficial, harmful) to the colony?
24. Is the British Commonwealth of Nations an (effective, ineffective) organization?
25. Is communism "the wave of the future"?
26. Were the Confederate States of America doomed from the start?
27. Were the Crusades (beneficial, detrimental) to those affected by them?
28. Is Cuba a real threat to the United States?
29. Were the Dark Ages dark (in Europe, in non-European countries)?
30. Is democracy the wave of the future?
31. Can the world's deserts be reclaimed?
32. Can East Germany and West Germany be reunited without war?
33. Were America's Founding Fathers (cynical realists, noble idealists)?
34. Were the Founding Fathers (patriots, traitors) in the American Revolution?
35. Was the French Revolution an irrepressible conflict?
36. Is the American frontier closed?
37. Can Germany be reunited?
38. Is Gibraltar obsolete?
39. Was the Glorious Revolution aptly named?
40. Is Great Britain still great?
41. Can President Johnson's Great Society be realized under our traditional free-enterprise system?

42. Is heraldry (meaningful, meaningless) in the modern world?
43. Are (high school, prep school) history courses "pap"?
44. Can historians be impartial?
45. Are our history textbooks slanted?
46. Do our (high-school, college) history textbooks promote (communism, democracy, socialism)?
47. Do our history textbooks discredit the American Way?
48. Does (history make the man, man make the history)?
49. Is history bunk?
50. (Can, Does) man learn from history?
51. Does history repeat itself?
52. Was the Holy Roman Empire holy?
53. Are the Jews "God's chosen people"?
54. Is the proper study of mankind (man, God)?
55. Is man worthy because he exists?
56. Is the concept of monarchy anachronistic in today's world?
57. Is the Monroe Doctrine merely a scrap of paper?
58. Is the moon America's next frontier?
59. Can Negro Africa be saved?
60. Was the New Deal a stacked deck?
61. Is the Panama Canal obsolete?
62. Is the past dead?
63. Is the past (an enslaver, a liberator) of men?
64. Do the paths of glory lead but to the grave?
65. Is patriotism old-fashioned?
66. Can the Polar regions be made habitable?
67. Was United States President ____________ (a do-nothing President, a scheming politician, a great man)?
68. Is Puerto Rico ready for statehood?
69. Is race a myth?
70. Is rank "but the guinea's stamp"?
71. Is Red China a civilized nation?
72. Is revolution (a right, a risk)?
73. Can violent revolutions be avoided without violence?
74. Do scientists need to study history?
75. Is South Africa doomed?
76. Can South America be saved?
77. Is Southeast Asia worth saving?
78. Will the Soviet Union bury the West?
79. Is the expression "States' Rights" (meaningful, meaningless) today?
80. Is a United States of (Africa, Europe) (desirable, undesirable; possible, impossible)?
81. Has the United States of America begun to decline?
82. Is Utopia on earth (desirable, possible)?
83. Are wars inevitable?
84. Is the West in a period of (decline, growth)?
85. Can the West live in peace with communism?
86. Is western civilization doomed?
87. Are non-whites the "white man's burden" (in Africa, in India, in the United States)?

PROPOSITIONS OF POLICY

1. Should America's Negroes be given one of the fifty States?
2. Should Canada be annexed to the United States?
3. Should canals like the Panama and the Suez be under international control?
4. Should ancient Carthage have been destroyed?
5. Should Central America be united under one government?
6. Should the American Civil War be forgotten?
7. Should Cuba be annexed by the United States?
8. Should East Germany be (joined with West Germany; declared an independent state)?
9. Should Europe be unified under one government?
10. Should (Haiti, Puerto Rico) be granted statehood by the United States?
11. Should historians (indoctrinate, propagandize) in their writings?
12. Should our (schools, colleges) require for graduation courses in (state, United States, world) history?
13. Should historians defer to (minority, pressure) groups?
14. Should the (United Nations, United States) have sent military aid in the abortive Hungarian Revolt against the Soviet Union?
15. Should Indian reservations be abolished?
16. Should Manhattan Island be returned to the Indians?
17. Should underdeveloped nations--such as those in Africa --have equal rights in the United Nations?
18. Should our national capital be moved to a more central location?
19. Should (nobility, royalty) be abolished--e.g., in Great Britain?
20. Should Negro Africa be united under one government?
21. Should the Philippine Islands become one of the United States?
22. Should the polar regions be placed under the control of the United Nations?
23. Should Red China be recognized by the United States?
24. Should Red China be admitted to the United Nations?
25. Should straits like the Dardanelles and Gibraltar be under international control?
26. Should college and university students be allowed cut-rate world tours?
27. Should the Southern states be occupied by federal troops in order to insure compliance with (the Supreme Court public school decision of 1954; the Civil Rights Act of 1964)?
28. Should the Soviet Union be expelled from the United Nations (e.g., for failure to pay dues)?
29. Should the Union of South Africa be boycotted by the United States?
30. Should the United States actively support emigration of American Negroes to Africa?
31. Should the world's scientists go on strike in the interest of disarmament and peace?

OBJECTS

Evaluation of an article useful in the study of archaeology, genealogy, geography, or history--for example,

A. A globe
B. A magnifying glass
C. A slide projector
D. A wall map, including the mechanism used for raising and lowering the map

POLICIES

A policy, in effect or proposed, of an association, organization, or institution--local, state, federal, or international; public or private--devoted to some aspect of archaeology, genealogy, geography, or history--e.g.,

A. A policy of one of our Service Academies with reference to interpretation, teaching, or writing of history
B. A policy of the British (or other) Museum
C. A policy of a church regarding the interpretation, teaching, or writing of history
D. A policy of Utopia's Department of (archaeology, geology, history)
E. A policy of a regional or national historical association or society
F. A policy of the National Geographic Society
G. A policy of the Smithsonian (or other similar) Institution
H. A policy of a state's Department of Education regarding the adoption of history textbooks or the teaching of history in secondary schools
I. A policy of the United Nations with respect to the writing of historical material
J. A policy of a patriotic organization--e.g., the U.D.C., the D.A.R.--with respect to the interpretation of history and the preservation of historical artifacts and/or records

1 2 3 4 5 6 7 8 9 10 11 12 13 14 15 16 17 18 19 20 21 22 23 24 25 SH 74 73 72 71 70 69 68 67 66 65